H. J. BLACKHAM

Political Discipline in a Free Society

THE SUSTAINED INITIATIVE

Well, Burke is right—but Burke is often
right, only he is right too soon
CHARLES JAMES FOX

London
GEORGE ALLEN & UNWIN LTD
RUSKIN HOUSE   MUSEUM STREET

11396.

JC 131

PRINTED IN GREAT BRITAIN
in 10 pt. Pilgrim type
BY SIMSON SHAND LTD
LONDON, HERTFORD AND HARLOW

POLITICAL DISCIPLINE IN
A FREE SOCIETY

whether there is an absolute morality or is
it relative — if there was an absolute
morality, & Gout/society remains within
the boundaries, then political decisions
must be moral —
What is the pursuit of Gout — what do they
want to achieve —

If Gout. does what the majority of the people
want then is this a moral decision

BY H. J. BLACKHAM
Six Existentialist Thinkers
The Human Tradition

PREFACE

THE CHAPTERS of this essay in revision are strung on old radical slogans of the movement of thought which has made the running and is now loudly declared, in various terms, to have forced the pace and to have headed in the direction of doubt and disaster. Although this is nonsense, there is no sense in pretending that eighteenth century faith in enlightenment and emancipation, or in reason and nature, is active and persuasive today in Western industrial democracies. The social enthusiasm of that time cannot be recaptured, but to look back on what happened then and later and to gain a vision of what is now practicable is the source of new energy to supply a flagging political impulse.

Current social analysis tends to be gloomy. We are tormented by dilemma and confused by paradox: on the one hand, we are overorganized and stifled, on the other, we are not organized enough to keep anything under control; unprecedented expenditure on security buys unprecedented insecurity; and all this unbearably familiar kind of thing. Whether these frustrations induce sluggishness or anger, scepticism or anxiety, the consequences are uniformly unhealthy.

There is no remedy in shrugging off these contemporary judgements of society, however loose and ill-founded many of them may be; they make the intellectual and moral climate of the time. Therefore, echoes of them reverberate throughout this book. Dominating these undertones, the essential theme is that we can bring things under due, not undue, control if we learn how to learn from political experience, and that enlightenment on this theme, how to learn from political experience, is the main present business of political philosophy.

Science is the conspicuous example of having to learn how to learn from experience and of success in doing so. It used to be thought that the methods of science might be applied equally successfully to political thinking: Bentham, or some other, was to be the political Newton. Undoubtedly, progress in political thinking was made on these lines. But the techniques of learning from political experience have not been and cannot be quite the same as those which have enabled us to find out what goes with what and what follows what.

Political knowledge is not a science, for it is knowledge in the social field of what one wants, of what one can get, and of how to get it. This is not a universal public knowledge, and in so far as people want different things in the social field, it cannot be so. But it can be a knowledge derived from a shared experience initiated by a shared intention, and in so far as it is so it is a personal knowledge with a public aspect, not the same for all, but under test and objective control all the same, not fantasy, not even mere opinion, nor mere self-interest. Cumulative learning from social experience in this way, whether it unite or divide, is the only intelligent method of vigorous democratic self-determination, and its necessary conditions ought, therefore, to be a subject of critical study in an enlightened democracy.

The first two chapters are mainly retrospective, and give as good reasons for hope yesterday as for none today; the third is an interlude; and the second half of the book is an attempt, in consideration of what has been done and what has happened, to see and to show what ought now to be thought: to construct a political imperative which can be acknowledged because there is no alternative so reasonable and none more practicable, and which is not too general to be useful nor too specific to claim general assent.

CONTENTS

CHAPTER I

Liberty, Equality, Fraternity

ARGUMENT

EDMUND BURKE, champion of the resistance in the eighteenth century to an exchange of faith in God for faith in man, appears today not as intellectual hero of a lost cause but as vindicated prophet and spokesman of the English political genius. The ideas of 1789 seem to have brought little good to anyone, least of all France, and the ideas of 1848 have issued in a cold world war tense with mischief, a wrecking malevolence in train for a war verily to end war.

This reading of history is not exactly refuted, but the invective daily pumped up against imperialist warmongers and against capitalists and landlords certainly does exhibit a different view of things, and does recall what used to be said in some quarters about kings and priests. Both sides can sling their slogans till paradise unites with utopia. Only a sober return to history justifies the ways of early rationalists and radicals to modern man.

The rationalists and radicals in question, not only Tom Paine and Rousseau, but also Diderot and Condorcet, Bentham and even Hume, and many others, earlier and later, were hardly of the same party, and certainly not of the same intellectual family, but they fought against a tradition and they fought already in a tradition, the cause of free inquiry for the sake of reliable and useful knowledge, the cause of common sense and humanity. Burke was not on their side.

The idea that man is the maker of man, through the remaking of institutions, which in one form or another inspired eighteenth century thinkers, and rationalized the confidence in themselves of the ascendant bourgeoisie, found less favour with nineteenth century thinkers (typically contemptuous of the bourgeoisie) who were preoccupied more with the laws of history than with the law of the constitution, and saw the generations as players cast for their roles, not lords of their destiny, even when such masterful spirits as Bismarck and Cavour were on the stage, and the proletariat had nothing to lose but their chains.

Today, social invention and historical destiny seem as played out as old theocracy as a source of confidence. There is found no reason for faith in God, nor man, nor history. , *no morality*

I. A CONSERVATIVE INTERPRETATION OF HISTORY[1]

Conservative thinkers in the United States and in Europe have been in heart for some time, with reason. There has been much to encourage them, if they look at some of the gloomy consequences of radical policies, and notice hesitancy and confusion in thoughtful radical quarters, and speculate about the inarticulate popular cravings which keep an archaic religion actively afoot with the fastest go-ahead industrialism. There has been much to encourage the thought that radical philosophies are being finally discredited by their results in the eyes of all fair minded people who are able to reflect and willing to learn.

An extreme statement of the conservative view might go so far as to say (if its author did not stop short with the suggestion) that at the Renaissance European man began to go wrong. He set out full of the fatal folly of the Prodigal. He abandoned a patriarchal culture bound under tradition and hierarchy to the past in veneration and obedience, a centripetal society centred in the stillness and eternity of man's inward being. He chose the unlimited expansion of his intellectual and sensual appetites, and the physical exploitation of the earth. He put settled things in question, turned hopefully to the future, set boundless reliance on himself. He chose a centrifugal society expanding without limit and in all directions.

The French Revolution and the Russian Revolution are fatally linked to this rebellion, and show its destructive character; so are the reckless exploitation of resources and defacement of beauty under *laissez-faire;* so are the scientific inventions which force the pace of social change into uncontrollable acceleration; so are the attempts to reap the whirlwind by centralized power and rational planning. The equalitarian doctrines and emancipating programmes of revolutionary reformers have resulted in impotence to control the appetites which have been released and the uncalculated resultant forces which have developed.

Politics (the argument goes) based on the abstract individual, enlightened and emancipated, taught to forsake his natural duties and to claim his natural rights, have issued, as they were bound to issue, in total governments and total wars. Men cannot meet on the level of their appetites. Liberty, equality, and fraternity as the sovereign truth of human association can be enjoyed only on the conditions established in an order of society which provides what is needful and exacts what is due: subordination as well as equality, obedience as well as liberty, veneration as well as fraternity. The liberties, equalities, and loyalties which are traditional and constitutional,

which have some relation to the facts of nature but whose chief
virtue is that, being acknowledged, they put unquestioned limits to
the insatiable craving of appetites, are the only ones which can be
sustained, because they alone give permanent satisfaction: affections
and loyalties of the family, of 'the little platoon', of mutually dependent patriotic classes under a beloved national leader. The argument, in sum, is that the pursuit of liberty, equality, and fraternity
ignores the permanent necessities of the concrete human condition;
proceeding either from envy and hatred or from humanitarian sen-
timentality, radical agitation works the unspeakable mischief of
loosening the bonds and thereby losing the blessings of human community.

This is of course a religious social philosophy, for only religious
sanctions and religious hopes will curb human appetites and induce
that sense of the ultimate vanity of this world and that trust in
Providence which justify acceptance of restrictive time-honoured
ways in place of the emancipation which even if it does lead to the
waste land at least promises on the way glittering prizes to the few
and to the many some of those desirable things which people of good
fortune have been able to have and always found reason to hold.

Throughout the nineteenth century the conservative creed was
voiced in Europe and America[2] in every generation with distinction,
but without hope. Such thinkers could prophesy woe. They could
proclaim truth. At least they would not bow down in the house of
Rimmon. As Sir James Stephen put it, if one has to accept the fact
that the people will follow the course of emancipation to the bitter
end, one need not rejoice and subscribe to the articles of the new
religion: 'The waters are out and no human force can turn them
back, but I do not see why as we go with the stream we need sing
Hallelujah to the river god.'

In our time, conservative hopes have risen again; the waters have
turned,[3] the vaticinations have been vindicated,[4] the masses are vul-
garized, standards have been swept away, governments have become
omnicompetent and yet are impotent to control the forces which
have been released. The time has come when second thoughts have
their chance to prevail. Is the ruin, then, not complete? If the
Prodigal has destroyed his Father's house, can he still return?

Although this philosophical conservative[5] says he wants to undo
the work of the French Revolution (whatever that can mean), he
does not propose, and says he would not want, to return to the
ancien régime. Untold harm, he thinks, has been done, but salvage
work is not hopeless. There is disillusionment and division among
radicals to temper further danger from that quarter. There is inertia

in the average human being to count on, and the craving for stability, continuity, permanence. There is still a survival of religious faith, private property, constitutional provisions; and these can be strengthened. The natural leaders of society can be appealed to, and educated; and education can be restored to traditional lines, respectful of discipline, sound learning, standards, achievement. Those who discuss ideas and ideals in books and on the air can raise the prestige of such words as 'authority', 'hierarchy', 'catholicism', 'aristocracy', 'tradition', 'absolutes', 'dogma', 'truths', and discredit such words as 'liberalism', 'naturalism', 'scientism', 'individualism', 'socialism', 'equalitarianism', 'progress', 'pragmatism', 'protestantism', 'personality'. The proletariat can be humanized through property-owning and co-partnership schemes, perhaps with a premium of plural votes for those who participate; and local community can be fostered under local leadership. Not least, rewards can be strictly joined again to endeavour. Family life, strict marriage, patriotism, and national pride can be encouraged. The characteristic virtues of an aristocracy, a middle class, and a working class can be prized and treated with parity of esteem. In such ways, the violence, envy, and avarice to which men are prone and by which they are destroyed may be confined again. In such ways, a barrier may be erected against the rationalistic planners of a classless society. In such ways, ancient ends may be restored which tranquillize and satisfy men's hearts, and save them from vice, indolence, boredom, frustration, and bitter discontent. In such ways, humanity may be turned from the presumption of innovating legislation and recover sensitiveness to the changes worked by an inscrutable Providence. In such ways, the brash confidence of rationalists and fanatics may be induced to give way to the humility and charity consonant with the generous complexity of human existence.

The indictment need not be drawn in hortatory rhetoric, nor in (obviously) Catholic terms. Sometimes the retrospect sounds an elegiac note.[6] Man used to think of himself as a rational soul in quest of virtue, or as an immortal soul in quest of salvation, until, with the eighteenth century, he learned not only to doubt his faith but also to question altogether the utility of metaphysics: he gave up grand views, ceased to ask *why*, contented himself with his great success in learning *how* and achieving practical ends, took to heart Bacon's dictum that knowledge is power, and began to think of himself as an economic or political ego in quest of wealth or of empire. Yet the old standards live on, ghosts sitting crowned with their laurels upon the graves of Humanism and Christianity.

Or, finally,[7] historical Christianity is effectively dignified by being used to parody or bastardize post-Renaissance humanism. The *philosophes* thought they had turned their backs once and for ever on the middle ages and all superstition, on ancient history and the crimes, follies, and passions of mankind; they thought they were giving their generation an enlightened modern scientific outlook. In fact, what they were doing was merely to degrade Christianity into secular terms, preaching the worship of Reason or Nature or Humanity, the salvation of the individual by emancipation, and the predestination of the species to perfection in time. This Protestant secularism was in due course reformed by the dogmatic, hierarchic Orthodox secularism of Marx, which found Providence in historical necessity and held there was no salvation outside the dispensation of the dictatorship of the proletariat, with beatitude in the classless society. But secular Christianity is less credible, and less creditable, than the original gospel, and has led to worse crimes, follies, and passions.

Whatever the mood or the precise terms of the judgement, it is widely insisted, and without regret, that secularism with all its works is discredited, that it has unhappily enjoyed a long period of ascendancy, and it is high time to hoist over all its sayings and doings the sufficient epitaph: TRIED AND FAILED.

2. 'THE MYTH OF THE FRENCH REVOLUTION'

Insolently ignorant arguments laced with unanswerable truths are sometimes offered and swallowed as a wonderfully restorative draught which will make everybody feel better. Too much recent conservative writing by persons with intellectual reputations to lose has been of this kind. There are conservative moralities and immoralities, and also those of a radical complexion; but only grotesque misrepresentation will make history reinforce the pretence that conservative thought appeals to the affections and radical thought to the appetites. The Whig interpretation of history[8] had more manliness.

Modern conservative thinking was brought into existence by the French Revolution and developed as counter-revolutionary thinking, as modern Catholicism is a development of the counter-Reformation. Neither is necessarily opposed to Renaissance humanism, and each may find its characteristic ideal in the Baroque age not the middle ages, in French classicism not epic and romance, in *l'honnêteté* not chivalry. Although it was brought into existence by the French Revolution, it is unnecessary at this time of day, and even absurd in the light of modern historical scholarship, but still the rule, for conservative thinking to date and derive modern evil from that complex of events and the ideas and ideals which developed in Europe during the preceding century and a half. Throughout the nineteenth century, all parties made their case by arguing from what happened in 1789-1799 and calling it the French Revolution. Exceptionally, de Tocqueville, steeped in the realities of his country's history, and as genuine a liberal conservative as ever felt in his own pulse and thought with his own brains, exclaimed against the absurdity and mischief of the opposition between those who made a stand for order, morality, and religion, and those who loved liberty and equality before the law, since these were all holy things, inseparable aspects of one ideal upon which in its entirety the whole dignity and happiness of mankind entirely depended.[9]

Looking back through the passionate, tangled, exhaustive debate which began more than a hundred years before the Revolution and was prolonged throughout the nineteenth century and till now, the greatest debate in all history, one may perhaps maintain a proportionate view by keeping always in sight three aspects, since less than ever is there a hope of seeing the Revolution steadily and seeing it whole. (1) The Revolution was only a legal adjustment to social changes which had already taken place. (2) The Revolution was effected by the masses in the streets. (3) The Revolution expressed a universal aspiration.

(1) 'The revolutionaries drew a line at the end of the *ancien régime*, subtracted the negative factors from the past, and added up the sum of what was positive, to be carried forward on the next page. A class of officials and professional men moved up from the minor to the major posts in government and dispossessed the minions of an effete Court; this was what the bourgeois revolution meant. The peasants relieved themselves of their seigneurial dues: this was the meaning of the abolition of feudalism.'*

The Third Estate in the National Assembly of 1789 sought with the aid of liberal-minded elements in the other Estates to rectify a discrepancy of law and fact. They were doing the work of the country in trade and industry and in government administration and the professions; they knew what they were doing and what obstructions impeded the efficient doing of it, and what privileges and emoluments were enjoyed by those who did nothing of it. Burke put it crudely in one of his more percipient statements: 'Jacobinism is the revolt of the enterprising talents of a country against its property.' Lord Acton thought the National Assembly the best legislature of modern times. Their 'Declaration of the Rights of Man and of

* Alfred Cobban: *The Myth of the French Revolution*, p. 20; London, 1955.

Citizen' may have been the death certificate of the *ancien régime*, but there is nothing more revolutionary in it, read historically,[10] than the will to establish equality of right, equality of law. Liberty and equality are inseparable in the document and are words for the same thing, equality of law: there was no intention of aiming at equality of means, of property. Whatever the ambiguity of language, abolition of anachronistic feudal privileges and of government interference with manufacture and trade was the unambiguous demand. The actual bureaucratic administration of the country had already become efficient, and when the flames and smoke of the Revolution had passed away remained intact. That aspect of the continuity enables Professor Cobban to speak of 'the myth of the French Revolution', by which he means 'the idea that there was *a* French Revolution, which you can be for or against. . . . A whole generation packed with significance for good and evil is summed up in the phrase the French Revolution' (p.22).

(2) The Third Estate might temporarily have been overridden by the remnant of authority in the *ancien régime* but for timely popular violence[11] in the streets of Paris. This frenzy was not the Revolution but it served the interests of the bourgeois claimants then and later, until after bitter experience of being excluded from any share in the fruits of the successive insurrections in which they had suffered (culminating in the savage reprisals of Thiers against the communards in 1871)[12] the French workers were forced to rely solely on themselves, and to this day put all their hopes in the proletarian revolution, and regard the Revolution of 1789 as betrayed and abortive. French politics have remained vexed by the three irreconcilables which have taken the place of the three Estates: the ascendant bourgeoisie, the Catholic counter-revolutionaries, and the malcontent workers.

(3) Although the Revolution expressed and achieved the crowning access to power of the middle classes, and began a long, bitter, sordid, still dangerous class struggle with the workers, it also expressed, if it did not achieve, the universal aspiration to something more noble than class ascendancy, the liberty, equality, and fraternity of true human community, a sovereign truth, an unquenchable ideal.[13] Always, the suffering of injustice, with the demand for justice, has overtones of universality: what is suffered is evil and should not have to be endured by anybody; what is demanded is good for all. Justice then seems natural, and oppression a violation of nature. Community of interest against the oppressor or oppressive laws seems community of interest *tout court*: all are equals and brothers in the demand for liberty. And in calling on all peoples to

assume their natural rightful sovereignty, the French people offered their example and help to brothers and equals in the sacred cause of the sovereignty of the people and the regeneration of society. When in fact the dynastic despots of Europe set their armies against the new republic and made 'a war against that example', against that 'system', that 'armed doctrine' in which 'the acknowledgement, directly, or by implication of any kind of superiority'[14] would be fatal to all forms of the old regime anywhere, the revolutionary ideals took fire with religious patriotism, and in due course it was the Republican army which embodied and symbolized the Revolution and guaranteed it against the return of the dispossessed, even when under Bonaparte it became to other peoples not the champion of natural rights but new nationalistic chauvinism.

3. THE RATIONAL ROOTS OF RADICALISM

(i) *Beyond the eighteenth century*

The critics of secularism[16] and all its works are of course quite right to go back to the eighteenth century if they want to exorcize the demon of radicalism from mankind, for it was then that the secular idea of Europe firmly replaced the medieval idea of Christendom. To ridicule eighteenth century philosophers for abstract thinking about man and society, however, is itself ridiculous, although Burke did it at the time, and even Hume. Once the question of the purpose of social institutions had been raised, it could not be settled by saying (as Burke said, long before the Revolution) that such questions ought not to be raised at all because if one started to look at institutions in the light of their supposed origins or demonstrable consequences, nothing could stand, political society not more than revealed religion, not God's work itself. Burke's warning (in 1756) against 'the extreme danger of letting the imagination loose upon some subjects' and of examining everything 'by our ideas of reason and fitness' was obscurantism some two centuries too late. Abstract thinking about man and society had become necessary because, so to speak, the individual and society had fallen apart. Abstract thinking did not force them apart and do violence to human realities;[17] on the contrary, abstract thinking was required to reconcile them, to discover and possess the conditions of the permanent union of the thinking individual with his fellows in society, to justify the laws and duties, the authorities and traditions, which he was required to accept. The fundamental questions of political philosophy had begun to demand answers.

The disgusted despair of Descartes and of Locke with the education they had received is symbolic of the new orientation: they turned from the uncertainty and the uselessness of traditional learning to seek reliable knowledge and to seek it for the conduct of their lives. Descartes turned his back not only on traditional learning but also upon the inconclusive scepticism of the sixteenth century; he used the principle of doubt resolutely to clear his mind of *all* ideas from whatever source, and positively to re-stock it with only indisputable certainties.

The impulse of free inquiry, the demand for *libre examen*, of which the cartesian *cogito* is only the most dramatic, as well as the most technical, starting-point, was the mainspring of the widespread European movement which is called in cultural history the Enlightenment. The individual thinker prosecuting his inquiry put his trust in reason and nature, and was thereby sundered from authority and tradition, even the most sacred authorities and immemorial traditions. At first, this was only a sifting of credentials, since reason and nature had prior claim to be of God, and confidence in the divine unity of reason and nature was the ground of the new empiricism: the 'works of God'[18] were more authoritative and less disputable than the 'word of God' had proved to be.

The attack on authority and tradition is inseparable from the inquiry into the foundations of knowledge. Descartes' *Discours*, Locke's *Essay*, and, much later, Mill's *Logic*[19] were all aimed at a way of thinking which could be used to defend established systems and institutions, to inhibit original thinking, to sterilize experience, and to preclude experiment. The questioning of knowledge was bound up with a questioning of morals, of politics, of religion. In so far as received ideas and opinions seemed increasingly archaic, irrational, unnatural, customs and institutions could not remain unaffected.

Locke is the representative thinker of the transition, for he touched the ascendant movement at all points and reproduced in classical statements the current modernity in philosophical and social thinking, though still struggling out of medieval dogmatic slumbers and bearing trails and traces of the dream, proceeding with caution and not to conclusions, a pointer not a 'gun',[20] the climate of opinion not the maker of an epoch. Thus he continued to use the language of 'natural law', although his case against innate ideas had destroyed the notion of moral maxims imprinted on the mind. 'Natural law' and 'the social contract'[21] were ancient concepts that in this way acquired new meanings in new contexts addressed to the purposes of the time.

Locke stated his political theory in terms of the social contract because to stress and develop this element in traditional political notions was the current way of insisting on intelligibility and utility as the justification of institutions, ignoring or expelling the other element in medieval concepts, that of divine ordinance, immemorial custom, imposing inviolable allegiance. Locke in exile had become versed in the claims of the sectaries, which raised the issue with absolutism; and the consciousness developed by this debate recovered the Greek idea of politics as a sphere of deliberate making, the most radical idea, that *society and* government were created by a deliberate act of free and equal men for their mutual benefit. In general it may be said that the contract theory anticipated the ideal of parliamentary law which superseded it, law whose authority derives from freely negotiated agreement and which represents a specific adjustment of wills and interests, and repudiated the older idea of law as not made but declared, a law of nature inscribed in the mind or revealed in immemorial custom. In Locke this movement of ideas is seen in transition, still carrying notions of natural law and customary law and the duality of sovereign monarch and subject, but qualified by an implied agreement to respect individual property rights and personal liberty, announced in the doctrine of the trusteeship of the monarchy and the conditional allegiance of the subject. The question of who has the right to govern is seen shifting to the question of what the government shall do. The change in the intellectual climate is taking place which will encourage discussion of the rights of man.

The shades of political theory reflected in the various uses made of the contract idea and of the repudiation of it in the debates of a whole epoch might be collected into three contrasting colours: (i) law as a divine ordinance imprinted in the mind or revealed in an immemorial sacred custom; (ii) law as a human contrivance, a convention; (iii) law as a natural phenomenon, an experienced regularity. Use of the contract idea really belongs only to the second category. And only the second category leaves room for more than explanation and subordination, leaves room, that is, for Hobbes, Locke, Paine, Rousseau, Hume, Bentham, who are as different as thinkers and persons can be but are alike in 'considering human beings as they are and laws as they might be'.[22]

The new construction was founded on a newly found confidence in the harmony of nature, including human nature, and the unity of reason, understood not as a common stock of fundamental unquestionable maxims imprinted in the mind,[23] but as a body of coherent clear and distinct ideas bearing the credentials of evidence and utility. This new confidence in the rationality of God and man (troubled but not yet destroyed by the problems of theodicy) led to the characteristic eighteenth century notion of 'man in general', whose opinions and standards could be plainly justified by their intelligibility and utility, that is to say, by the appeal to common experience and common sense.

By the end of the eighteenth century,[24] the ideas of practical men reflected these pioneer thoughts; the many rising industrialists felt they owed their success to the steady application of rational principles to all problems, and with that confidence went a contempt for traditional attitudes and ancient prejudices. And practical men were then equally ready to apply such principles to politics and the problems of society, and with that readiness went a contempt not only for the monarchical and feudal survivals of traditional politics, but also for the personal politics of the eighteenth century which had become a cynical spoils system precisely for lack of modern political institutions and principles. The time of the Utilitarians had come. The American Revolution dealt the death blow to the *ancien régime*.[25]

(ii) *Eighteenth century models*

These essays in the formulation of political principles for modern society, although most of them follow some version of the contract theory and go back fancifully to the origins of society and the institution of government, are not concerned, like *Leviathan*, with the problem of anarchy, the security of each man against his neighbour; they are concerned with the problem of misgovernment, the control of the ruler by the ruled.

Tom Paine put it more vividly than anyone in the opening pages of *Common Sense* (1776), the trumpet call to victory in the revolutionary cause, the prelude to the Declaration of Independence, even to Washington 'sound doctrine and unanswerable reasoning'. Paine rejected Locke's theory of a contract between government and subjects, since society is instituted in the original compact by individuals who thereon decide to create a government, and the government remains in their hands. Following the formula 'society is produced by our wants and government by our wickedness' (and therefore 'government, like dress, is the badge of lost innocence'), he designed government for freedom and security in the simplest way by imagining the setting up of government on the first peopling of any country or of the world. They enjoy liberty, they need security, and they therefore form a parliament which at the outset is the plenary assembly of all. As the people multiply, it becomes convenient to elect representatives for constituent parts:

'and that the *elected* might never form to themselves an interest separate from the *electors*, prudence will point out the necessity of having elections often; because as the *elected* might by that means return and mix again with the general body of the *electors* in a few months, their fidelity to the public will be secured by the prudent reflection of not making a rod for themselves. And as this frequent interchange will establish a common interest with every part of the community, they will mutually and naturally support each other, and on this (not on the unmeaning name of king) depends the *strength of government and the happiness of the governed.*'

Gont. reflects individualistic beliefs

This principle of creating and maintaining an identity of interests in rulers and ruled is the key concept in all the rationalistic thinking of the time about society. Rousseau in the *Contrat Social* (1762) had attempted to formulate the universal principles of true society.

'Since no man has natural authority over his fellows, and since Might can produce no Right, the only foundation left for legitimate authority in human societies is Agreement. (Bk. i, chap. iv.)
Some form of association must be found as a result of which the whole strength of the community will be enlisted for the protection of the person and property of each constituent member, in such a way that each, when united to his fellows, renders obedience to his own will, and remains as free as he was before. (Bk. i, chap. vi.)
So long as a number of men assembled together regard themselves as forming a single body, they have but one will, which is concerned with their common preservation and with the well-being of all. When this is so, the springs of the State are vigorous and simple, its principles plain and clear-cut. It is not encumbered with confused or conflicting interests. The common good is everywhere plainly in evidence and needs only good sense to be perceived. . . .
What sets theorists on the wrong tack is that, seeing only those States which have been badly constituted from the beginning, they are struck by the impossibility of applying such a system to *them*.' (Bk. iv, chap. i.)

The preoccupation of the age with constitutions was not only the result of living in 'States which have been badly constituted from the beginning', but also the activity of minds versed in newtonian mechanics, minds looking for principles, interested in construction, in autonomous systems. If an engine was clumsily designed and worked ill, like existing 'common botched and inaccurate governments' (Hume), you took it to pieces, studied it, and redesigned it for efficiency, for utility.

Hume is an instructive case, because he is a cautious empiricist, as moderate and as scornful of abstract theories as Burke himself. He argued that in historical fact political obligation was not founded upon a social compact; all titles to power and property if looked into would be probably found to depend upon force and fraud, and political obedience rested in the first place on long custom, veneration, and affection, and, in reflection, on the benefits of an established order. His own theory of society is empirical and realistic. With Shaftesbury, he thought that men were naturally social, and with the eighteenth century he thought they ought to be sociable; it was their duty to make themselves useful and agreeable members of society. The long-term interests of everybody were bound up with society, but men were prone to take short views and to act impulsively, even against their interests. Recognizing this, they put in office men whose immediate interest was made to consist in enforcing the laws of society.

'Men are not able radically to cure, either in themselves or others, that narrowness of soul which makes them prefer the present to the remote. They cannot change their natures. All they can do is to change their situation, and render the observance of justice the immediate interest of some particular persons, and its violation their more remote. These persons, then, are not only induced to observe those rules in their own conduct, but also to constrain others to a like regularity, and enforce the dictates of equity through the whole society.'*

By this device the real will and permanent interests of each man are secured against others and against himself by men no better than himself. The rough and ready spontaneous social order, reinforced by reflection, is stabilized, regulated, guaranteed by device.

Moreover, the device is perfectable. Hume, the empiricist, thought that politics was a science, that a perfect constitution might be not only devised, but also achieved and handed down intact, as the greatest human blessing, to the latest posterity. You should not insist on reason when the bulk of mankind prefers to be governed by authority, you should not engage in political experiment, you should not tamper with an established social order, you should not think society can be improved in design like an engine: nevertheless, what you should not attempt in practice you can do in thought, and what could possibly be thought of more useful to mankind than the idea

* *Treatise of Human Nature*, vol. ii, bk. iii, pt. ii, sect. vii.

of a perfect commonwealth, for who knows when or where the occasion may not offer to put it into effect, on the dissolution of some old government, perhaps, or on the formation of a new society in some distant part, or, anyhow, as a model for all moderate reforms or trembling innovations which may gradually lead to perfecting an existing constitution.

Thus Hume, the empirical conservative who anticipated the part of Burke against the rationalist radicals, in his own acute persuasive way reaffirmed all they wanted to say, and pointed to the very historical occasions when what they were saying would have been said to some purpose: the collapse of the French monarchy, the independence of the colonies in the New World, the reform of parliamentary representation in Britain.

Burke also used the language of the eighteenth century: he spoke as freely as Rousseau of reason and nature, of utility and of the union of utility with justice, of natural law and the natural order, and of the social contract. But he rejected with abhorrence the use which radical thinkers made of these terms; his moral world and theirs were as light and darkness. For him, the natural order was historical society, not a system of rational principles drawn from nature; reason was a product of history, the collaboration of the best minds of every generation with Providence, not mere ratiocination, nor the conclusions of common sense; the utility of institutions was proved by historical survival, not by 'ideas of reason and fitness'; the social contract was partnership in the Providential historical order, not a bargain whose fictitious terms could be used to threaten the forfeiture of society or to absolve the citizens of political crimes.

The natural order of society, on which government was founded, could be seen in the family, in the local community, above all, in heritable landed property, in 'connexion' and 'party' in the eighteenth century sense, in the dependence of man on man and class on class. In such relationships, rational self-interest was rooted and moralized by restraints and responsibilities and flowered in legitimate satisfactions. This historical hierarchical order was natural society which embodied a permanent objective reason not to be subverted by will or caprice, transient feelings and appetites, and not to be replaced by abstract rights of individuals, which would substitute an irresponsible numerical democracy for a representative parliament where the nation in little deliberated on the general good in the light of the general reason of the whole ('the great danger of our time, that of setting number up against property'). The parties to the social contract were not abstract individuals intent on guarantees for their natural rights, for the very meaning of civil society was the surrender in trust of all such rights; the real parties to the contract were the men who were living in the actual context of their social relationships, bound, humanized, moralized by the nexus of obligations and loyalties which guaranteed the satisfaction of their legitimate interests. This human relationship, this partnership, this participation in the Providential order of nature, this subjection to a sovereign reason paramount to all forms of legislation and administration, this was society, inherited from our ancestors, invested with more than human dignity, and holding us by the most solemn obligations. To protect it from invasion by any form of human wilfulness was our most sacred duty. To attempt to release human beings from this natural Providential order of their being, from the moral harmony of these inter-personal social relationships, to bring them out of it as so many individuals and to collect them again in an orderless aggregate under laws devised to give them equal rights, this was mad impiety and incurred the untoward consequences of presumptuous folly.

Burke's whole mind was set against any attempt to devise and impose an order on human affairs instead of to recognize and reinforce the Providential order, the order of nature and objective reason. There was no need to contrive in society an artificial harmony of selfish interests if in fact society already was for all reasonable and modest men a moral harmony of legitimate interests.

This stand did not preclude reforms, since the present operations of Providence demanded the co-operation of the living even more certainly than the fruits of past co-operation demanded to be preserved. What was to be resisted was the demand of appetite, of will, the innovations demanded by a perverse discontent with the conditions of human life. The reform of abuses, the sowing of seed, the laying of foundations, might be entirely profitable, and even necessary; but the abolition of workable institutions, clearing the ground for mere plans, this was a monstrous unnatural thing, the unstable evil whose authors defied the indestructible moral order of the world and brought themselves only the unvailing sorrow of remorse.

Burke recognized that Rousseau was 'nothing if not a moralist', but none of Rousseau's contemporaries can be expected to have understood him, and if Burke had known him better he would not have loved him more. Rousseau called his principal political treatise *The*

Social Contract because he wanted to insist that the sole principle of legitimacy in governments and of obligation upon subjects is agreement, but his theory of society is not contractual, for the compact which constitutes civil society has only one clause, which enacts the total surrender of all individual natural rights to the whole community. There are no specific terms of the contract (such as specified natural rights), but the compact is violated unless the laws are enacted by the whole community and are of such a kind that each can will them as equally binding on all. The laws thus have the rational universality of Kant's moral imperative, and indeed Kant was directly influenced by Rousseau here.[26] The union of the individual with society on this plan was in an identity of wills, the union of the permanent wills of all individuals.

At this general level Rousseau's thought is not alien from that of Hume or Burke, but he went farther than they would have gone, and outside contractual theory, in insisting on the continuous active participation of all the ruled in giving or refusing assent to the rules, as the condition of legitimacy in government. For Burke, the House of Commons as it was seemed virtually representative enough to be the nation in little, competent in conjunction with the Crown and the House of Lords to form the general will, the public interest. For Rousseau, representative institutions however strict and delegates however bound by mandate were at best a totally inadequate substitute for the direct participation of all in the acts of legislation. Moreover, it was as individuals that citizens should deliberate and vote, not as involved in any corporate interest or subjected to any extraneous influence: the social compact created civil liberty and equality, and it was the business of legitimate government to maintain them by maintaining the conditions of the compact.

Thus, although Rousseau's premises might be considered orthodox, and not unlike those of Hume and Burke, he took them seriously in a way they did not, and pressed them to radical conclusions.[27] Probably not because he was more rationalistic, or gallic, but for personal reasons. Rousseau in the eighteenth century was what Kierkegaard was, or Nietzsche, in the nineteenth, the great exception, an extreme case, exemplifying in his own life the problem of the age, the conscious separation of the modern personality from traditional institutions. With his whole soul he loathed contemporary society. As an orphan, a social misfit, a complicated being, a genius, a paranoic, Rousseau was driven into solitariness, which alienated his friends in that sociable age; and he longed the more for a society in which he could still be himself and united with others. At the same time, what he hated in society was not simply its early rejection of himself, but more directly what he saw as an acute psychologist and a calvinistic moralist: man as a puppet of the vain opinions bred by existing social relationships, the unedifying spectacle of the social pantomime. This of course is the age-old theme of the moralist, but there are times when it attracts, and deserves, prophetic denunciations.[28] There was nothing of the recluse or the sour moralist about Diderot or Baron d'Holbach; Diderot, like Hume, was ever a useful and agreeable member of society: but Diderot's most powerful piece of writing, *Le Neveu de Rameau*, depicts with the vivid visualness of mime the universal moral corruption which was the real social world, from which not even the philosopher, not even Diogenes, could be immune. It was to insure him against the degradation of having to play a part for his living in this world of postures and gestures jerked by vain opinions, like Rameau's nephew, that Rousseau insisted on Emile's learning a trade, by which he could hope always to maintain his independence.

Since it was for this society that Emile and Sophie had to be educated, they could be educated only by taking them out of it. They were not to be educated for their station and its duties in this society, but as 'man in general' and for the human condition. They had to be given immunity from the vain opinions which ruled society before they could be allowed to enter it. Robinson Crusoe was the ideal for their education.

In such an age, Robinson Crusoe societies were the political ideal, societies as self-dependent, as peculiar, as primitive in virtues as possible. Such societies could be only small rural communities, uncorrupted by money and commerce and the progeny of vain opinions and needs produced inevitably by a cosmopolitan trading nation.

With such ideas and ideals, Rousseau, although he loathed the present, could not look forward to the future. The inevitable trend of the times was against him. So far from improving, the further societies moved from the simpler primitive elements in their traditions the worse their corruption; and more and more societies still relatively simple would follow the same path: the future could be only the wider spread of degradation, moral entropy. There was nothing in such an outlook to make a revolutionary, and in fact Rousseau was less revolutionary than Burke, who did not begin to understand him. The old was better than the new, the further one remounted to antiquity the better; let a people cherish their oldest customs and be very wary and chary of changing anything.

How is it that Rousseau with such old-fashioned, unpopular, impracticable ideas and ideals, as he himself knew them to be, had so vast an influence, was comparable only with Tom Paine as a propagandist of new ideas at this time of ferment, heavy with the portents of social change, was perhaps the most influential writer of all time? How is it that this pessimistic reactionary, of all men, could be a prophet of the Revolution? Tom Paine succeeded by the simplicity, clarity, and timeliness of his ideas and the metaphorical vivacity of his style, creating an impact of ideas in images, an unrivalled pamphleteer. Rousseau could not approach him in this, but he was read with absorbed attention.

Apart from the romantic side of Rousseau, which was his alone, which was both timely and creative, which added another dimension to his thought and appeal, which enchanted and enchained his women readers, he was exciting for his political ideas in spite of their pessimism, and he appealed to the times in spite of looking backwards. He was the clever doctor, the acute diagnostician, who gave his opinion and named his remedy, with the air of one who knew there was no other hope and did not pretend to think his patient would be able to take the prescription. The sickness was not original sin; it was the corruption of manners and morals by vain opinion: the opinions of a nation are born of its constitution, and its morals derive from its opinions. Men are what they are because they are what their laws and education make them. Given good institutions, virtues are natural, that is to say, emulation in excellence is spontaneous. This is proved by the ancient world, pre-eminently by Sparta and by Rome: men loved their country and did and dared everything for its sake. Modern society is corrupted by money, by luxury, by the enslaving dependence of man on man and class on class. If you want a remedy and look for practicable proposals, the practicable can be only what is in fact practised, for any proposal for the improvement of what is practised would soon be assimilated to that practice. Half-measures are not practicable: men can have institutions which make them spontaneously good, or those which make them wholly corrupt. How do men get the education, laws, institutions which make them free, virtuous, happy? In so far as they have been lucky enough to have been given institutions suited to their situation by some legislator of genius, a Lycurgus, a Numa.

The eighteenth century was an age of practical projects; its thinkers were inventors, and they looked hopefully to the despots of Europe to carry out their schemes. Rousseau was a would-be-legislator-of-genius who for want of being a prince had to write about his ideas. Political and economic thinkers and advisers at that time were in a position rather like that of the modern town and country planning movement: a more or less unsuitable inheritance had to be reclaimed and redesigned for pressing modern needs.

Rousseau, having gained fame by *The Social Contract*, became something of a consultant, a practitioner. In that capacity, when consulted by the revolting Polish Assembly and by the revolting Corsicans, Rousseau went to work, not as an abstract theoretician, not as a municipal engineer with a grid-iron paper plan, but like Patrick Geddes in India,[29] with a detailed study of the existing situation, the customs, habits, history of the people, in order to elicit from the total situation its best possibilities in relation to the general principles of *The Social Contract*, with a warning of the inevitability of gradualness.

Rousseau is thought of today not as an eighteenth century political Geddes, but, rather, as an enemy of the human race,[30] father of our Hitlers, our political religions, our police states, the worse half of our democratic inheritance. No doubt there is much in his writings to give colour to this thesis. Probably his ideas for the regeneration of patriotism, on the evidence of his advice to Poland, were workable only in such terms as Mussolini or Hitler invented; but he himself would have disowned them and sought affinity rather with Hegel and with Sorel. His own disciples were not the capitalists for whom and the dynamic society of the future the Revolution made way, but the fanatics Robespierre and St Just who dreamed of putting back the clock to antiquity, for whom the Revolution had instituted the republic of equally independent small proprietors. The abortive but symbolic constitution of 1793[31] may reasonably be used to sum up Rousseau's practical political influence.

Rousseau was 'nothing if not a moralist'. The really influential part of his political thought, which as a system was a fantastic ruin,[32] was the general principle that men are morally ruined only politically and can therefore be morally saved only politically, that they always are only what the laws make them, and with that the principle that legitimate law is always the general will, the unanimous, or, at second-best, the majority, opinion of the whole people as equally independent individuals deliberating upon the general good. These were profound and revolutionary views, no doubt, as Diderot said of his own views, 'devilishly ideal', and perhaps amounting to an indictment of the human condition (Burke's justification), but they were informed by close acquaintance both with ideal social possibilities and with the evils of a society founded on appetites in which it was as difficult to practise virtue as in Hobbes's state of nature. At any rate, when Rousseau is among those blamed for an emancipating programme which has delivered over the world to the claims of unregenerate appetite, the answer is that he saw no possibility of a tolerable society that was not explicitly founded on the general will, that is to say, not the empirical will of the unregenerate individual, nor the sum of such wills, but the universal will of the higher permanent self, the kantian moral law, the public interest. And when he is blamed for the lead into totalitarianism, he gives his own answer: 'When a man renounces liberty he renounces his essential manhood. . . . There is no compensation possible for such complete renunciation.'*

4. THE ENGLISH FRUIT: UTILITARIANISM

The radical complex of ideas opposed by Burke, reviving the Greek idea of politics as a sphere of deliberate making, and using the old juridical idea of society as a contract, but shifting from the idea of a contract between monarch and people to the idea of the institution of society by a contract of equally independent individuals for mutual security and prosperity, included the notion that human behaviour is conditioned by human institutions, and rejected the belief that institutions were ordained either by divine ordinance or by human nature. Consequently, if the oppressive sectional interests created for themselves by rulers were thought away and the full mutuality of the original contractual situation recovered, the spontaneous general interest would be restored. Equally independent citizens deliberating on their common concerns would keep the rulers whom they appointed, subject to recall, from developing any alien sectional interest of their own. The identity of all interests in the public interest, including an identity of interests between rulers and ruled, would be consciously restored and consciously secured. On these conditions, there would be a spontaneous practice of virtue (otherwise more or less impracticable) because no interest at variance with the general interest would be allowed to take root. The notion of identity of interests, with its necessary conditions, is the central idea of the whole complex.

This complex of ideas is found in its fullness and richness in Rousseau; and it is tempered by his plain recognition that the necessary conditions of the necessary identity of interests can obtain only in simple face-to-face communities. Hume, on the other hand, who knew there was no pristine purity to restore and who could not be expected to admire contemporary rusticity,[33] thought that existing institutions established more or less satisfactorily a working identity of interests and that attempts at improvement should be made only with a trembling hand. Jeremy Bentham who said that he differed

* Social Contract, bk. i, chap. iv.

from Hume[34] in being anxious to show what *ought to be*, not content to account for what *is*, had no such illusions about a satisfactory working identity of interests. In showing what ought to be he provided rules and methods for the changes proposed.

Bentham attempted to make a science of morals, law, and politics by making a few simple assumptions. He assumed that men seek pleasure and avoid pain, and that the State exists to regulate human behaviour with a minimum of interference in order to create a harmony of selfish interests. If pleasure is what is good for its own sake (or what men call good and desire as good for its own sake), then equal amounts of pleasure are equally good whoever enjoys them, and the greatest happiness of the greatest number is the greatest good and the chief end of action. The borrowing and application of this criterion, the principle of utility, which proposed an ideal of the best society, brought order into chaos. It reduced moral and political questions to questions of fact capable of being settled by investigation: does the proposed action, law, or the existing institution produce in all probability more inconvenience than advantage, measured in terms of general happiness? With this objective attitude went a behaviouristic approach to politicians. The great men and families of the land who monopolized public office and kept politics personal could be treated not as Burke treated them, with veneration, but as Bentham treated them (on paper) like rats in a laboratory.*

As a student of law Bentham had early recognized the need for reform, both to introduce order into the chaos of laws and to extirpate the vested interest of the corporation of lawyers in obscurity and in costly procedures, the first example of those 'sinister' interests opposed to the general interest which it became his lifelong interest not merely to denounce but radically to prevent. He began by offering his inventions, intellectual and practical, to enlightened despots and oligarch parliaments, and thereby learning the hopelessness of reform by such means ended as a democrat and theoretician of the radical movement.[35]

'All establishments have commenced in times of ignorance: the first institutions could only be attempts more or less defective; but when experience renders their inconvenience sensible, the spirit of routine opposes itself to reform, and also prevents our perceiving the true sources of the evil': this is the Enlightenment looking at its

---

* 'The most favourable opportunities for legislation are those in which the two methods are so combined, that the punishment immediately follows the omission of the duty, and the reward its performance. This arrangement presents the idea of absolute perfection.' (*The Rationale of Reward*, chap. iv.)

inherited institutions, and going to the roots. But was not the British constitution matchless, the envy of the world?

'On no occasion, in no place, at no time, by no person possessing adequate power, has any such end in view as the establishing the greatest happiness of the greatest number been hitherto entertained: on no occasion on the part of any such person, has there been any endeavour, any wish for any happiness other than his own and that of his connexions, or any care about the happiness or security of the subject-many, any further than his own has been regarded as involved in it. . . . Among men of all classes, from the beginning of those times of which we have any account in history—an universal struggle and contention on the part of each individual for his own security and the means and instruments of his own happiness—for money, for power, for reputation natural and factitious, for constant ease and incidental vengeance. In the course of this struggle, under favourable geographical circumstances, this and that little security has been caught at, obtained, and retained by the subject-many, against the conjoined tyranny of the monarchy and his aristocracy. No plan pursued by anybody at any time—the good established, as well as the bad, remaining the result of an universal scramble, carried on in the storm of contending passions, under favour of opportunity—at each period, some advantages which former periods had lost, others, which they had not gained.'*

If indeed 'men are in every respect what the laws make them to be', there is some hope of altering the course of affairs which this reading of history reveals if one goes systematically about it. The politics of the time (Burke's politics) were still personal, county politics, in the hands of men of landed interests and local connexions. These politics of county 'interest' and 'connexion' and of the spoils of office and place, the politics of which Walpole had been an acknowledged master, had not absolutely excluded the possibility of spells of sound administration, but the rise of new interests and the growing complexity of affairs required political method. Bentham, though providing theoretical justification and direction for the radical movement, was no agitator, but the father of modern social legislation and its requisite procedures and institutions.

Nevertheless, agitation was required, since the effective part of the people in the constitution was diminishing fast, and 'that things should continue long in their present state seems absolutely impossible':

* *The Book of Fallacies.*

'in this faculty on the part of the many of creating uneasiness in the bosoms of the few—in this faculty on the part of those who suffer from abuses of creating uneasiness in the bosoms of those who profit by them—in this invaluable, and, except in America, un-exampled faculty—rests the only chance, the only source of hope.'*

The opposition of Bentham's political theory to Burke's, so opposed as it is at almost every point, and entirely in spirit, is nowhere more irreconcilable than in this reliance on the people to control the rulers, since Burke had come to think: 'The source of corruption is in the minds of the people; so rank and extensively seated is that corruption that no political reform can ever have any effect in re-moving it.'[36]

Of all human evils, Bentham argued, the evil of misgovernment is the most calamitous, since it is irresistible, for it turns against men the very means of their security and the condition of self-help. Therefore the constitutional part of law is by far the most im-portant and the most difficult: on this depend the quality and be-haviour of all officials. In order to put in office only men of powerful talents, public spirit, and great energy, they must be chosen by those whose interests will be affected by what they do, and they must remain answerable to these electors and removable and punishable by them, and their interest must be made to coincide with their duty. These were Tom Paine's principles, and it is on the example of America that Bentham relies. There is, he says, no possible rational argument against this leading principle of any constitution except impracticability, and the groundlessness of this objection has been demonstrated by the experience of the United States, which has shown the world the aptitude of the people and the practicability of democracy to produce general happiness.† He goes on to say that in any case this constitutional principle must be the model, because it offers a reasonable promise of permanence, whereas every other form of government has in its essence the seeds of its own dis-solution.

The composition of a political assembly will be dependent in this way upon the constitution, but even if it is fully representative it

* *The Book of Fallacies.*

† 'No other constitution is there, or has there been, under which, in anything like so small a degree (slave-purchasing and pertinaciously slave-holding States always excepted) the interest and happiness of the many have been sacrificed to those of the ruling and influential few: no other, under which what yet remains of that sinister sacrifice, will, with so little difficulty, and sooner or later with such perfect certainty, be abolished.' (*Leading Principles of a Constitutional Code for any State.*)

C

still is not capable of forming a general will unless it follows a proper methodical procedure.* In 1791 Bentham wrote an essay on parliamentary procedure for the National Assembly in Paris,† in which he showed how material the methodical manner of framing, moving, amending, debating, and voting upon a resolution was to the rational determination of the will of the assembly, exemplifying his argument by an analysis of the confused results of French practice compared with the results of English practice; and in order that not only the will of the assembled legislators should be methodically ascertained, but also that the legislators should be adequately informed of the will of the people as affected by a proposed law,[37] he showed how it should be made known to the public and time allowed for the relevant facts and representations to be presented to the legislators by the interested parties, and objections to the Bill published as amendments.

Whether or not the French had as much need of their schoolmaster as he supposed, their Declaration of Rights presented him with a broad target for his particular kind of pedagogic pedantry. 'Right' was an unmeaning word without a law to enforce it. In any case, the prefixing of a declaration of rights to a constitution showed a shocking lack of understanding. As a result of painstaking examination of innumerable laws and their operation, Bentham had classified all laws as (i) laws which take away from liberty in their immediate operation, and (ii) laws which in the same way destroy, in part or in whole, the operation of the former.[38] Therefore, in the nature of the case, fundamental law is an abstract digest of detailed laws, not a preliminary declaration. And such a declaration was useless.

'In short, when you have made such provision, that the supreme legislature can never carry any point against the general and per-

* 'Political liberty depends everywhere upon the free action and frequent and genuine manifestation of the public will: but the free action and genuine manifestation of that will, depend upon the mode of proceeding observed in going through the several steps that must be taken before any such result can be produced.' (An Essay on Political Tactics.)

† 'A political assembly, selected from the whole body of a great nation, were about to meet for the first time. Everything that concerned them was yet new to them: everything was yet to create. They were in the situation of a manufacturer, who besides the work that was the object of his manufacture, should find himself under the necessity of making the very tools he was to work with. The presenting the new manufacturers with a new set of tools, with a description of their uses—tools whose temper has been so well tried—was the object of the present design.' (An Essay on Political Tactics, note to chap. vi.)

severing opinion of the people, what would you have any more? What use in their attempt to bind themselves by a set of phrases of their own contrivance? The people's pleasure: that is the only check to which nothing can add anything, and which no other can supersede.'*

Therefore, ' "natural rights" is simple nonsense: "natural and imprescriptible rights", rhetorical nonsense — nonsense upon stilts'. He called it 'bawling upon paper' and 'terrorist language' — by contrast with the language of plain sense, of science.

For Bentham, although he could and did use strong language about the powers that be, was no revolutionary. He thought security more important than equality. He wanted to put an end to misgovernment and to establish the permanent conditions of good government by methodical reforms.

'One great merit in a good administration is that it proceeds gently in the reform of abuses — that it does not sacrifice existing interests — that it provides for the enjoyment of individuals — that it gradually prepares for good institutions — that it avoids all violent changes in condition, establishment and fortune.'

And when people say that anybody has a right to something, for example, that the poor have a right to the assistance of the community,

'then it is necessary to determine how this assistance ought to be levied and distributed: it is necessary to organize the administration which ought to assist the poor — to create the officers who ought to inquire into their necessities, and to regulate the manner in which the poor ought to proceed in availing themselves of their right.'

And he goes on to say:

'The relief of indigence is one of the noblest branches of civilization. In a state of nature, when we can form any idea of it, those who cannot procure food, die of hunger. There must exist a superfluity for a numerous class of society, before it is possible to apply a part of it to the maintenance of the poor. But it is possible to suppose such a state of poverty — such a famine that it will no longer be possible to supply bread to all who want it. How, then, can we convert this duty of benevolence into an absolute right? This would

* *Anarchical Fallacies.*

be to give the indigent class the most false and dangerous ideas: it would not only destroy all gratitude on the part of the poor towards their benefactors—it would put arms in their hands against all proprietors.'*

5. BURKE'S APOLOGIA

Burke was not a mere reactionary. He was not, for example, a High-Flyer, nor a Jacobite, nor a tory squire. He was not a renegade whig; he was and remained a parliamentarian, wedded to the settlement of 1689; he was to the end an 'old' whig, a moderate whig. In his spirited apologia *Appeal from the New to the Old Whigs* (1792), he insisted on the moderation of his politics. His moderation, however, was absolute, and intransigent: 'For there is no medium besides the medium itself.' Those who were not with him were against him; and not merely against him, against the country; in the last analysis, against God. At first, they might be misguided men, but persistence with opened eyes meant they were bad men, and then: 'There is no safety for honest men, but by believing all possible evil of evil men, and by acting with promptitude, decision, and steadiness on that belief.' That is the mainspring of his polemics. His moderation consisted in forcing the issue. Either you are loyally for the constitution or you are in favour of abolishing it for some scheme of imaginary perfection; and in that case you are out to abolish morality itself.

Burke is the patriot of a country which the radicals have renounced, and by doing so they have made themselves outlaws, under no authority, without morality, incapable of society: 'Our country . . . consists, in a great measure, in the ancient order into which we are born. . . . The place that determines our duty to our country is a social, civil relation.' The fascination of Burke is that he embodies and generates in the new age the old time; in helping to bring Europe to birth he revives the idea of Christendom; he expresses in the language of the age of reason the mystique of the age of faith. His position is based on five premises.

(1) The terms of morality cannot be changed, neither subtracted from nor added to; there are no inventions possible in morality; our duties are not subject to our wills. (2) These terms include the social relations historically established into which we are born. In England, the constitutional balance of crown, lords, and commons represents a moral harmony which is also a moral obligation.[39] The PEOPLE is not one element in this composition, still less an aggregate of all individuals; it is nothing less than the whole body acting with

* *Book of Fallacies.*

the co-ordinated movement of its several members. Every individual has his station and its duties in this nexus of social relations. These relations are outside our will and not subject to votes, since the votes of a majority of the people cannot alter the moral any more more than they can alter the physical essence of things. Only the consent of all the parties can alter the constitution. But no clear start is ever possible: we are inevitably born into relationships not of our own choosing, and to put in question the duties, trusts, engagements, obligations involved in such relationships, to dream of more rational arrangements, is in itself to abandon morality and destroy society. (3) This moral order is divinely provided: no possible good is to be obtained outside it. The basic Christian virtue is humility, submission to the terms of morality, doing our duty in the place assigned us without any thought of evasion or rebellion, without seeking easier terms for our appetites and desires. (4) This moral and divine order is also natural. The constituted authorities are natural authorities, the subordinates are naturally subordinate, and they are protected more than they are restrained. A natural *élite* is maintained in the offices of rulership and leadership which they are qualified to fill, and a natural social discipline is enforced. An aristocracy, so far from forming a separable interest alien from the general interest, is a constituent and essential part of the general interest: to give no more importance in the social order to such men than that of so many units is a horrible usurpation. (5) The only alternative to this moral order is the reign of appetite. If the many are loosed from their natural bonds of moral and social dependence, they do not become independent; they become the natural prey of impostors, the criminal elements who are always ready to seize power and to keep others out by violence. The many can always and easily be led to think they have more to gain by resort to arms than by industry, obedience, and frugality, but the defiance of authority is the hopeless defiance of reason and nature, for morality is as unchangeable as physics, and rebellion against natural authority and necessary obedience brings only enslavement to ruthless masters: if the coactive and coercive force of conscience does not reinforce our natural affections and loyalties and hold us in due subordination in a lawfully constituted hierarchy, we only allow ourselves to suffer present violence and ultimate perdition.

This argument appealed to the panic fears raised by the French Revolution, but it evaded altogether the main contentions of the radicals. Apart from his religious presuppositions, in which his whole argument was rooted and without which it withers away, there are three closely related points on which Burke fails to meet his opponents.

(1) The existing terms of morality were the results of past violence. That did not matter, as Hume recognized,[40] so long as they were in fact accepted, so long as they represented a still existing balance of power and were upheld by public opinion. But these terms were not something other than will, and therefore to make the sanctified will embodied in an established order rule out every question, all search for a rational principle of social order, to make the idea of inherited immutable obligation forbid the ideal of living agreement as the basis of morality, was disingenuous, if not plain error.

(2) It is in the appraisal of the actual state of affairs that the profoundest political differences occur. Burke found in the civil society of his time the source of all that was good and best, it was a partnership in every virtue and in all perfection. Rousseau found it an inescapable source of mutual depravity; and Bentham found in it a liability to calamity (misgovernment) worse than the insecurity of exposure to all natural risks: in both cases the evil was unnecessary, for its source was human and the remedy was prescribed. The remedy was clear and practicable. Hobbes had shown how men gained security one from another under a ruler; it was now necessary to complete this security by instituting control of the ruler: reciprocal control was the solution of the political problem. Granted with Plato and Aristotle (and Rousseau) that the good life could be lived only in the good society and that men could design their society for this purpose, following reason and nature, the treatment of the problem by Hobbes and Bentham was quite different in spirit from that of the Greeks. Plato had distinguished three alternative forms of the political situation: to do injustice and have to suffer it (Hobbes's state of nature); to be able to do injustice and not have to suffer it; neither to do nor to suffer injustice. The first, anarchy, was obviously intolerable. It is for the moral philosopher (Plato) to show why the scond which is desirable to most men is not in fact preferable to the third. Meanwhile, men, and classes of men, seize their opportunities of practising the desirable second alternative. It is not the business of the political philosopher (Bentham) to defend or to denounce their action, for his business is to show how it can be prevented, to devise the conditions on which men are not able to do injustice without having to suffer it.

If Burke is moralizing the second alternative as historically established and is insisting that it is the general interest and that to challenge it is to destroy the very notion of rights and duties, and if

Bentham is saying that these dominant interests are 'sinister' interests which frustrate the general interest which could and should be made to prevail by methodical ascertainment of the general will, and if Burke answers that this general interest is 'sinister' interests writ large and the total ruin of society, then, the same colour is being identified by one as black and by the other as white, and there seems no possibility of further argument.

(3) The radical alternative to Burke was not anarchy, a surrender to appetites followed by the ascendancy of the worthless and the ruin of all. The government of affairs was indeed a business, and it was possible and proper to make more businesslike arrangements: there were methods by which public offices could be kept filled only by men of ability, integrity, and energy, and without these methods there was no certainty they would be. When Burke argued that any government is administered only by men, that men will make mistakes, and mistakes may be aggravated by misfortune, and if that happens when people's minds have been unsettled by radical ideas, instead of waiting for a change of men, they will become disgusted with all public men and parties, and stake all hope of reform upon an alteration in the machinery, and that then radical ideas will come home to roost in a common ruin, he assumed that all methods of government are equally liable to produce misgovernment, that no machinery of government can be designed to minimize the liability to misgovernment by its operation in selecting, controlling, and replacing the agents of government. On the other hand, the radicals argued that a society founded on agreement and basic satisfactions (general happiness) and a government whose interest is made wholly to consist in maintaining that agreement and increasing those satisfactions, is both mechanically feasible and morally desirable, and greatly to be preferred to an inherited system in principle unjust and tending to produce misgovernment because concentrating power in the hands of those with privileged interests to defend and augment.

All the same, Burke's rhetoric was not 'nonsense upon stilts'. His objection to abstract reasoning about morals and politics, although untimely because there was then no way forward, no way out of the impasse created by his premises, was basically sound. Equally important, his argument was justified (in so far as it was justified) by his Christian faith, and is inseparable from it.

Anybody can see that existing power relations historically established may be moralized and humanized by the modifications of time and usage, and that they are altogether to be preferred to the raw relations instituted by new violence. But then it becomes extremely important to find ways and means by which to assimilate to that morality new claims and newly recognized dues, answering to shifts of power, changes in status, and growing enlightenment. If, however, you think that to wish to change your duties is the beginning of all evil, that to dream of unacknowledged rights is to conjure up the insatiable clamour of all appetites which throws the mind into the ferment of conflict or imprisons it in the sore pre-occupations of competition and shuts it out from grace which is only to be had in the stillness of due submission and becoming humility: then, like Pascal,[41] you will prefer peace to justice because peace may produce the fruits of the spirit, whereas justice is end-lessly postponed and the pursuit of it is the occasion and the excuse for all fret and strife. This is the ethos of a believing community. Burke denounces with contempt and fear the levelling spirit of John Ball, and the jacquerie and jacobins of all the ages, and his defence against them was to recall all men to the duties of their station, like Piers the Plowman, with moral equality here and divine justice hereafter. The issues are in God's hands, the redress is in heaven. This might in good faith be the basis of Langland's social philosophy, when the faith of the believing community on which it depended was not seriously in question; but when the seriousness of the age consisted in putting that faith in question, it was disingenuous to in-sist on Christian humility as the basis of political philosophy. In such a case, those who hold the faith can make their appeal honestly only on the terms of the epicureans or of the stoics, to come out of the world of strife and competition and live with moderation in the company of like-minded friends, or to choose for oneself uncondi-tionally the part of resignation. Europe in the eighteenth century was no longer Christendom, and Burke was guilty of the wilfulness he so sternly condemned. In Hobbes, Hume, and Bentham, and in Locke and Rousseau, one sees the shift of morals from a religious to a political basis; and this is capital. The ethics of Christian humility remain the ethics of the Church, the believing community, but the ethics of society are grounded in agreement, in mutuality, in the reconciliation of interests and the predominance of the general interest, guaranteed by social controls and sanctioned by satisfac-tion.[42] That is the meaning of all the talk of the rights of man, of happiness, and of liberty, equality, and fraternity.

Burke's eighteenth century language obscured his medieval posi-tion. Those who would revive him today are dreaming of a Golden Age: they are further, far, from addressing themselves seriously to serious problems of their time[43] than the eighteenth century rationalists whom they revile for utopian thinking. They can exploit a theme, they can score personal debating triumphs by playing on ignorance; they cannot restore Christendom, that is to say, a religious basis for social morality. Even a sober writer on *The Moral Basis of Burke's Political Thought** misses the point in his title. Burke's political thought is in the highest degree moral, certainly, but the moral sub-structure rests on religious foundations, and it is not opposed to the political thinking of the rationalists as moral to non-moral: it was opposed to theirs in taking different foundations for morality, which was, and remains, a capital distinction. Theirs was a political foundation, which set aside religious assumptions. Christendom had dissolved and society had become individualized, but moral behaviour was as natural and normal as necessary (dependability, faithful fulfilment of duties and engagements) if basic securities were politically guaranteed on a footing of mutuality. They either explained society by these principles or they designed society on these principles. On these principles, what were supposed to be natural propensities might have latitude only limited by what was required to allow others a like indulgence. The psychological assumptions might be extremely crude. Let each pursue pleasure and avoid pain. Let each be the sole judge of his own interests and be free to pursue his own happiness in his own way. Then, on this basis of equivalence, each to count for one and no one for more than one, a minimum of necessary legal restraints would secure a harmony of interests and the greatest happiness of the greatest number. The springs of action in this political model operated also the economic model that was being perfected at the same time. Mandeville exhibited the model in his *Fable of the Bees*: by the division of labour and the mechanism of the free market all were engaged by self-interest in mutual dependence and each in pursuing his own profit automatically produced the goods or services required to meet the needs of others. This self-regulating system, dependent on the automatic mechanisms of the market and the ballot box for producing and distributing goods and services and appointing and controlling rulers and officials, making the utmost use of available resources in material and personnel for all the purposes of society, and thus securing maximum satisfaction as the supreme sanction which reinforced its operaions, was the theoretical idealization and inspiration of a new world which definitively displaced the congeries of communities enclosed in the theocratic system of Christendom. This is what happened; and nobody can strike a balance of advantage and disadvantage.

The crude psychology of Bentham's system was already dis-

* Charles Parkin: Cambridge, 1956.

credited, for Shaftesbury and Hume had corrected Hobbes, and Rousseau was abundantly a more subtle and modern psychologist than any of them, even in social psychology. But Bentham's simple abstractions[44] served the needs of the time in social theory more adequately than the more adequate psychology, something not unknown in science. And all of them based their morals either on a political foundation (Hobbes, Rousseau) or else on natural propensities (differently specified) reinforced and regulated by political arrangements. This capital difference between a religious and a political foundation for morals cannot be too strongly emphasized: it is the difference of incompatibles, theocracy and democracy.

6. THE MODEL APPLIED

The notion that Burke was a reactionary, an isolated figure, the voice of a lost cause, resisting modern ideas and the inevitable trends which they heralded and shaped, is today challenged; and it is suggested that he spoke and speaks for the age-old characteristic English way of thinking and feeling about political questions. However that may be, it was Bentham's thought-model which on the whole prevailed in the nineteenth century and Bentham's methods which were adopted.[45]

The grand design of *laissez-faire* democracy, based on natural laws and rational methods, was the fullest employment of productive energies in all industrial and professional tasks as well as in all public offices, by the reward of only efficient self-dependent and dependable persons, and by the punishment with loss of independence of all those who proved undependable or failed in self-dependence. Extreme defenders of this drastic system of social individualism have always said that it has never properly been tried. That is true. But it does not follow that only human perversities or vested interests have stood in the way of a fair trial. The simplicity of the system leaves out too much that has to be reckoned with in all practical policies. Nevertheless, this thought-model had, and has, validity. The reform of parliamentary representation, the reform of commercial laws and institutions for the facility of enterprise and business, the opening of the public service to competition, the dismantling of privilege and the emancipation of the individual were measures inspired or hastened by this ideal. Reform never went so fast nor so far as the Radicals wanted: the monarchy, the Lords, the Church establishment survived; universal franchise and the ballot were delayed. But such survivals and delays are in the nature of politics; and the survivals were more or less adapted to the new conditions and the postponed instalments were milestones on the in-evitable gradualness of any undertaken journey.

The Reform Act of 1832 initiated the modern age of social legis-lation.[46] The statutes which followed (the Poor Law, Factory, Edu-cation, Public Health, Constabulary, and Local Government Acts), although there were ancient precedents, brought in a new phase of creative parliamentary activity in the course of which the govern-ment assumed the monopoly of parliamentary business. This social legislation did not differ in design from the political and commercial reforms: the purpose in both cases was to prosper the self-dependent and dependable person, in the former case, the worker, the ultimate agent of production. Beginning with the bold report of the Royal Commission on the Poor Laws (1834), there was a great series of inquiries inspired by parliament, by means of which the related aspects of the social problem were looked at throughout the nine-teenth century. The creed of individualism was a mockery unless the self-dependent and dependable worker was enabled, for himself and his family, to keep in health and in work, to save, to get suitable education, and to enjoy his property in peace. These simple pre-suppositions required far-reaching complex public measures: the policing of the country, large-scale engineering works for sanitation and water supply, building regulations, factory laws, educational provisions, facilities and guarantees for insurance and saving. To these large needs the Benthamite formula was largely applied: in-vestigate, legislate, inspect, report. On the whole, the best practice was discovered and publicized, and eventually by compulsion made the standard for the country. But this process of consolidation, simplification, and standardization of both law and administration was complicated and delayed by the diversity of conditions in the various industries, by the number and variety and inadequacy of local authorities, by vested interests, and by political rivalries. More or less, a coherent social system adequate to modern needs based on simple agreed principles applied by uniform and efficient methods was achieved piecemeal in the course of the nineteenth century, combining more or less judiciously the voluntary principle and compulsion, local and central authorities, expert and amateur.

'More or less' must be used to qualify an achievement which was composed of old and new elements, paternalism and individualism, traditional ways and rational methods, yet emerging into coherence by propagating success. Undoubtedly, the legislative and administra-tive foundations of our modern highly organized welfare state were definitely laid in the nineteenth century under the dispensation of political and economic individualism,[47] and the most decisive social changes in our history took place then and not before nor since. The Fabians were the direct heirs of the Benthamites, and were associated with the Liberals as the Radicals had been with the Whigs until the Labour Representation Committee was formed in 1900; but the social service state was not a simple result of the pressure of organized Labour nor of the mass vote, for it followed consistently from the measures adopted deliberately to enable the worker to be industrious and thrifty, self-dependent and self-advancing, a competent and competitive agent of production. The premises of individualism could not be established in practice unless and until the worker enjoyed fundamental protection and opportunity, was sure of the rewards of self-help, could separate himself from the destitute, could count on the safety of his savings, could keep himself in health, could be safe from depredations, could educate his children, could be preserved from being driven to overwork. Such elementary social securities, made necessary by the destruction of the old communal self-sufficiency and the collection of masses of individuals in factories and towns, required administrative innovations on a national scale. Later on, the pressure of organized labour and the seduction of mass electorates, grievous experience of prolonged mass unemployment, and the expediencies created by two world wars in which the people as a whole were actively involved, facilitated and accelerated the development of social services, but deepdown their roots were embedded in the requirements of an industrial system based on individualism.

By mid-century[48] radical and liberal thinkers were dismayed to find that individualism engendered collectivism. Already, the great collectives were sketched-in which in our time have been filled out: the trade union and the big corporation, the political party, the bureaucracy, the pressure group, the State. The individual was beginning to feel imprisoned within these collectives, for their effectiveness demanded complete loyalty and he found it increasingly difficult to maintain his independence. The thinking of the eighteenth century, so short a time before, had been directed to the emancipation of the individual, as a citizen of the world, arranging his own private affairs and taking a hand in the management of public affairs, unorganized, a representative of 'man in general'. Social institutions were to be remodelled to suit the rational aims of the emancipated and enlightened individual, and already the new order was turning into its opposite; the emancipated individual was in danger of becoming more enslaved than ever, and by the logical development of the initiative and ideals of individualism, for trade unionism was the means of self-help, the political party was the necessary result of a universal franchise, big business came out of competition, the dominance of a standardized mass public opinion followed universal literacy exploited by a commercial press and the assimilation of habits to a uniformity of goods and services, the nation state was organized in the competition for world trade and empire, and the bureaucracy was required by the unavoidable enlargement of the area of public responsibility and public interest. Each of these developments has a literature of protest and lament, but in each case the causes of what was deplored were beyond control, worse, were inextricably bound up with the ideals and purposes of the liberal and enlightened previous generation. Thus social freewill was displaced by social determinism,[49] individualist rationalism by historical thinking, Condorcet by Comte, Bentham by Marx — as Kant by Hegel. Men were, indeed, 'in every respect what the laws make them to be', only the laws are not devices and institutions of their own making, but the laws of nature and of history. Social intentions and acts were intelligible only by historical interpretation, and rational only in so far as in conformity with historical necessities.

The uneasy observation of the unforeseen consequences of individualism was not a clear if reluctant recognition of inevitability, and whilst the sun gradually flooded a new phase of political reflection it continued to shine on yesterday's thinking, and the day before yesterday's. Collectivist trends were attributed by critics to mistaken or perverse policies. Meanwhile, the work of emancipation and enlightenment went on also; the wheat and the tares grew up together. The nineteenth century was, in mid-career, a period of large transformations, and the sense of this, a sense of the complexity of issues and the inevitablity of big social changes, moderated opinion: one-sided minds[50] had reigned earlier, or were to prevail later. Peel, Gladstone, Disraeli were deeply conservative yet moving minds, attached to the institutions of the country yet ready to move with the times, and they formed and led the main administrations in the creative political work of the century. The young Mill was fascinated by the idea of combining Bentham with Coleridge (the heir of Burke). Comte had partly defined theoretical Positivism as the outcome of a union of opposites, Condorcet and de Maistre.[51] Acton combined loyalty to the Catholic Church with Croce's passionate dedication to the irreplaceable religion. Matthew Arnold's persiflage as a social critic expressed his mission to moderate the pretensions of everybody, to make room for the play of mind, to make current

and make prevail the best that has been thought and said, to argue
that perfection must be the perfection of all sides of our humanity
and of all parts of our society.

In spite of confusion and of doubts, the programme of the
eighteenth century thinkers was carried out, the work of enlightenment and emancipation went on, and still goes on: the emancipation
of slaves, of women, of children, of colonial peoples; the humane
and scientific treatment of the destitute, the deprived, the sick,
mental and physical defectives, lunatics, and delinquents.

7. THE MODEL DECRIED

The inadequacy of the political premises of Radicalism had early
been pointed out by some radicals: the assumption that to get rid of
the dominance of 'sinister' interests, to establish the sovereignty of
the people, would be to restore the general interest, and thus to solve
the political problem outright. Paine had assumed that the complicated checks and balances of a liberal constitution were simply required by, and perpetuated, an unnecessarily bad situation: correct
the initial position, abolish the independent position and alien interests of hereditary rulers, and there was no need for complications;
control by the people was direct and efficient. Turgot, the able and
progressive minister under the *ancien régime*, in a letter to the
English radical Richard Price, complains of this assumption by
republican writers, 'for certainly every individual has his rights, of
which the nation cannot deprive him, except by violence and an un-
lawful use of the general power'.

Later, J. S. Mill, in his *Logic* (bk. vi, chap. viii), pointed out that on
logical grounds Bentham and James Mill were in error in making
accountability (in order to ensure the identification of the interest
of the government with that of the people) the necessary and sufficient principle of good government: some absolute governments
had been good governments, in this sense. He excused his father and
Bentham by saying that to make parliament more representative
was in the given circumstances of the time requisite for increasing
the sense of identity of interests between rulers and ruled. Elsewhere, he elaborated this apology for extreme Radicalism.* But he

* 'It is very conceivable that such a doctrine should find acceptance from
some of the noblest spirits, in a time of reaction against the aristocratic
governments of modern Europe; governments founded on the entire sacrifice
(except so far as prudence, and sometimes humane feeling interfere) of the
community generally, to the self-interest and ease of a few. European reformers have been accustomed to see the numerical majority everywhere un-
justly depressed, everywhere trampled upon, or at the best overlooked, by

himself felt strongly the need for an analysis of 'the general interest' for any properly philosophical theory of government. He was impressed by Comte's criticism of the *philosophes* for their abstract treatment of social questions, neglecting the all-important context of historical development in which existing institutions were to be studied before they could be understood and reformed. Society could not be resolved into a number of equivalent individuals sharing a general interest which was safe in the hands of their appointed representatives accountable to them, and violated if left to the mercy of independent rulers with 'sinister' interests of their own. Nor was 'the general good' necessarily the resultant of the individual pursuit of enlightened self-interest in a commercial market. In the early years of his critical reaction against Benthamism, he was ready to follow Comte, in thinking that 'the general good' might consist primarily in the maintenance of such historically continuing needs of society as Permanence and Progress adequately and consciously represented and maintained in abiding institutions. He was enthusiastic about Coleridge's new version of Burke's conservatism (or of Plato's utopianism), the heritable landed interest standing for permanence, the industrial and professional classes for progress and social mobility, and the 'clerisy' for culture and civilization.[52] He learned also at this time to recognize that some regular social conditioning, education in the principles and spirit of the constitution, social cohesion engendering and engendered by patriotism, adherence to something settled in the social order which evoked unquestioned loyalty and was the accepted basis of calculations and of hopes and aims (which he thought in the modern world would not be ancient laws nor religious beliefs but, rather, individual freedom and political and social equality embodied in appropriate institutions) were all necessary to the good society. His fears that the sovereign people might mistakenly seek to take into their own hands the specialized functions of legislation, executive government, and

governments; nowhere possessing power enough to extort redress of their most positive grievances, provision for their mental culture, or even to protect themselves from being taxed avowedly for the pecuniary profit of the ruling classes. To see these things, and to seek to put an end to them, by means (among other things) of giving more political power to the majority, constitutes Radicalism; and it is because so many in this age have felt this wish, and have felt that the realization of it was an object worthy of men's devoting their lives to it, that such a theory of government as Bentham's has found favour with them. But, though to pass from one form of bad government to another be the ordinary fate of mankind, philosophers ought not to make themselves parties to it, by sacrificing one portion of important truth to another.' (*Mill on Bentham and Coleridge*, ed. by F. R. Leavis, p. 85; London, 1950.)

administration over which they had indisputable authority, and for which they had no competence, and his fears of the reductive pressures of a uniform and despotic Public Opinion did not worry him into a retreat from radical principles but braced him to embrace their consequences and to prepare against the dangers of the new world which the Radicals had helped to bring to birth but which had been fathered by no school nor party.

Not only the political assumptions but also the economic assumptions of the model were eventually put in question. Malthusian gloom enveloped the speculations of the economists at the beginning of the century, and ruled out the idea of economic equality: if the profitable employment of land, capital, and raw materials was limited, the profitable employment of labour was limited, and if the supply of labour exceed this limit nothing could prevent the wretchedness of the labourer. The illimitable expansion of trade and industry as the century went on seemed to prove that the premise was unnecessary which had yielded this pessimistic conclusion. On the other hand, the optimistic conclusion from the main economic assumption that in a state of free competition, in the long run, all resources would be kept fully and most advantageously employed also lacked its operative premise. The world of pure competition like the frictionless world of Newtonian mechanics was an ideal postulate for the formulation of uniformities, but the world of actual economic behaviour was more complicated than the world of actual mechanical operations. The natural market of free trade for competitive industry became as highly organized as everything else: to the pulls and pressures of supply and demand were added those of monopolies and trade unions, fiscal and monetary policies, social and national exigencies. After the first world war, John Maynard Keynes was writing *The End of Laissez-faire* (1926); and ten years later, his major essay in revision *The General Theory of Employment, Interest, and Money* (1936), a title chosen to point the contrast with the *classical* theory. Nearly twenty years later than this, an equally liberal and intelligent American economist, John Kenneth Galbraith, has published his analysis *American Capitalism* (1952), in which he proposes 'the concept of countervailing power' for the classical concept of pure competition, and in which the title of one of his chapters is 'The Abandonment of the Model'.

This pilgrim's progress of the orthodox, who had resisted so long all temptations to rewrite the gospel (the typical employment of the damned and the deranged in the sociological underworld), really began with the Slough of Despond in the 1930's, the chronic mass unemployment which afflicted all the industrial capitalist societies. 'Autarky' was the word invented in those years to give the assurance of doctrinal mastery in the alarming experience of international struggle for an increasing share of diminishing trade returns. The precarious liabilities of a money economy having been revealed, the world knew that the automatic self-regulation of the trade cycle of inflation and deflation could not be trusted any more. Whether or not economists can and will quickly enough gain reliable knowledge and statesmen and businessmen can and will find the skill and public spirit to run successfully a managed economy still remains to be seen. But 'the abandonment of the model' has taken place, the big corporations, public or private, have come to stay, and insecurity in the midst of theoretically dubious but amazing empirical success is the climate of capitalism in the country of its most confident exponents.[53] Economic and social thinking are ceasing to be concerned with the preservation of the conditions of a system which secured the steady expansion of wealth and opportunity and are becoming preoccupied with the preservation of individual freedom and the public interest in a pattern of powerful organizations which hold the monopoly of wealth and opportunity.[54]

Not only were the political and economic assumptions underlying the model soon put in question, but also the underlying human assumptions were vigorously attacked. The aridity of a merely business creed which made utility and efficiency the ultimate standards of judgement and reduced all values to market values and all motives to the commonest appetites was scorned and denounced by intellectuals and aesthetes and social prophets throughout the nineteenth century. Germany was the source of early criticism. The individualism and, in its early form, the dualism of social contract theory had failed to do justice to the unity and majesty of the State, and it was this idea which in the nineteenth century was explored and exploited in theory and practice in Germany. The German metaphysicians of the grand manner in the evolution of their high school gaits or in romantic exercises on the great horse might be expected to look down on the pedestrian utilitarian philosophy of the English. 'Man does not aspire to happiness; only the Englishman does that.'[55] The sneer might not be unmixed with resentment at the pioneer advancement of England into national wealth and political empire. But there were English thinkers who found their moral home in Germany. The gospel of Thomas Carlyle was learned there, and its bottom secret was abandonment of the ignoble pursuit of happiness.

D

Coleridge was the other pioneer of the infusion of German thought into England. Both influenced the young Mill when he was feeling most oppressed by the one-sidedness of the doctrine in which he had been bred.[56] Matthew Arnold, operating the categories of Hellenism and Hebraism, and lightly scourging Barbarians, Philistines, and Populace, is relying on Germany when he comes to his most positive ideas for the future and enlarges on the creative role of the State.[57] Blake, Ruskin, Pater, Wilde, Morris, Carpenter, all the wits and artists, were rebels and critics, returning to the middle ages or the renaissance or to classical antiquity or projecting themselves into utopia, in order to escape from the age of Progress.

Perhaps disgust is the occupational disease of the intellectual. Perhaps he is only the playboy of the western world, a moral orphan not the social mentor. At any rate, his alienation from the regnant virtues and values of bourgeois society inevitably made his work increasingly destructive or esoteric.[58] Bourgeois virtues and values are being displaced by those of the masses. The alienation of the artist and the intellectual continues, though changed. Some think that it is the prime symptom of social malaise.

8. NEW MODEL

The evident inadequacies, political, economic, and cultural, of *laissez-faire* democracy demanded an alternative philosophical model, for the trouble was with the basic assumptions and the total ethos of the system. In the new thinking, the ideas of historical development and collectivism displaced the ideas of rationalism and individualism.[59]

Whereas the rationalist radicals had designed their model on the assumed behaviour of the individual, in order to reform society on a rational plan, the philosophers of the new model set out to explain the phenomenon of historically determined social change, in order that conduct and policies might be brought into conformity with rational understanding of the laws of history. These laws of social change were the laws of a cosmic model, and no model of human device however soundly constructed on mechanical principles could survive in opposition to them. The theoreticians of *laissez-faire* democracy had not produced an industrial nor a political revolution, and could not do any such thing: all they had done was to rationalize what they had found going on; but superficially. To make a proper analysis required an historical survey and the formulation of developmental laws. Intelligent action and rational control were limited to conformity with such laws.

The confluence of such currents of thought in Marx influenced the stream of tendency decisively, though by underground channels. It was Marx who fully took over the aims of the radicals and the promise of the new economic machine and embodied them in a system of thought with which he intended totally to replace the liberal politico-economic system. He derided the naivety of utopian socialists and liberal democrats, but he was himself utopian and liberal. Social change depended on technological change in methods of economic production. Analysis of the existing phase of mass production by machines in factories owned by capitalists showed what the next phase was bound to be. By the survival of the fittest in a competitive system, ownership would be concentrated in fewer and fewer hands, and the sectional interests of these private owners would ignore the consumer needs of the masses who anyhow were prevented by the law of wages from having the money to buy what they produced or its equivalent. This central contradiction, with the inevitably increasing misery of the masses and monopoly of the owners, must sooner or later result in the proletariat's taking the economic machine into their own hands, and for that purpose in their smashing the military and bureaucratic machines which the possessing economic class used to operate the State in their own interest. Thus the bourgeois revolution was followed inevitably by the proletarian revolution, which was historically decisive, for the result would be, once for ever, the establishment of the general interest at the hands of the proletariat who *alone* were interested, and solely interested, in community production for community consumption. Thus contemptuously rejecting the abstract individual and abstract general interest of the rationalist radicals, Marx recovered for radicalism the dynamics of concrete interests of actual classes, and promised to radicalism, as an historically determined achievement, the independent individual and the general interest whole and undefiled.

The triumph of Marx was later; the nineteenth century was the reign of his philosophical master Hegel. In the last decades of the century, the professorial socialism dominant in German universities since Fichte and Hegel came to Britain, for the Neo-Hegelians who then displaced the Utilitarians as the ascendant school, if not themselves socialists, encouraged the type of political thinking which favoured socialism and bred socialists.[60]

Hegel's immense philosophical preoccupation with the self-consciousness of modern man, human disintegration by specialization into aspects and functions of culture (science, art, religion) as well as into classes and individuals, collected and posed again in its historical complexity the problem of man in society which the British philosophical conservative burked. Like Rousseau, he romanticized the Greek commonwealth and the legislator of genius, and found here in the imagined coincidence of individual will with universal purpose the clue to the restoration of unity in totality. The State does not exist by contract for the utilitarian purpose of protecting property and personal freedom: its existence, interests, and capabilities transcend those of the individuals who compose it, and who enjoy genuine individuality, objective interests, and ethical capability solely in virtue of their membership of it. The political union of a nation state under a strong central government which left everything else free enabled the citizen consciously to identify himself with his people and therein with the ongoing life of humanity moving to a consummation of self-conscious unity and totality. Such an absolute government is divine, self-sanctioned and not made. The universal will with which it is the supreme happiness of each to be identified is not the mere will of the ruler nor the will of a majority; it is the disinterested public opinion which does not make laws but reveals them. Such a general will is not fabricated in a general assembly by the machinery of representation and methods of procedure; rather, it is the voice of experience, the counsel of the Aged and the Priests, elements purged of the appetites of active interests; and the law itself no longer merely defines individual privileges and so-called liberties, but subordinates and organizes, and corrects and completes itself. Three social classes are fitted to embody an absolute political order of this kind: the peasantry, the industrial classes, and a nobility wholly devoted to public duties. The bourgeois, with his tendency to reduce all law to contract and all values to money and to disregard all ties but the cash nexus, is the symbol of degeneracy; and with him is branded the radical who agitates for political rights and would reduce the government to impotence, or impose majority rule, unstable and incapable of creating the organic unity of the State.

Hegel's theocratic nationalism might be identified with the political absolutism combined with a free culture which under the domination of Prussia became the pattern of German social life. Germany was the progressive example of the nineteenth century,[61] as England and France had been earlier. If her political absolutism was not universallly admired, her universities were unrivalled in prestige and attraction, and her pioneer social services were studied and copied. And even in the haunts of liberalism there was new thinking about the positive role of the State. In England, neglecting the schools, one could not do better than choose Matthew Arnold (fortified by his practical experience of Prussian education) to represent vividly and humanely this new phase in social thinking. The service state, not the police state, the civil unity of the nation, was to be the organ through which choice spirits drawn from all classes, generous and humane souls, lovers of man's perfection, detached from class prepossessions, might work upon the whole body politic. The State is the focus of national culture and the promoter of its development, through men who combine a passion for education and the public service to which they devote their lives and their best thought, with that profound belief in the possibilities of human nature and the value of human personality which is the heart of the democratic creed. To such men, education and the public service, both growing more liberal with each generation, and embracing a larger and larger proportion of the best and brightest spirits of the time, are the chariot-wheels of civilization, the meaning of which is not power or wealth, or even the conquest of nature, but simply the adorning and ennobling of the spirit of man.

Others, pre-eminently Croce, polarized Hegel's thought in a liberal interpretation of history.

'There is no philosophy of history in the sense of a pre-determined plan or of a Hegelian dialectic, but there is an ever developing ever renewed pattern grouped about the central, eternal, truth of liberty as a moral ideal and a moral need, never to be finally forgotten or suppressed, never satisfied with less than its real personal force and liberating quality. The eager critical constructive labour of the mind in liberty is the historical force, the irreplaceable religion. Politics can never be static, a perfected administration founding a free culture as in Germany; they must be for ever dynamic, ethical: in the nature of things political liberty is a good never established, a perpetual moral task.'

The nineteenth century tide of philosophic faith has ebbed in the West, and perhaps elsewhere. Where the army advanced exultantly there is a neglected graveyard. We have seen the prophecies. About the year 1870, the people of Europe saw

'. . . a State that had rejected popular government, based itself on authority, taken its rulers only from above, and was obtaining such triumphs as no other state in Europe had the ability or the audacity to challenge; a state perfect in its mechanism and in its administrative work, and a people that was the best taught and the richest in knowledge and learning of all the peoples of the world, and before whom there was unfolding as well a vast field of activity in economic production and commerce.'*

We have seen the German Empire. We have seen the proletarian revolution. We have seen the national leaders and the 'ethical' state, the new republic.

Not only that: the theories have lost their intellectual rank. The biological analogy deceives nobody now, the philosophy of history is aged and destitute, the grand cosmic abstractions are logically disgraced with the assumptions of the rationalists they displaced. Hegel was perhaps the most prolific of philosophical fathers, but his progeny have had their day and the family is extinct.[62]

9. THE PRESENT DISCONTENTS

There is, then, neither paradise nor utopia; and the thinking which borrowed a meaning for the world from paradise or utopia is bankrupt. That would not matter much, that might be a good thing, if any reasonable confidence remained in any method of controlling human affairs, if we had not already seen tried out all the hopeful ideas. We are terribly frightened, because we know we have lost or destroyed ancient restraints and hopes and have released tremendous energies which are forcing the pace and scale of social changes we are powerless to prevent. We have no longer any reason for faith in God's providence, in man's power of social invention, nor in the laws of historical development; there is every reason for our having lost the faith we have had in God, in man, and in nature. The undoubted powers we increasingly own by means of science and collective organization are powers by which we are threatened, of which we are victims. The liberal emancipation which destroyed the old collectives which were systems of restraint, humanized by age-old customs, dignities, consolations, and gratifications, and which was to have produced an enlightened society of free and equal individuals, inevitably did produce the new collectives which are organized appetites, the nation state, the trade union, the political party, the giant corporation, and which engender and maintain destructive conflict by the logic of their function, institutionally compelling the individual to become the victim of his insatiable appetites, thus standing on its head the rationalist's concept that in society men enforce on one another the long-term and permanent interests which they share, making the harmony of laws prevail over

* B. Croce: *History of Europe in the 19th Century*. Trans. H. Furst (London, 1934), p. 255.

the jungle of appetites. If there is a philosophy of history it is bitterly ironical, for it has to explain how societies put an end to the state of nature and proceed to reproduce its terrors and dilemmas some thirty, some sixty, some a hundredfold.

Science, which was to have done away with superstition and magic and the arbitrary ascendancy of the privilege of birth, and was to have given men the sure means of meeting their needs and solving their problems, has become itself a problem, not only by its impact on military technology but also in its large-scale unintended consequences. The theories of historical development, the scientific proletarian revolution, the self-regulating democratic industrial system, the slow progress of social evolution, cannot be relied on to solve or banish these problems. Governments become more nearly omnipotent over their subjects and more nearly impotent in the face of economic fluctuations and the menace of total war. The individual is imprisoned within the collectives which give him the only power he has and create the vicious system of which he is a helpless victim.

Without science, that is to say, without either a reliable and efficacious method or the assurance of reassuring knowledge, man is left a prey to all the primitive fears of a world of which he is no master; and in this case the fears are aggravated by a thoroughly awakened self-consciousness, and a too clear-sighted view both of the nature and extent of human helplessness and of the dangers which are all too likely to prove disastrous.

This is not a speculative view of the present situation. The symptoms of panic, gross or subtle, are widespread. There has been a revival of interest in gloomy prophets not much heeded in their nineteenth century day, in particular, Kierkegaard and Nietzsche, with the displacement of the optimistic Idealism of European philosophy by an Existentialism which insists that a man is a problem, and which is preoccupied with the actualities of the individual's situation and the permanence of his predicament, the problems, limits, and contradictions which constitute his inescapable, perhaps irredeemable, lot.[63] There is a revival of interest in religious faith, not only in Christianity but also in Buddhism[64] and in religious speculation largely inspired by Jungian psychology. Within Christianity, there is an end to Modernism, a revival of confidence in regard to science, a rediscovery of the relevance of biblical concepts and biblical language to the rediscovered human predicament,[65] a fresh and tentative protestant approach to the modern world with the recently stale resources of theological salvation.

Then there is the Revolt of the Moderates,[66] the disillusionment

with or fear of political parties or governments, the will to support
no party and no policy consistently and wholeheartedly, the revolt
which makes it difficult for a democratic government to deal realistically with serious problems, apt to set up a vicious downward spiral
into anarchy. With these go the young men for whom the lesson of
modern life is caution, who are therefore prepared to buy security
with conformity, whose low-pressure doubt is perfectly compatible
with orthodoxy. In their justification is the modern linguistic
analysis at work in the land of political theory, which has systematically reduced each stately ancestral pile to a heap of silly words.[67]

On the English side of the Atlantic the legend of the 'angry young
men' continues the story, in so far as they are angered by the lost
ideals of socialism or the miserable deceptions and boring futilities
of humanism. The Outsider, sickened by the social reverberations
which come from a hollow core, seeks to galvanize his will to will,
to inspire himself with an indefinite idealism.[68] Finally, without deriding abstract art, one can mention 'the demon of progress', the
tendency to destructiveness and sterility, the breaking of the nuptial
tie with the natural world.[69]

The chiaroscuro of the contemporary scene includes the healthy
disregard of the masses for all serious ideas by which nervous minds
represent to themselves the state of the world, and the still sanguine
thoughts of partisans whose minds run on programmes and polls.
One can agree that malaise is the natural state of the intellectual,
living under the pale cast of thought; but when all is put into the
picture, it is seen to be true that in this scientific age those who are
playing with magic or flirting with faith or just keeping their fingers
crossed are justified by the failure of scientific theory to offer now
any reliable method of control or any reassuring prospect; whereas
neither the careless and ignorant masses can contribute anything but
their indifference and drift nor the confident doctrinaires anything
but headstrong blindness. The utopias are all nightmares, the gospels
are all sells.[70]

NOTES: CHAPTER I

1. *A Conservative Interpretation of History:*
   Russell Kirk's *The Conservative Mind* (London, 1954) is a source book for
   this theme. Another, from a Catholic point of view, is Erik von Kuehnelt-
   Leddihn's *Liberty or Equality* (London, 1952). Irving Babbitt's *Democracy
   and Leadership* (Boston, 1924) is the view of a cultural critic of democracy
   who does not use the religious argument.
      On the historical side, Carl L. Becker's *The Heavenly City of the
   Philosophers* (New Haven, 1932) is a lively attempt to show that
   eighteenth century *philosophes* were followers of thirteenth century

schoolmen, rebuilding the City of God with more up-to-date materials, but in the same style. J. L. Talmon's *The Origins of Totalitarian Democracy* (London, 1952) has sign-posted the route from eighteenth century premises to twentieth century conclusions. Charles Frankel's *The Case for Modern Man* (London, 1957) includes a spirited defence of the *philosophes* and a rehabilitation of the tradition of the Enlightenment, against the defeatism and religious revivalism of characteristic contemporary 'liberals'. Herbert W. Schneider's *Three Dimensions of Public Morality* (Bloomington, 1956) is a critical re-examination of 'Liberty, Equality, Fraternity', the political faith of the Enlightenment, with a first chapter on present claims and counter-claims. Another good American restatement is Henry Alónzo Myers's *Are Men Equal?* (New York, 1945; Ithaca & London, 1955).

B. E. Lippincott's *Victorian Critics of Democracy* (London, 1938) studies an earlier phase of conservative reaction. See also Walter E. Houghton's *The Victorian Frame of Mind, 1830-1870* (New Haven & Oxford, 1957).

The origins of the debate, the transition from Bossuet to Voltaire, is the subject of Paul Hazard's *La crise de la conscience européenne, 1680-1715* (Paris, 1935). A profounder but more specialized treatment is R. W. Meyer's *Leibnitz and the Seventeenth-Century Revolution* (Cambridge, 1952).

A psychological study of the theme is to be found in Peter Nathan's *Retreat from Reason* (London, 1955), and a sociological study in Pitrim Sorokin's *The Crisis of our Age* (New York, 1946). A Protestant exploitation of the theme is J. V. Langmead Casserley's *The Bent World* (Oxford, 1955).

2. *and America:*
   see H. A. Myers, op cit., pp. 115-23.

3. *the waters have turned:*
   Langmead Casserley, op. cit., p. 209.

4. *the vaticinations have been vindicated:*
   Russell Kirk, op. cit., pp. 31-2.

5. *Although this philosophical conservative:*
   for this paragraph, see Russell Kirk, p. 411 to the end.

6. *an elegiac note:*
   discernible in Basil Willey, especially in *Christianity Past and Present* (Cambridge, 1952).

7. *finally:*
   the first part of the paragraph is Carl Becker's picture. The general theme of the whole section is contemporary rewriting of history by resurgent conservatives who have assimilated the liberal ideal and stand in four-square opposition to marxist communism, ignoring democratic socialism as 'a book without words'.

8. *The Whig interpretation:*
   Macaulay certainly believed that radical thought appealed to the appetites, but then he did not idealize the *ancien régime*.

9. *exclaimed against . . . the opposition:*
   in a letter to Eugene Stoffels. Tocqueville's masterpiece, *L'Ancien Régime et la Revolution* (J. P. Mayer's ed., Paris, 1952-3), is still irreplaceable.

10. *read historically:*
    Georges Lefèbvre's *The Coming of the French Revolution* (trans. by R. R. Palmer, Princeton & Oxford, 1947) is a summary account of the origins and first phase of the Revolution, with an analysis of the Declaration; sig-

nificantly, the Vichy authorities destroyed this book, a fruit of the life-work of the foremost living historian of the Revolution.

11. *timely popular violence:*
the composition and action of the revolutionary crowds in Paris from 1787 to 1795 has been studied by George Rudé, *The Crowd in the French Revolution* (Oxford, 1959). For a vivid and unforgettable (if imaginative) impression of the revolutionary impact of a French popular uprising, there is nothing to match Lamartine s *History of the Revolution of 1848* (Bohn's Standard Library, 1849). Christopher Hibbert's *King Mob* (London, 1958), a graphic account of the Gordon Riots of 1870, exemplifies the same phenomenon in England—with which *Peterloo* by Donald Read (Manchester, 1958) is an instructive comparison. See *The Victorian Frame of Mind*, pp. 54-8, for Victorian fear of the masses; also Graham Wallas's *The Life of Francis Place, 1771-1854* (1898), pp. 244, 266, 274, 290. Instructive background is provided in Alexander Somerville's *Autobiography of a Working Man* (1848; reprinted 1951), pp. 256-83.

12. *savage reprisals of Thiers:*
Mill wrote to Charles Dupont-White in 1871 a protest against the frightful abuse of power in wishing to massacre or deport anyone who has desired the least of the changes in the programme of the Commune. 'Political unity on these terms means only violent suppression of the working class by the old established methods of tyrannical monarchy, carried by a class to an extreme which a single monarch would not dare. The respite from agitation will not be used to find the way to satisfy the legitimate aspirations of the workers, but to sleep and forget the matter as under the empire, until one wakes up to general revolt.' (*Letters*, ed. H. S. R. Elliot, vol. ii, p. 320). For the Commune, see *The Paris Commune of 1871* by Frank Jellinek (London, 1937).

13. *an unquenchable ideal:*
the *locus classicus* for this aspect at the time is of course Wordsworth's *Prelude*, especially (de Selincourt's ed., London, 1933), bk. vi, 352f.; ix, 200f.; x, 690f.

14. *'a war etc.:*
the words are Burke's. *Letters on a Regicide Peace* (Letter, October, 1796).

15. *The Rational Roots of Radicalism:*
The most comprehensive and profound treatment of the ideas of the Enlightenment is Ernst Cassirer's *The Philosophy of the Enlightenment* (tr. by Koelln & Pettegrove; Princeton & London, 1951). On the political side, Kingsley Martin's *French Liberal Thought in the Eighteenth Century* (ed. by J. P. Mayer, London, 1954) still holds its place by its vigour and scholarship. Basil Willey's *The Eighteenth Century Background* (London, 1949) is a standard work. John Morley, like Kingsley Martin, is in the tradition himself, and his *Diderot and the Encyclopedists* (London, 1878) is one of the best of his studies of the period, and still useful.

16. *secularism:*
the point is that the undying heart of conservatism is the belief that politics are inseparable from religion; this belief may be disguised as the notion that impersonal laws not human wills ought to prevail. See below, pp. 40-1, and chap. 2, sects. i & v. Also, Russell Kirk, op. cit., p. 125, and Langmead Casserley, pp. 37-40; 55.

17. *abstract thinking did not force them apart:*
see, e.g., R. W. Meyer, op. cit., esp. pp. 15, 21, 45-6.

18. *'works of God':*
the phrases (from Bacon) are used by Basil Willey in *The Eighteenth Century Background*, pp. 3f. The new rational approach to religion is fully treated in Roland N. Stromberg's *Religious Liberalism in Eighteenth-Century England* (Oxford, 1954). The Socinian influence, which was strong in Locke, is documented by H. John McLachlan in *Socinianism in Seventeenth-Century England* (Oxford, 1951). A useful study of the transition of thought within the Church of England 1660-1700, is G. R. Cragg's *From Puritanism to the Age of Reason* (Cambridge, 1950). The special influence of Leibniz in asserting with emphasis the unity of theology with science, on the ground of the competence of human reason to provide a rational account of man, God, the world, and revealed Christianity, is studied by W. H. Barber in *Leibniz in France, 1670-1760* (Oxford, 1955). The part of Bayle in challenging the new synthesis is well brought out, pp. 73f; 89. An extreme and supreme example of this characteristic turning from 'the word of God' to 'the works of God' is Tom Paine.

19. *Mill's* Logic:
The foundations of Mill's thinking include this basis to which he frequently returns: that an epistemology which gives independent status to intuitions, if allowed, would sanction any custom or institution: criticism must go to the roots. This was as true of current opinion as of immemorial custom. Mill writes:

It is easy for anyone to imagine an ideal public which leaves the freedom and choice of individuals in all uncertain matters undisturbed, and only requires them to abstain from modes of conduct which universal experience has condemned. But where has there been seen a public which set any such limit to its censorship? or when does the public trouble itself about universal experience? In its interferences with personal conduct it is seldom thinking of anything but the enormity of acting or feeling differently from itself; and this standard of judgement, thinly disguised, is held up to mankind as the dictate of religion and philosophy, by nine-tenths of all moralists and speculative writers. These teach that things are right because they are right; because we feel them to be so. They tell us to search in our minds and hearts for laws of conduct binding on ourselves and on all others. What can the poor public do but apply these instructions, and make their own personal feelings of good and evil, if they are tolerably unanimous in them, obligatory on all the world? (*On Liberty*, Everyman ed., p. 140. Mill's technical treatment of necessary truths is in his *Logic*, Bk. ii, and in his *Examination of Sir William Hamilton's Philosophy*.)

The epistemological question, at least in this practical sense, is the fundamental division between conservatives and radicals. In Mill's time, Matthew Arnold was raising again the banner of 'right reason' against him in *Culture and Anarchy* (see Lionel Trilling's *Matthew Arnold*, p. 265); as Walter Lippmann today against our empiricists (*The Public Philosophy*, 1955). For Victorian dogmatism, see *The Victorian Frame of Mind*, pp. 144-54.
In the passage above, Mill identifies dogmatic religion with dogmatic philosophy; but in the seventeenth century Bossuet discerned in the intuitions of philosophy a socinian confusion of the divine and the human, and for him toleration would have been a *trahison des clercs* (Hazard,

op. cit., pp. 285, 313). Arnold, denying Hebraism its exclusiveness and reducing religion to one cultural discipline amongst others, left his 'right
reason' without a rule, a mere discursive play of mind. Walter Pater loosed
the intuition from all bonds, and idealized pure disinterestedness, universal
sympathy, as the perfect humanism (*The Renaissance*, esp. 'Sandro
Botticelli' and the famous 'Conclusion'). Not less influential over young
minds in another country was Leon Brunschvicg, against whom, fairly or
not, Sartre has borne witness:

As democracy tolerated all opinions, even those which aimed expressly at
destroying it, republican humanism, which was taught in the schools,
made tolerance the primary virtue. Everything would be tolerated, even
intolerance. Hidden truths had to be recognized in the silliest ideas, in the
vilest feelings. For Leon Brunschvicg, the philosopher of the regime, who
all his life assimilated, unified, and integrated, and who shaped three
generations, evil and error were only false shows, fruits of separation,
limitation, and finiteness. They were annihilated as soon as one overthrew
the barriers which compartmentalized systems and collectivities (*What
is Literature?* p. 159; London, 1950).

The war and the occupation, Sartre says, made his generation rediscover
the absolute at the heart of relativity and the irreducible reality of evil;
and he demands a dogmatic humanism. The wheel completes its cycle.
And the moral? Not the way of retreat, not an advance into new dogmatism; simply and firmly, Mill's 'universal experience', with reasons
given, and, of course, open to challenge.
See *Are Men Equal?* p. 134 for the curse of non-empirical thinking. For
the transition from British Utilitarianism to American Pragmatism, see
Philip P. Wiener's *Evolution and the Founders of Pragmatism* (Camb.,
Mass., 1949).

20. *a pointer not a 'gun':*
the phrase is borrowed from John W. Yolton, *John Locke and the Way of
Ideas* (Oxford, 1956), who has provided a valuable study of Locke's
epistemology in relation to his practical preoccupation with religious,
moral, and political issues, showing how the 'new' doctrine was not so
new but in Locke's work excited attention and stimulated the many
radical movements of the century.

21. *the social contract:*
a critical study of the notion and use of 'the social contract' is J. W.
Gough's *The Social Contract* (sec. ed., Oxford, 1957). This constituent of
medieval political thought was extracted and used by liberals to insist on
volition, consent, agreed purpose, in a context which presupposed the
dualism of sovereign and subject (Locke). It thus became the tool, or
plaything, of political thinking which everybody used in his own way for
his own purpose, not only for making or reforming a constitution but also
for conserving one or for justifying a juridical order. In this way the
radical thinking emerged which eliminated dualism and the sacredness of
rights and customs (Locke) by attributing sovereignty to the people, not
only legislative authority but also sovereignty over the constitution. This
view did not triumph in the USA.

22. *'human beings as they are and laws as they might be':*
the phrase is Rousseau's in the prefatory note to the *Social Contract*.

23. *maxims imprinted in the mind:*
for the assumption of the Enlightenment that Reason—a few simple self-evident truths—is the same in all men and equally possessed by all and should therefore be the guide of life, see Arthur O. Loveday's *The Great Chain of Being* (Boston, 1936) pp. 288f. See Yolton, op. cit., for a thorough discussion of the grounds and nature of these universal ideas in the arguments of the time. For the problems of theodicy, see W. H. Barber's *Leibniz in France*, esp. pp. 70, 166; and *The Philosophy of the Enlightenment*, pp. 258-74.

24. *By the end of the eighteenth century:*
see J. H. Plumb's *The First Four Georges*, pp. 124f (London, 1956) also G. R. Elton's *The Tudor Revolution in Government*, pp. 370, 423 (Cambridge, 1953), for the administrative contrast with earlier and later times.

25. *The American Revolution:*
the founders of the US were aware of the significance of their historical role; e.g., Alexander Hamilton in the first paper of *The Federalist*: 'It has been frequently remarked, that, it seems to have been reserved to the people of this country, to decide by their conduct and example, the important question, whether societies of men are really capable or not, of establishing good government from reflection and choice, or whether they are for ever destined to depend, for their political constitutions, on accident and force.' See also Richard Price's *Observations on the Importance of the American Revolution*, 1785.

26. *Kant was directly influenced by Rousseau:*
see Ernst Cassirer's *Rousseau, Kant, Goethe* (Princeton, 1945). Rousseau was always for Kant the thinker who, in the realm of ethics, 'awakened him from dogmatic slumber', who had confronted him with new questions and stimulated him to new solutions. See also Cassirer's view of Rousseau in *The Philosophy of the Enlightenment*, pp. 258-74.

27. *radical conclusions:*
on Burke's repudiation of those who drew practical conclusions from general principles, see Gough, op. cit., pp. 196-7; and 112-13. Once the contract idea had been used to establish the sovereignty of the people, it was useless as a check to the sovereignty of the ruler: the shift had been made in anticipation from the medieval polity to modern democracy. Preoccupation with 'social contract' and 'natural law' (both inherited from medieval thought) characterized a period preoccupied with constitution making or reform and with the foundation of knowledge. These ideas wither (they linger on) once the devices, techniques, and procedures of democracy and the epistemological foundations of empirical science are sufficiently established.

28. *prophetic denunciations:*
for the work of the *philosophes*, Morley's *Diderot* is still valuable. He suggests that their task was to make Catholicism itself civilized and moral, following the complete failure of tradition and authority, and that these writers were inspired by a zeal for political justice, for humanity, for better and more equal laws, for the amelioration of the common lot, which in energy, sincerity, and disinterestedness has never been surpassed.

For the social hierarchy and pageantry as a source of moral corruption, cp. also Adam Smith's *The Theory of Moral Sentiments*, pt. i, sect. iii, chap. iii.

29. *Patrick Geddes:*
    see *Patrick Geddes in India*, ed. by Jacqueline Tyrwhitt (London, 1947).
30. *an enemy of the human race:*
    see esp. Talmon's *The Origins of Totalitarian Democracy*, pp. 38-49; and chap. 2 below, pp. 79-82 and notes.

Talmon's critical summary of Rousseau here, admirable though it is, seems to me to be vitiated by hindsight and to make no concessions to Rousseau's confusion of thought. Obsessed as they were with the 'sinister' interests entrenched in power, contrasted with the 'natural' or primitive mutuality of society, with their horror of faction and admiration of public spirit derived from classical reading, and with no possible experience of the devices of democratic government subsequently learned gradually and empirically, radical political thinkers of that time might be excused for thinking that to think away the 'sinister' interests in power entitled the thinker to rely on spontaneous public support for equal rules equally enforced. The *Social Contract* is the paradigm of this thinking. After all, Hume, the conservative and empiricist, who did not share the radical view of the Establishment as a confederacy of sinister interests, found it necessary to elaborate reasons to show why the prime, permanent, general, evident, avowed interest of men in doing and maintaining justice does not spontaneously prevail (*A Treatise of Human Nature*, bk. iii, pt. ii, sect. vii). Naturally, one would not want to hail Rousseau as a prophet of the Open Society, but one would hardly be justified in denying the title to Condorcet, and Condorcet himself, even in hiding from the Terror of Rousseau's disciple, does not hesitate unreservedly to give Rousseau the honour of having established political theory on permanent foundations (*The Progress of the Human Mind*, ed. Hampshire, London, 1955): 'After long periods of error . . . no longer permissible to forget or combat', pp. 128-9. Condorcet, a student and author of constitutions, recognizes the foundation of the rights of the majority and the limits of those rights, and repudiates the elaborate devices of 'liberal' constitutions as insufficient remedies for a factitious problem, without ever being in danger of letting go the individual rights which are for him the *raison d'etre* of society. It is not reasonable to expect radical thinkers to be more reasonable without further experience. The historian of ideas does not do wisely nor well to remember too much of what has been learned only since the period of his study. It would be more to the point to give Rousseau the benefit of a modern philosopher's acceptable reformulation of the substance of his contention in the *Social Contract*, a redemption that has no apologetic intention and no apparent reference to Rousseau at all: *Three Dimensions of Public Morality*, pp. 63-6; and *Are Men Equal?* p. 136.
Mr Talmon is certainly an able and industrious historian, but is it unfair to quote at him Marc Bloch's distich?

Robespierristes, anti-robespierristes, nous vous crions grâce.
Par pitié, dites-nous, simplement, quel fut Robespierre.

31. *but symbolic:*
    as a rallying point of the Left, and as a definitive form of the Declaration of Rights. See A. Aulard's *Histoire politique de la Révolution Française*, pp. 628-9; 782-3.
32. *fantastic ruin:*
    the confused and passionate elements in Rousseau's political philosophy

seem to be the following: (i) hatred of oppression, the evil men do; (ii) love of solitude and fear of the demands of society; (iii) exaltation of the moral above all other interests, especially the intellectual; (iv) admiration of public spirit, especially in the antique models, Fabricius and Regulus, Agesilaus and Lycurgus; (v) total surrender to society, willing the general will (Kant's universal), unites the moral individual with the moral society, in which the self is realized and transcended.

This may be a fanatical and hateful philosophy if made rigorously consistent and taken seriously, but then so is many a system that enjoys the highest respect. Rousseau's passions and inconsistencies and humane insights make him human and tolerable—and still improving.

33. *admire . . . rusticity:*
for a characteristic example of Hume's horror of the uncultivated, see his letter to the Rev. Thomas Percy, *New Letters of David Hume*, ed. Klibansky and Mossner, no. 110, p. 198 (Oxford, 1954).

34. *differed from Hume:*
on this point, see Elie Halévy's *The Growth of Philosophical Radicalism*, p. 12 (tr. Mary Morris, London, 1934). This is still a standard work on Utilitarianism, but a more recent valuable study is John Plamenatz' *The English Utilitarians* (Oxford, 1949).

35. *ended as a democrat:*
Halévy op. cit., pp. 251-64; and Wallas, *The Life of Francis Place*, pp. 126-34.

36. *'The source of corruption . . . removing it':*
William Wyndham's argument against parliamentary reform, borrowed from Burke, and quoted by Bentham in the *Book of Fallacies.*

37. *a proposed law:*
cp. Sir Courtney Ilbert in India, chap. iv, p. 141 below.

38. *classified all laws:*
this exemplifies not only the empirical approach of the Utilitarians but also their characteristic view of law (as of punishment) as a necessary evil; which is in the strongest possible contrast with the medieval notion of law, the law of nature representing the will of God and embodying man's own true interest. For a curious glimpse of the transition from the medieval to the utilitarian view, see Locke's *Second Treatise on Civil Government*, sect. 57. Cp. Tom Paine, 'government, like dress, is the badge of lost innocence', p. 21 above.

39. *the constitutional balance:*
see note 29 in ch. 2 below.

40. *as Hume recognized:*
in 'On the Original Contract'.

41. *like Pascal, you will prefer peace to justice:*
Pensées (ed. Brunschvicg) sect. v, 294, 298, 299, 325, 326.

42. *sanctioned by satisfaction:*
Mill wrote in his Diary for April 8, 1854, (*Letters*, ed. Elliott): 'Moral regenerators in this age mostly aim at setting up a new form of Stoicism or of Puritanism—persuading men to sink altogether earthly happiness as a pursuit. This might be practicable in the ages in which myriads fled to the Thebaid to get into any solitude out of such a world, but must be a failure now when an earthly life both pleasant and innocent can be had by many and might by all. What is now wanted is the creed of Epicurus warmed by the additional element of an enthusiastic love of the general good.' This was written more than fifty years after the *philosophes*, but

in such matters the transitions can hardly be pointed on so large a time-scale. Cp. Halévy, op. cit. p. 477.

43. *addressing themselves seriously to serious problems:*
no more unhistorical misreading of the radicals of the period is possible than Professor Butterfield reveals in his remark: 'It is not social institutions that make men worse than they might have been, as people used to say—social institutions however bad, are better than nothing and have the effect of making men appear a little more virtuous than they really are' (*Christianity and History*, p. 34, London, 1949). The remark is fatuous, anyway; but what the radicals meant by saying that social institutions had made men worse than they might have been was more nearly what Bentham meant by saying: 'men are in every respect what the laws make them to be'. It was, and still is, necessary to fight for the recognition of this primary truth. There is no need to accept it as the last word; but most words are idle until it is recognized.

44. *Bentham's simple abstractions:*
see Halévy, op. cit., pp. 28, 34.

45. *Bentham's thought-model ... prevailed:*
Halévy, op. cit., pp. 512-14.

46. *the modern age of social legislation:*
for documentation, see *English Historical Documents, 1833-74*, ed. G. M. Young and W. D. Handcock (Oxford, 1956). For the part played by Bentham's thought and Bentham's disciples in the creation of the modern English service (welfare) state, see G. M. Young's *Victorian England: portrait of an age* (London, 1936), esp. p. 170; Wallas, *The Life of Francis Place*, pp. 185, 330. For the historical perspective, and a parallel with the administrative revolution of the 1530's, see G. R. Elton's *The Tudor Revolution in Government*, esp. chap. vii.

47. *under the dispensation of political and economic individualism:*
'a generation that had the enterprise and industry to assemble the facts, the honesty to reveal them, and the energy to set about the task of reform has been held up to obloquy as the author, not of the Blue Books (Royal Commissions and Committees of Inquiry 1830's' 40's 50's) but of the evils themselves': T. S. Ashton on 'The Treatment of Capitalism by Historians' in *Capitalism and the Historians*, ed. F. A. Hayek (London, 1954) p. 36. These essays in the revision of economic history set out to redress the balance. See also W. Hardy Wickwar's *The Social Services* (London, 1936). Those for whom independence was the end, chose the State as an important means. Those who acted without the State, aimed at the dependence of man on man and class on class.

48. *By mid-century:*
1875-95 is given by Mr Wickwar, op. cit., as the great divide between early Victorian radicalism and modern collectivism; bad times as well as positive developments contributed to the drastic reduction within state-defined limits of the application of the old principle of 'paying one's way for oneself'. Dicey's *Law and Opinion in England* (2nd ed., 1914) is the classic work on the inter-relation of Benthamite individualism and collectivism in the nineteenth century; and Sir Roland K. Wilson's *The Province of the State* (London, 1911) reaffirms the strict principles of radical individualism.

49. *social determinism:*
for the depressing effect of social determinism and of materialistic deter-

minism on the Victorians, see Houghton, *The Victorian Frame of Mind*, esp. pp. 71, 337f.

50. *one-sided minds:*
see Mill's Diary for January 18, 1854 (*Letters*, ed. Elliott). See Bagehot's essay 'The Character of Sir Robert Peel' (1856) for a picture of the constitutional statesman at work at this time.

51. *Condorcet and de Maistre:*
Système de politique positive, iii, p. 614.

52. *Coleridge's new version:*
On the Constitution of the Church and State, according to the idea of each (1830).

53. *insecurity . . . in the midst of success:*
Professor Galbraith, recognizing that pessimism today is infinitely more respectable than optimism, is himself confident that the insecurity is the insecurity of illusion, that the anxieties which afflict conservatives and radicals alike, for different reasons, are in both cases the result of holding on to inapplicable ideas. *American Capitalism*, pp. 8, 34, 90.

54. *monopoly of wealth and opportunity:*
for a cry of alarm from a man with inside knowledge, see T. K. Quinn's *Giant Corporations* (New York, 1956).

55. *only the Englishman:*
Nietzsche, of course.

56. *the young Mill:*
see the early letters to Carlyle and the essays on *Bentham and Coleridge* (ed. F. R. Leavis, London, 1950).

57. *Matthew Arnold:*
in *Culture and Anarchy*.

58. *his alienation:*
see, for example, Sartre's essays in *What is Literature?*

59. *an alternative philosophical model:*
for a comparison between the Enlightenment and the German Aufklärung and its continuation in the historiography of the nineteenth century, see W. Kluback's *Wilhelm Dilthey's Philosophy of History* (New York, 1956).
The nineteenth century discovered Vico, an early eighteenth century pioneer in the humanist philosophy of history. Victor Cousin lectured in 1828 on Bossuet, Vico, and Herder as 'historians of humanity': 'Religion also forms, according to Vico, a part of the state and of society; while according to Bossuet the state forms part of religion. According to Vico, religion relates to humanity, but according to Bossuet, the services of humanity are entirely at the disposal of religion; the point of view has completely changed, and this was, in my opinion, an immense step in the progress of the science of history, of which the ultimate aim is to cause everything to re-enter into humanity.' (Quoted by M. H. Fisch and T. G. Bergin in their edition and translation of Vico's autobiography. *Vico: his autobiography*, Cornell, 1944, p. 76.)

60. *bred socialists:*
see the excellent study by Adam B. Ulam, *Philosophical Foundations of English Socialism* (Camb., Mass., 1951).

61. *Germany was the progressive example:*
for a comparative summary, see Sir Ernest Barker's *The Development of the Public Services in Western Europe, 1660-1930* (Oxford, 1944) pp. 69,

E

75, 78, 83-5, for the Prussian lead in social insurance and education.
62. *the family is extinct:*
of course marxism is not extinct, but it survives as a sterile orthodoxy.
63. *an Existentialism:*
not a school, nor a movement, but a characteristic contemporary type of
philosophy; see my *Six Existentialist Thinkers* (London, 1951).
64. *Buddhism:*
for example, the remarkable sale of Christmas Humphrey's *Buddhism*
(Penguin Books, 1951) and the growth of the English Buddhist movement.
65. *the relevance of biblical concepts:*
see Reinhold Niebuhr's *The Self and the Dramas of History* (London,
1956).
66. *Revolt of the Moderates:*
Samuel Lubell in a work with this title (New York, 1956) demonstrates by
an analysis of voting and a sampling of opinion-trends the establishment
of a 'middle road' conservatism as the dominant political force in the
country (the evidence is that the people are swinging their votes—'groping
for a policy' is Mr Lubell's interpretation). He is himself optimistic about
the political results of this trend, and thinks that it means the people are
rediscovering the art of government and are going to solve their problems
and make their adjustments empirically (p. 250). He is aware, however, of
the dangers (the discrepancy between this trend and the institutions and
traditions of political life in the American democracy; complacent neglect
of government and public affairs) and he ends: 'The time to worry is
when all is "moderation".'
The plebiscitary votes for de Gaulle, useful as they were in saving the
country from the unmitigated disaster of civil war, have ruined the
political schools of thought and disciplined parties, that is to say, political
rationalism. This is a sad deterioration, even if it was anticipated by the
discredit of 'the system' brought about by irresponsibility of the parties.
Intractable problems, the strength of the Communist Party (not a democratic player) and public apathy, have their heaped share of blame, which
does not all lie at the door of the party system, nor of the parties.
67. *a heap of silly words:*
see T. D. Weldon's *The Vocabulary of Politics* (Penguin Books, 1953).
68. *seeks to galvanize his will to will:*
the reference of course is to Colin Wilson's *The Outsider* (London, 1956).
69. *the tendency to destructiveness and sterility:*
Sartre's *What is Literature?* P. Wyndham Lewis's *The Demon of Progress in
the Arts* (London, 1954). Gabriel Marcel's *Homo Viator* (tr. Craufurd,
London, 1951) pp. 75, 93, 161-2, 268. Perhaps Mr Francis Bacon is the best
representative of this terrorist destruction of the humanist tradition in the
arts, because he expresses his rejection from within.
70. *the gospels are all sells:*
Peter F. Drucker's *The End of Economic Man* (London, 1939) argued that
disillusionment with the old dreams and promises made the masses
desperate and destructive and brought about the disintegration of rational
ideals, above all, man as a community of responsible free and equal persons. Fascism was the result of the fatal tendencies to fantasy thinking
(the demand for Utopia) and to destructive passions when Utopia does not
come and things go wrong. Religious, political, and now economic,
promises had failed to realize the free and equal society.

Herbert Schneider in *Three Dimensions of Public Morality:* 'Liberty is in danger of going toward what Hobbes described as its inevitable culmination, "the war of all against all". Equality is in danger of sanctioning tyranny and cruelty, while fraternity is apt to cloak bigotry. The three ancient spectres—war, tyranny, fanaticism—which have haunted the growth of civilization for ages have now returned to oppress us more savagely than ever. A generation ago we had been taught not to fear these ghosts of savagery; today we have learned, and not from books, that these terrors still lie ahead of us and threaten our ruin' (p. 41).

CHAPTER II

The Sovereignty of the People

ARGUMENT

IF HISTORY, including the history of ideas, brings out anything, it is the due and undue persistence of the past in the present. A system may be dead and done with, but its residues do not quickly decompose and any soul it may own haunts its successor. Theocracy was not established ten centuries, and in the nineteenth century had been dead two centuries when it is found in the most unlikely places, in Whig liberalism and in rationalist positivism—and its disguise in modern marxism is an open secret.

The antithesis of theocracy is individualism, which would be incompatible not merely with the rule of God but even with rule of any kind if it were not assumed that individual interests are somehow spontaneously in harmony. Since this is obviously not so, or not obviously so, the assumption requires the assistance of other suppositions. There was the neat idea of Mandeville that private vices are public virtues, or of Adam Smith's 'invisible hand' that leads to social ends which were no part of selfish intentions. On the political side, there was the idea of republican law, that the general interest would prevail once dominant sectional interests had been removed and prevented from re-establishing themselves. When in fact faction prevailed, a problem was set which proved amenable only to the institution of faction as political party under the rules of parliamentary government.

The party government solution, resisted and regretted by so many theorists, who deplored party rule or who wanted to give the people their rightful sovereignty whole and indivisible, is, however, perhaps only an interim solution. In so far as a political democracy is not yet a homogeneous mass upholding the same general interest, it is a divided society represented by rival parties. If the popular party can win a succession of elections by promises to the indigent many, it can bring into existence the homogeneous mass society. The alternative is a see-saw of the two parties or a fragmentation into factions, both of which make nonsense of politics and open the way to dictatorship.

Everyway, the result is that the constitutional solution may solve too much, since it threatens to resolve politics into totalitarian ad-

ministration, of which Tocqueville and Marx had different visions.

I. THE RULE OF LAW

The dominant theme of modern political history is the sovereignty of the people: how and why the various forms of popular government got established as contenders for the *ne plus ultra* of politics. Nationalism is the counterpart of this theme, and the two are intricately interwoven.

(i) *Theocracy Ancient and Modern*

Sovereignty and nationalism are distinctively modern issues, forced by modern occasions and modern movements. By contrast, they did not trouble the consciousness of medieval thinkers. For this reason, it is anachronism to go back to St Thomas Aquinas to find 'the first Whig', and to quote from him, as Lord Acton did, 'the earliest exposition of the Whig theory of the revolution'.[1] To be sure, the whiggishness of the language is unexceptionable; but St Thomas, piecing a great inheritance at the end of the thirteenth century, was formulating the rules of a sublime abiding order whose humane ethos depended on not raising questions and not forcing issues which have had to be raised and have been fought out. This was the whiggery of Burke, justified in St Thomas, the whiggery of proviso: provided that the Christian faith be not in question. This was nearly three hundred years before Thomas Cromwell dated the foundation of the modern secular state with the Acts of Supremacy which made law by statutes of parliament embodying the wills of living men. By this, even more than by his consummation on modern lines of the Tudor revolution in administration, he made a breach with the ideas and ideals of the medieval past.*

St Thomas had laid down that a law to be valid must be authorized by the whole people or by their legitimate and accepted guardian, must give effect to or at least be consistent with natural justice, must be designed by reason as means to the common happiness, and must be promulgated to all; and he was not afraid to show how his four conditions were to be applied in practice on such crucial questions as

---

* 'The establishment of the royal supremacy over the Church, the expulsion of the Pope, and the assertion of the unlimited sovereignty of statute destroyed the foundation of medieval polity and society and put something new in their place. Thomas More knew well why he opposed the voice of Christendom to an Act of Parliament, and Thomas Cromwell knew equally well what his assertion of the omni-competence of Parliament meant. They both knew they were witnessing a revolution.' (G. R. Elton, *The Tudor Revolution in Government*, 1955, p. 424.)

property and war.[2] He took over from Aristotle preference for a mixed constitution (a blend of autocracy, aristocracy, and democracy) and from the Stoics and Roman jurists the notion of natural law as the regulative principle of positive laws; but he assimilated all this to a divine dispensation in which God alone is sovereign: they are elements, necessary or useful, in the realization and regulation of a theocracy.

The justification of those who claim St Thomas as 'the first Whig' is that they too want a theocracy, not the rule of priests but the reign of God through the 'sovereignty of the developed conscience' (Acton).[3] Those political forms and devices are preferred which have proved most serviceable in safeguarding the sovereign rights of the conscience so that duty may be done unhindered by man:[4] the mixed constitution, separation of Church and State, division of powers, plurality of interests. With this usually goes some form of 'natural law' thinking, insistence on the absoluteness and paramountcy of the moral law.[5]

Theocrats of this description include those liberal conservatives or conservative liberals who have striven to avoid forcing to a conclusion the issues raised by the revolutions, English, American, and French.

Thus Guizot and the so-called 'doctrinaires' after the French Revolution denied sovereignty to any man or number of men and spoke about 'the sovereignty of reason' or the 'sovereignty of conscience'. Guizot, a liberal Catholic and an historian as well as a politician, held that representative government is the permanent truth of politics, and as an historian he tried to demonstrate it.[6] This truth, he argued, was the idea of 1789, and he believed it was the faith and hope of his time that, after several false starts, the permanent foundation had been laid in 1830 after the July revolution, with the accession of the citizen king, Louis Philippe, and the establishment of a mixed constitution. Rightful law was not a question of human will but a question of eternal truth, the moral law: it was, therefore, the discovery of competent men engaged with good will in the search. These representative men were to be elected for their competence, and, therefore, elected by those who were competent to select them (some 300,000 Frenchmen at this time); and they were to be made and kept responsible by the division of powers, the publicity of debates, and the freedom of the Press. (Guizot here reproduces the characteristic eighteenth century confusion between respect for public opinion and regard for effective representation, and does so on the explicit assumption that the few are chosen by the few not to execute will but to exercise reason in the forum of the nation.) The sovereignty of the people, unless it was unanimous, was a contradiction from the outset; it had no greater right than the force of numbers, and turned out to be the domination of inferiorities over superiorities, of all tyrannies the most violent and unjust, but fortunately the most transient because the most impracticable. It had a temporary justification when it erupted like a force of nature to break up an inequality which had become excessive or a power which had become absolute: it was not a principle of government but an agent of destruction. Guizot's own regime suffered this destruction in 1848 in the name of the sovereignty of the people; and the exercise of that sovereignty was as temporary as he said it must be.

Auguste Comte was not a theocrat, since his creed of scientific positivism dismissed unanswerable first and last questions, but he provided a modern secular model of medieval theocratic polity and a comparison with Guizot is instructive, for they were contemporaries who accepted the Revolution, devoted themselves to thinking about the post-revolutionary problems, and sought in history the principles for a permanent basis of modern society.

Like Guizot, Comte accepted the principle of the sovereignty of the people as merely destructive; it had served a turn and could have no constructive possibilities — unless temporarily, to sanction experimentation and provisional institutions until a true and permanent hierarchy should be established. Like Guizot, he wanted the rule of a law independent of and paramount to human wills, the will of one, of few, of many, or of all. Like Guizot, he relied for the discovery and promulgation of this law on a competent *élite*. Like Guizot, he relied on the acceptance of this law by the masses in virtue of its demonstrable reasonableness.

Yet Comte rejected Guizot's regime (1830-48) with contempt, as a mere interregnum, indeed, a vacuum. He was not merely dissatisfied with Guizot's practical conduct of affairs (as others were): he denounced as false and obstructive the prevailing view that the parliamentary system of government was the ultimate issue of the Revolution. A refutation of this blind confidence in constitutionalism was required. The revolution of 1848 provided it — or so he thought at the time. Constitutionalism as the fruit of the Revolution, as a permanent basis for society was a notion to be destroyed. Why?

Comte's political thinking, though disfigured, maimed, and blinded by crazy egotism, is fascinating and respectable. Fascinating, because he flourishes with sublime confidence every weapon then in play, having precisely deprived it of its lethal power: he is a *philosophe* who longs and looks for the elimination of the middle classes and the extinction of men of letters; he is an historicist who founds his hopes on the proletariat and denies them any active class interest or historical political role; he is a Catholic who looks back to the golden age before the Renaissance, but replaces theology with science; he is a progressive who makes science the key to the future and for whom science is virtually complete and specialism is retrograde idiocy; he is an authoritarian who concentrates against the concentration of power; he believes that (his) ideas will transform society definitively, yet assigns to reason a subordinate role. His thought is respectable, nevertheless, because he is not a fantastically inept eclectic in all this, but a bold and original thinker, with insight into social dangers and social needs of the time.

The reason why parliamentarianism and the universal franchise were, in Comte's view, dangerous aggravations of disorder was that they sanctioned and institutionalized the protestant sacred right of private judgement, encouraging any and every vanity and inanity and speculative futility, encouraging intrigue and the scramble for political power, along with the scramble for wealth, encouraging faith in political solutions of all problems. This anarchy sooner or later led to authoritarianism of a blind reactionary character, restoration of the *ancien régime*; and the dreary and senseless oscillation perpetuated itself. The most that could be expected of parliamentarianism was a moderation of this perpetual futile oscillation by its reduction to rule. Since the dissolution of the medieval order there had been five centuries of passionate and useless struggle, which with the French Revolution had become a chronic state of crisis. Guizot's parliamentary régime, putting power into the hands of the selfish and greedy bourgeoisie, had merely provoked the opposition of numbers to wealth. It was time to reconstruct society on the permanent foundation of universal principles. Such principles were to be learned from history. Comte named Condorcet as his predecessor. Of the Introduction to Condorcet's *Sketch for a Historical Picture of the Progress of the Human Mind*, he says: 'These few immortal pages leave really nothing to be desired in regard to the position of the sociological question at large, which will, in my opinion, rest for all future time, on this admirable statement.' This fervent approval was directed to Condorcet's assumption of uniform general laws underlying the development of mankind and corresponding to the laws of individual development, and his proposal to formulate them so as to furnish the means to make further progress certain and rapid. 'If there is to be a science for predicting the progress of the human race, for directing and hastening it, the history of the progress already achieved must be its foundation.' Such a science Condorcet had failed to establish because he had failed to discern the general laws of historical development, and had merely linked the progress of virtue with the progress of reason, that is, of science. This failure Comte set out to remedy. Condorcet's general vision of universal co-operation as the result of enlightenment he fully shared, but Comte's understanding of how the orderly and progressive reign of natural laws could and would supersede the capricious and futile chaos of human wills was much more precise.

The restoration of authority, if it met the prime social need of the time, could not be a revival of legitimacy nor the advent of a strong man; it must be the establishment of the intellectual and moral authority of those competent to discern and to demonstrate the laws of history. This authority of the scientific philosophers must establish itself by the power of demonstration and with the credentials of evident disinterestedness: moral authority was strong and respected in so far as it was, and so long as it remained, destitute of political power. The philosopher-king, anyhow a utopian solution, would be a monstrosity. This separation of moral authority and political power was the masterpiece of medieval political wisdom, the one discovery of permanent validity, subsequently lost, on which the final organization of society principally depended. The greatest modern political error had been the concentration of all authority in the hands of a political sovereign. The constitutional correction of this error by a division of powers within the government was merely a mistaken substitute for the genuine principle, since it weakened authority without removing the confusion of authorities which was the source of the mischief. 'The disposition to seek in political institutions the solution of all our difficulties whatsoever is a disastrous tendency of our time. Naturally arising from the concentration of powers, it has been aggravated by the constitution-making of the last half-century.' Instead of seeking a solution in legal institutions, and thus perpetuating unsettlement in a vain search, men should try to discover the principles of society and establish the power to apply them.

Modern society was founded upon work and talent, industrial organization and the division of labour.[7] Its natural leaders in government and administration were to be looked for in the hierarchies of industry and commerce. But before these could form a new and true patriciate they had to be socialized: as an oligarchy, they were pursuing alien and ruinous interests of their own. Therefore, society depended for regeneration upon the support of a public opinion derived from unsophisticated, uncorrupted elements, chiefly, women and the proletariat. An interim regime was necessary and required a dictator, probably to be drawn from the ranks of the proletariat.

This unsophisticated public opinion had to be enlightened and guided and enabled to prevail. This was the work of the moral authority whose demonstrations and example and educational programme were the source and stay of the new and permanent social order. All progress consisted in the development of order; it was the continuous extension of liberty, not in the anarchic direction of liberal individualism, but in the direction of conformity to natural (scientific) law, resulting in the gradual expansion of human powers.

In the order of ideas, positivism, that is to say, empirical science, had superseded the earlier phases of speculative reason and of theological dogma. Science was completed and synthesized in the social knowledge gained from history, for it issued in a general conception of the future deduced from satisfactory explanation of the whole past, and proved by the requisite transitional regime, demonstrated as the only and sufficient solution of intractable current problems. Science for the first time made fully possible, and fully evoked, the operation of social sympathies; for, negatively, in reaching the goal of thinking it brought to an end the restless and futile preoccupation with intellectual speculation, and, positively, in discovering the laws and the means of human fulfilment it permanently established the rightful ascendancy of social feeling. Thus science, through its culmination in sociology, was consummated in the universal collaboration of men and women for human welfare and betterment: the organization of society was the natural fruit of the organization of science. Understanding of the laws of his nature in social development exalted social feeling and gave man the incentive with the scientific means to concentrate all his powers on the common welfare, entering into the collaboration of present, past, and future generations in the partnership in every virtue and in all perfection.

Comte's idea may be summed up as the concentration of all human effort upon the service of humanity in conformity with the natural laws established by the sciences, leading inevitably to the maximum freedom and expansion of human faculty, as the common political, scientific, and moral tendency and ideal. He believed it would prevail because it drew attention to, and thereby reinforced, the spontaneous tendency of development, because its demonstration would be convincing, enlightening, and inspiring to the disinterested (and disinherited) elements in society, because it gave everyone his appropriate place and part in society, and therefore his fulfilment, because it did away with arbitrary claims and sterile powers, and because even to conservatives and even to revolutionaries it did offer the only solution of their problems, testing them by the promise of satisfaction to all that was legitimate in their hopes and aims. Thus a preponderant body of public opinion in due course would demand and support the constructive programme, which would itself provide the test of good faith and evoke the public spirit to protect and carry it through. And thus would be cleared up once for ever the social chaos produced by the disruptive ideas of 1789, the mental chaos produced by mixing up theological, metaphysical, and scientific ideas, and the moral chaos produced by identifying intellectual and moral authority with political power.

Comte unwittingly provided the epitaph on his own political philosophy. 'Greek philosophy merely indicated, as every Utopia does, the social need of the age, and prophesied its satisfaction.'

Theocratic ideals were of course prevalent in the English debates in the seventeenth century (with which Guizot was familiar). A party in the Long Parliament before the civil war broke out, the 'root and branch men', wanted Parliament to establish the calvinist presbyterianism in place of episcopacy, and during the civil war the views of those like Cromwell who cherished the ideal of religious liberty and thought that the separation of Church and State was the most scriptural way to make the sovereignty of God prevail, had the ascendancy in the Army Council. But if the disagreement at this time was mainly about religious issues and the forms of the divine sovereignty, it was not merely so, for there was the question of the king's sovereignty and the sovereignty of parliament, touching the rights and customs of property.[8] When the Revolution established in Defoe's phrase 'the divine right of freeholders', this was the Whig principle, *par excellence*; and although the language of Locke is the language of 'the judicious Hooker' and of St Thomas, it speaks to a different purpose; so that when Lord Acton says that Whiggism is 'the supreme achievement of Englishmen, and their bequest to the nations' and 'the leaven that has leavened the world', he is listening to the original sound, not to be the seventeenth century echo.

The fundamental law of nature to which Locke appealed was the self-preservation of each and all. Society was instituted by compact for that purpose. Each desires, and has the duty, to preserve his life, liberty, and estate ('property' is Locke's comprehensive word). Valid law gives effect to this desire: it is freedom, because it confirms and secures me in the enjoyment of my own, and restrains my neighbour only from injuring me. Legislators or executives who abuse their office and violate reason and natural law are open to the sanction of rebellion and liable to the punishment of removal. This is the ultimate sovereignty of the whole people in virtue of their common will in the compact which instituted society. Here the language of the old theocracy is used to express in terms of will and property the notions of the modern secular state. By the end of the seventeenth century interest in trade was supplanting interest in religion, and there was not long to go before Colbert pronounced the blessed words *laisser faire*[9] and men were not thinking much of any form of theocracy but, rather, of a society run on the inexhaustible energy of unregenerate self-seeking which worked for the common benefit by the natural mechanism of the market: on which all the intellectual, moral, and spiritual blessings of freedom would supervene.

Once the religious issues receded which so sharply divided the nation, the question of authority which they had occasioned could be thought of and discussed in general terms: the question of the basis and purpose of society. This led naturally to explicit recognition of the legitimacy of actual individual interests and to the general interest in society as the guarantee of these particular interests. That is to say, the notion of society as a general interest upheld by the desire of the whole people as the final and sufficient authority, without reference to natural law, became explicit. This notion of the whole people, forced into prominence by reflection on the purpose of society and the source of authority, although confused, and later obstructive,[10] was, as the parent concept of modern society, necessary and creative. Although it was convenient at first to think of the authority of the whole people in the traditional terms of a social contract whether with the monarch or between one and all in the institution of society, the contract notion and natural law were superseded by modern concepts, in England by the idea of utility, the language of Locke by the language of Hume. And Hume generalized the idea by making the authority of the people, of all people everywhere, the final arbiter on all questions of morals and of literature and the arts as well as of politics. The consensus of mankind as the final authority on questions not of science but of opinion, of conduct, of taste, and of policy was an appeal to numbers. But the authority of the majority was not merely the force of will and of number; its authority lay in its generality, its impartiality, its attention to general interest, its common sense, whether the language used was natural law, social contract, reason, common sense, or utility.[11]

(ii) *The Republican Myth*

The most serious and systematic attempt to organize the sovereignty of the people for continuous government, as distinct from invoking it as a constitutional sanction, was made in the second phase of the French Revolution. In their Declaration of the Rights of Man and Citizen, the men of 1789 were aware that they thus abolished formally the *ancien régime*, following the American example. They were not setting out, however, to achieve a democratic republic, to organize the sovereignty of the people. Although the conjunction in the Declaration of the sovereignty of the nation with equality of political rights would seem to have implied it, no such implication was seriously thought of until national events forced the issues.

These national events had already begun with the taking of the Bastille. This rising of Paris on July 14, seconded by risings throughout France, was the movement that accomplished the overthrow of the *ancien régime* and pushed the Assembly into the exercise of effective sovereignty. At the end of the first phase of constitutional bourgeois rule, the rule of *active* over *passive* citizens, it was a similar insurrection three years later, on August 10, 1792, on the defection of the monarch, that pushed the Assembly into a definitive abolition of the monarchy and into taking the initiative in establishing a democratic republic. August 10 was taken in Paris as the inauguration of the sovereignty of the people. The Legislature explicitly acknowledged this sovereignty in convening the Convention authorized to organize it, to provide the constitution of a democratic republic.

The constitution of 1793 is the most serious attempt in history to organize the sovereignty of the people. It put together the sovereignty of the nation and equality of rights announced in the original Declaration, and placed the sovereignty in the whole people, abolishing the distinction between active and passive citizens. Adopted almost unanimously by a national plebiscite, it announced the intention of the French people to carry the Revolution to a certain end, a democratically organized Republic, one and indivisible.

The Constitution and the discussion of it exhibit most clearly the republican myth which at that time possessed the minds of progressive political thinkers. The republican myth was the rule of laws, not men; in an extreme form, the identity of interests. Whilst the Convention was sitting and preparing the constitution of 1793, addresses were sent in from the Departments expressing loyalty to the united will of the nation and threatening the pretensions of any sectional interests. 'Republicans listen to and follow only the laws: egoism and factions are unknown to them.'[12] This purple hyperbole was dark with the fear that haunted these first ventures into modern popular government, in France, America, and England. The lesson of politics in antiquity had been that the bane of popular government is faction: the field is opened to factions, whose turbulence or tyranny drives the people into the arms of Caesar. (When Bonaparte wanted to be named Consul for life, he would not concede to the liberals re-establishment of the freedom of the Press, saying, 'I should have to govern again with a minority, a faction, and begin the Revolution over again, whilst all my efforts are bent on governing with the nation.') Horror of faction colours the political thinking of the time, and providing against faction is the main preoccupation in the making of constitutions for popular government. The devices and conventions by which faction might be institutionalized as a system of government were learned the hard way.

The clearest recognition of the inseparability of faction from popular government and of its ruinous effects unless controlled is in Number X of *The Federalist*, a classic paper attributed to Madison.[13] He says: 'By a faction I understand a number of citizens, whether amounting to a majority or minority of the whole, who are united and actuated by some common impulse of passion, or of interest, adverse to the rights of other citizens, or to the permanent and aggregate interests of the community.' Since faction in this sense was an unavoidable product of liberty and natural inequalities, it could be remedied only by control, not by prevention, if popular government was to be maintained. Disinterested legislation was not to be expected from parties in power. The only way to avoid partisan legislation was to secure that majority votes are not party votes: that is the problem that had to be solved if popular government were not to be utterly discredited and resisted. Experience had shown that no moral or religious motive imposed any adequate restraint. Contrary to the opinion of Rousseau, a pure democracy, in which the whole body of citizens administered their affairs together, would certainly be oppressive; and experience proved it. The only possible control of the effects of faction was to be obtained by a representative system drawn from a wide area. Then the representative Assembly is numerous enough and the constituencies large enough to reduce the danger of manipulation, and the multiplicity of interests represented will reduce the danger of a settled party majority. These safeguards were reinforced in a federal republic, both because of its greater extent and because of the separation of local and national interests.

This was a realistic and sophisticated appraisal, in contrast with which the constitution of 1793 was doctrinaire and naive; but both proceed on the assumption that a republican constitution can produce republican laws which will be just and equal because they are enacted by a majority of disinterested votes on every question.

The Constitution of 1793 as first submitted to the Convention was mainly the work of Condorcet, an eager student of the American constitutions, the only survivor of the *philosophes*, and the greatest political thinker of the time in France, not forgetting Siéyès. In the *Progress of the Human Mind*, there is a passage close to the heart of Condorcet's political thinking:

'We shall prove that this principle of the identity of interests, if it is made the criterion of political rights, is a violation of them in regard to those to whom one takes the liberty of not leaving the entire exercise of them; that this identity ceases to exist precisely in becoming a genuine inequality. We shall insist on this point, because this error is the only one which may still be dangerous, because it is the only one of which truly enlightened men may not yet be disabused.'*

Condorcet undoubtedly meant here that a restriction of the franchise was a violation of political rights, and therefore of the principles of the American and French Declarations. And his emphasis was probably the result of his prolonged study of American constitutions, with their restricted franchises. It is tempting to see in these words his comment on Hamilton's doctrine that there was an identity of economic interest (in respect of taxation) between landlords and the poorest tenants, artisans and the richest merchants, which rendered their independent representation in the legislature by members of their own class as superfluous as chimerical (*The Federalist*, No. 35). If this was the language of a truly enlightened man who genuinely believed in free institutions and was striving to organize popular government on a permanent basis, Condorcet's emphasis was in point.[14] But he was out of step with his time, he was looking beyond the Hamiltons and Guizots, the energetic and capable liberal-bourgeois-capitalists who were about to take the new states into their hands and to organize them largely in their own interests. He was insisting on the necessity of equality, and looking

* ed. Stuart and Hampshire, London, 1955, p. 145.

with extraordinary, if inevitably imperfect, prescience to the modern welfare state.

St Just, Robespierre's lieutenant, like Robespierre himself, was formed on Rousseau. His speech on Condorcet's draft constitution is a manifesto of Rousseau's political thought. After insisting on the power of laws and institutions to produce peace, plenty, and public virtue, simply by creating the conditions on which these benefits naturally flourish, he turned to a criticism of Condorcet's project.

A legislature composed of representatives elected by the Departments with an Executive Council of ministers elected directly by the people, defeated the sovereignty of the people in two ways: (1) the legislature thus elected was not the nation in little, one and indivisible, deliberating in the place of the nation as a whole, and reaching by majority vote a formulation of the general will, subject to the veto of the nation as a whole; it was a congress of delegates representing local interests; (2) the Executive Council elected directly by the people, instead of being the agent of the National Assembly, and dependent upon it, would inevitably gather to itself all power and prestige, would in fact be sovereign, an oligarchy interpreting for itself the national will. In sum, the general will is indivisible and the sovereignty of the people is destroyed if it is divided.

Condorcet's project was revised, mainly in this sense, by a committee of which St Just was a member.[15] The details have ceased to matter, but there are two points of interest in tracing, and learning from, this history of political ideas. (1) At this time, the sovereignty of the people was the criterion of government; two years later, when the next constitution was under discussion, the question had shifted from, How can the people exercise their sovereignty most fully? to, What system of voting will ensure the wisest elections? (2) The idea that independent responsible votes would give authority to the wisest heads to deliberate in common in the national interest remained the common but illusory constitutional ideal whether or not the letter of popular sovereignty was respected. Rousseau and his followers, unlike Locke and Hume and Bentham and theirs, were moralists who wanted to cure men of their private interests and unite them in a natural identity of public interests, but the idea of an identity of interests underlay the thinking of all of them because in thinking about the first principles of politics government was identified in purpose with the mutuality of society represented in a constitutional order which was a common interest. Since there was a genuine common interest in the security of each from oppression at the hands of his neighbour or of the sovereign, constitutional thinking was naturally preoccupied with confirming and asserting this identity of interest and preventing its infraction by faction.

St Just's theory of pure democracy exhibits the idea in its simplest terms—mainly because, athwart the stream of economic tendency, a fragile political dam, he dreamed like Rousseau of a society of equally independent small, mainly rural, proprietors, enjoying and upholding together the same private and public interests. The National Assembly, in his view, elected directly on a universal franchise was the nation in little deliberating in place of the whole nation, and its decisions were subject to the ratification of the whole nation. The decision of the majority of such an Assembly, when duly ratified, necessarily expressed the general will, and could never be oppressive, since it was the same for all. Under such a regime, minorities were, in effect, factions, conspiring to form alien special interests, and therefore properly to be overruled and ignored by majorities. If the procedures for the election of the National Assembly and for the voting of laws were duly observed, the sovereignty of the people would prevail, the general interest would be served, no alien interest would be allowed to form and flourish, the people would have security and encouragement in their legitimate interests, virtue would spontaneously spread and thrive and vice would be deprived of the opportunity to establish itself.

The horror of faction increased to morbidity after what happened to the Convention. The Constitution of 1793, although adopted by a nearly unanimous plebiscite, was never put into effect. It remained the rallying point of the Left for years to come, but at the time it was suspended for the duration of the emergency whilst the provisional Revolutionary Government exercised a necessary dictatorship under the pressure of events ('la patrie en danger'). There were factions in and around the Convention in this critical national situation. Jaurès has argued that death was the only possible arbiter of factions in that time when 'minutes were worth centuries'.[16] The unanimity of effective government had to be bought at the price of murder. The tragedy was not in these murders but, rather, in the cause of which they were the effects, namely, the failure of those who suffered to rally to the Revolution in its direst hour, the egoism of men. In the end, this example corrupted the Revolution itself, destroyed the confidence of the people in the Revolution and in themselves: they became willing to alienate their sovereignty.

The framers of the constitution which followed two years later were so determined to prevent a Right or a Left that they had the seats in the Chambers physically separated, required each member to occupy a seat determined by lot, and forbade him to occupy the

F

same seat more than a month; they also forbade the formation of permanent committees. The succession of civic oaths required under the Directory is further evidence of the fear of the diversity of opinions and of political activity, the frenzied fear of faction blown up into dread of the people. Bonapartism was in the logic of this attempt to expel faction from politics. He was determined, he said, to govern with the nation.

Thus the republican myth destroyed the First Republic in France through faction and the fear of faction.

2. WHO SHALL KILL WHOM?

The rule of law as the political ideal, whether held on theocratic or scientific grounds and thought of as the search for laws independent of and paramount to the wills of men, or enveloped in the republican myth and thought of as the general will, and whether idealized as regenerative, directing or conducting man to his only good, or as releasing the spontaneous public spirit of the citizen by bringing down dominant sectional selfish interests, or as setting up the selfish interests of everybody to work for society, this ideal, in spite of differences, confusion, and even conflicts, can be considered historically in its early naive forms as one undifferentiated type of theory which has encouraged one or more of such major policies as would make the king subject to the laws of the land, extend the franchise, demand or defend the freedom of the Press, or separate Church and State.

If policies which ignore, or seek to cure or to neutralize or to utilize ego propensities, by checking, balancing, or diffusing political power, are compartmentalized in one class, another is required for those which seek to concentrate, consolidate, and extend power. In this case, the question raised is not, What is the law? but the ultimate political question, Who shall kill whom? Not, How shall power be exercised? but, Who shall wield it? The writers who justify or describe this approach are not malevolent; they are close observers, and they grasp the nettle: this is how men and nations behave; therefore, no policy can succeed which is not based on this knowledge. The great names of Thucydides, Machiavelli, and Hobbes attest the influence, if the ill repute, of this body of thought.

There is a negative and a positive aspect of this thinking. Negatively, the argument would be: since men and nations can and do succeed by force and fraud, the only way to resist or outwit them is by superior force or fraud; to refrain from violence, to show trust, and to keep faith is merely to make oneself a victim ('the cully of my integrity' — Hume) and allows evil to prevail. Positively, the argument might be: by force and fraud great ends may be achieved which are otherwise out of reach, nations can be unified and made strong, empires can be created, men can be wound up to great achievement: greatness is the theme, political creation.

Although argument on these lines is not advocacy of injustice nor aggression, there is a fine distinction between studying the conditions of defence and survival in a world in which injustice and aggression pay and prevail and the contemplation of aggression and injustice as the ineluctable conditions of political power and of the achievement open to political power alone. Thucydides shows Pericles consciously assuming the responsibilities and guilt of empire building, and shows the fearful all-or-nothing logic of power-seeking in the Athenian bid for hegemony.[17] Machiavelli shows how the patriot statesman may do the state some service, if he loves Florence better than the salvation of his soul.[18] Hobbes, however, appalled by the anarchy of an imagined 'state of nature' and an actual civil war, shows the condition, which is absolute submission to absolute authority, on which alone it becomes reasonable to obey the indubitable and permanent law of nature, *Do not to another, that which thou wouldest not he should do unto thee.*[19] Power having been established, whether by conquest or by institution, whether the *pax romana* or *Leviathan* (which makes nothing of the difference), it becomes a datum for theorists of the rule of law, it can be moralized and controlled. All the political writers are dealing with one or another aspect of a total situation, a complex of problems. They and their prescriptions are not simple alternatives.

There is, of course, no simple orderly sequence in history: first, the build-up of absolute authority, then the extension of popular control, the triumphs of force and fraud followed by the rule of law, with equivalent theoretical explanation and justification. If Thomas Cromwell is deliberately applying the teaching of Machiavelli to the creation of the first modern nation state, the same teaching was still being applied to the same purpose some three hundred years later when Cavour and Bismarck pitted their wills and wiles against parliaments and popular movements (which they were as ready to use) as against rivals and adversaries abroad and at home. After Louis XIV and his ministers had done this work for modern France, the grievances which accumulated and exploded in 1789 were in vast volume grievances against the feudal aristocracy, not against the central bureaucratic administration of the king. The modern map has been made and remade by nationalism and imperialism, the clash and balance of powers: and the rule of law is not yet. Imperialism engenders and is limited by nationalism. British imperialism provoked the birth of a nation in the New World, as Bonapartism did in Europe, but the nationalism was in the minds of statesmen not in the hearts of peoples, and what was first brought into existence was a state, not a nation,[20] whether by the blood and iron of an autocrat or by the institution of 'we, the people'. And the Union of the federal republic, instituted by votes, was ratified later by blood and iron under the leadership of a man of the people, a model citizen, upholding with patient intransigence the rule of law against authoritarians and slave-holders (amiable and gifted men), forcing the issue on moral grounds, mobilizing behind a paper constitution the nationalism of a people, bringing to the work of state-craft the sanction of national character and popular decision, refusing to save the Union in the way advocated by Douglas, who would have deferred to the sovereignty of the people, and left the matter to be settled independently in the States by local majority vote.[21]

Nationalism itself has many faces, or, rather, it is a number of distinct and different, if distantly related, phenomena. There is the state-craft which forms a state and perhaps a nation out of a congeries of congeners. There is the arousal of a people to a fervent sense of identity and community, as in Revolutionary France beleaguered by the Powers.[22] There is the rebellion of native politicians, or of a people, against the sovereignty, or the oppression, of an alien power. There is a stubborn parochialism, or a factitious, revivalist archaism. Imperialism is not less different. At least, there is the difference between an imperialism tempered by an ideal of the rule of law, say, Roman imperialism, and an imperialism which is absolute autocracy, say, Russian imperialism which has never accepted Roman jurisprudence, the tradition of natural law.

There are lags and survivals, overlaps and anomalies, anticipations and anachronisms, abortive beginnings and chequered progress, the plenitude of confusion which is the natural historical landscape. In particular, the democratic nation state enjoys natural birth and healthy growth in England, springs from the head of Jove in America, and is several times abortive in France and Germany. Nevertheless, there are unmistakable general tendencies, and the achitecture of modern states bears in their historical styles characteristic common features. National sovereignty (not sovereignty of the people) is the principal common feature, but there are other principles perhaps more permanent than nationalism, and without which popularism has neither hands nor feet: personal loyalties, religious oaths, and kinship, as the bonds of political society, have long ago dissolved, and in their place we have the division of labour and the elected representative as the structural principles of the new building. These are structural changes destined to spread with industrialism to the ends of the earth. The division of labour and the election of representatives are the fundamental institutional inventions, which together with the fundamental intellectual invention, the logic of inquiry, have destroyed the *ancien régime* and provided the dynamic and the techniques for a universal human civilization. However, their universality is not yet. In particular, the elected representative is an ancient figure in the world, who may have no power or responsibility. If he is to be the dynamic figure in politics with power and responsibility, more machinery is required that was dreamed of in the republican myth or recognized by the Guizots and Hamiltons.

3. GOVERNMENT AS A DEVICE

England is the classical land of parliamentary institutions and party government. Party government, on the road to popular government, hardly begins until the nineteenth century, until the Reform Act of 1832. But important principles and institutional habits were well established in early times. The administrative device of an early legal-minded king of summoning representatives to Westminster to consent to taxation imposed an onerous duty which soon became a customary right;[23] the assembly of local notabilities at Westminster developed a corporate identity, and exercised the power of the purse. The violation of customary right by the Stuarts, their extravagant need of money, their high-handed unpopular ecclesiastical policy, their ineptitude in the choice of ministers and the handling of Parliament,[24] combined to force the issue of sovereignty in the seventeenth century. The Long Parliament was organized and managed not by the King's ministers, but by Pym.[25] It became a complex business machine. It was united in opposition, on the rights of property, until the Grand Remonstrance, when it split into a king's party and a parliamentary party, mainly on the issue of episcopacy versus presbyterianism, but hardly less on the prerogative, that is to say, on sovereignty, because of Pym's insistence that the king's ministers must be acceptable to parliament, that parliament must have confidence in, and to that extent control over, the executive. Liberty of conscience together with the right to be governed by parliament made up the 'good cause' for which the 'honest party' engaged against the king.

The interregnum was a period of infinite political discussion and of many constitutional projects, the seed-plot of the coming time for the whole modern world.[26] As the upshot of the fighting, the parliamentary army established itself as the power in the land, not the Parliament. But this army was a peculiar military machine, an armed body of political and religious thinkers engaged in incessant discussion of problems of church and state. If its presiding genius, Oliver Cromwell, failed to organize and manage his parliaments or to give effect to the sovereignty of the people called for by his radicals, and the axiom of current political argument,[27] if he fell back on Elizabethan ideas of the constitution before the issue of sovereignty had been forced, his contribution to the solution was nevertheless decisive, because he executed the legitimate sovereign, and because by failing with his parliaments and ruling with the army he reinforced the independence of parliament. After the Restoration, the King, having no independent army to count on, had to govern by his management of parliament, with the sore weakness of ignominious dependence on French money, in which he was outwitted by the astuter management in the constituencies and in parliament of Shaftesbury, the equal of Pym. James II by relying on the passive obedience of the dominant Anglicans for the exercise of his royal prerogative decisively demonstrated the limitations of that doctrine.[28] If the Glorious Revolution, and triumph of whig principles, crowned nothing more aspiring than intrigue and bitter factional rivalries, if all the parliaments of the time were tricked or packed or bribed, shabbily used in this shabby game, that is the nature of politics in their crudity, and the effect, at any rate, was to make the management of parliament the prize, the centre and object of intrigue, bribery, and personal and factional struggles; and this was the way to institutionalize power, personal and factional rivalries, and thereby to control the game of politics by providing rules.[29]

In the new regime, when the sovereign deliberately rejected faction and tried to ignore the party label in forming an administration, the attempt was vain.[30] Politics were still personal, based on local interests and connexions, on personal abilities and ambitions, and on the personal predilections of the sovereign. With the result that an able and ambitious politician out of office, like Walpole, could and did organize a more or less factious Opposition within the House and in the country, exploiting grievances and party spirit and the weaknesses of the king and the administration, forcing the king to seek and depend on a majority in the House. This pattern of Opposition,[31] by which forceful politicians took every opportunity to force their way into office, and took office on their own terms and with a personal following in the House and in the country, was the way of transition from personal to party politics, from support of the king's administration by placemen and honest independents in parliament to support of a party leader and his programme by a majority of the electors in the country.

The transition was slow and staggered, though ultimately certain from the time parliament had won the initiative and was established constitutionally independent of the king's will. Instead of the bulwark against tyranny it then became the bulwark of privilege. The political struggle centred in the competition to get into Parliament or to control elections.[32] Skill in weaving the complex and subtle web of patronage, the great chain of control, was the political art, and the attainment of office the political end. The constitutional establishment of Parliament, its limited business, and the growing prosperity of the country made this parliamentary game safe for a time,[33] as the uncertain role of the king and the power of the oligarchs made it inevitable. But Opposition to be effective had to organize interests and opinions out of doors as well as within the House, that is to say, in the City and in the counties; and in this they were breaching the system, since they brought into play the discontents of people excluded from the privileges and profits of the political and social system of the oligarchy. The king remained the head of the executive and the Court the focus of politics longer than used to be thought,[34] because Opposition was too personal and partial to be capable of designating ministers and deciding on measures, but Opposition favoured the development of party, organized largely out of doors, and mainly in the agitation for parliamentary reform, which in time concentrated power in the hands of a premier who was a party leader supported by an organized majority in the House and in the country.

(This conduct of politics, management of power by means of patronage, intrigue, and faction, developing into political organization, is far removed from the conception of making laws by the independent votes of all the citizens or of a majority (the politics of Burke in contrast with the politics of Rousseau, *Thoughts on the Present Discontents* versus *The Social Contract*), but it is not merely 'property' versus 'number', as Burke supposed, nor even the difference between politics conceived as the competition and the harmony of organized interests and politics conceived as the prevailing of disinterested opinion, for Burke and Rousseau and those who thought with them are thinking in the contexts of different phases of social development. Rousseau is preoccupied with the constitution of society, with first principles. So long as this is in question, political organization on personal, factional, or party lines is disastrous, is civil war. That is why Hume is so afraid of party.[35] He thinks of it as reopening the questions or maintaining the cleavages which made the civil war, and his counsel is pleadingly addressed to the healing motives of moderation and coalition. Burke, on the other hand, assumes that the constitutional question is settled and that the country is safe for the parliamentary game as he wanted it played; that party is not merely allowable but necessary, because it is not merely factional opportunism but the only effectual way of maintaining the constitution by bringing to bear on the conduct of the executive the check of responsible, informed, systematic, persistent, concerted and efficacious criticism, supported in the House and in the country by men who have confidence in each other because they know each other, have worked together, and share the same principles, opinions, and interests. And this party 'connexion' was necessary not only for Opposition to maintain an effectual check but also for manning Administration. 'Party is a body of men united for promoting by their joint endeavours the national interest, upon some particular principle in which they are all agreed.' This anticipated the constitutional part which party would play when some innovations in the constitution which Burke deplored would make it practicable.)

The demand for parliamentary reform, to make representative institutions genuinely representative, which became a political tide carrying all before it in 1832, was itself the first modern nationwide party issue.[36] Afterwards new methods of organizing the constituencies and the administration had to take the place of the old method of government by jobbery. At the same time, the nation's business created by the needs of an expanding industrial society forced itself on the agenda of a parliament previously occupied in providing the executive with the means of carrying on the king's business. Public opinion in the country, not in parliament, had been decisive on the question of parliamentary reform. Voting measures the force of public opinion, and, necessarily, a public opinion vaster in volume than the franchise, and election procedures institutionalize its political power.[37] Traditionally, the voting for parliamentary candidates had been thought of as a measure of confidence in men, rather than as an expression of opinion on measures.[38] Pledges had often been exacted in popular constituencies, and were often cried down as unconstitutional, although, as Fox pointed out, the representatives of pocket boroughs were nominees sent to speak for the interests of their patrons;[39] but a mandate on national issues of principle or interest could hardly be sought nor given until there were such issues and until the men and parties actively interested had to seek and to organize the vote of the responsible part of the population. Then the party system was set, organization of the constituencies and of the House on party lines proceeded apace by competition, and appeal to the people was decisive. That this institution of party government happened to be reinforced by the personal rivalry of Gladstone and Disraeli as party leaders with great national prestige may have been fortunate. At any rate, it raised the position of the people as arbiters; and the pressure of public business raised the position of the Cabinet, and gave it monopoly of the time of the House.[40] Politicians were still opportunist in their appeal to the people and in their interpretation of the constitution and, in particular, of the principle of the mandate, but the day of absolute representation, the sovereignty of parliament, was over: the sovereignty of the people was established.[41]

This sovereignty of the people as the outcome of a long and stormy constitutional development is a precarious authority in its effective control over policy, because it consists in the opportunity of the electorate on an adult franchise to choose the Prime Minister and the programme of the government at a general election, and this opportunity depends on there being not more than two alternatives offered, and on the constitutional obligation of the majority party to go to the country when their mandate is exhausted or if unforeseen issues of major importance come up for decision. Otherwise, effective sovereignty reverts to the House. Assuming an adult franchise, so long as the two-party system continues, with party discipline and solidarity, and in so far as the mandate principle is respected, and on condition that party leaders on both sides provide the electorate with honest and clear formulation of the issues, then, the electorate and the Cabinet maintain their interdependent ascendancy in the constitution; the House is deprived of its pre-eminence, and the people are sovereign.[42]

The historical outcome of constitutional development in England can be generalized to include parallel developments in the United States and in France and other political democracies. Such a generalization might describe these forms of government as devices to allow a regulated competition for a regulated exercise of political power, with the vote of the majority of the adult population as final arbiter, directly or indirectly, of men and measures. There are important differences in the rules for voting and in the rules for regulating and terminating the exercise of power, but in each case both legislature and executive and their measures have to be based on measured popular support and all public authorities exercise their powers under forms of popular surveillance and subject to limits and checks which institutionalize popular control.

A device is properly a deliberate contrivance for a desired effect. In this case, what is wanted? Simply, an agreed method of putting an administration in office which avoids recourse to force or fraud, a method of legitimacy? Or a method for obtaining the most efficient government available, by the competition of personalities, principles, and programmes, and by the tests of practice? Or a method of combining liberty with authority and responsibility? Or a method of organizing the general will, of giving effect to the sovereignty of the people?

Although paper constitutions are made and adopted, there is, of course, no sitting down in history to decide what is wanted from government and to devise the means by which it may be obtained. Legitimacy, efficiency, the popular element, the due combination of liberty with responsibility, together with other such aspects of government, are all important and related elements in a total complex. If any of them is lacking or is suppressed the whole is impaired; as it is when any of them is abstracted and given doctrinaire rights of sufficiency. History may be considered as the long working out of this truth. In the struggles for power, different aspects of government have been dominant at different times, reflected in different phases of political thought. Government by device, as distinct from absolute governments, in which law is the ruler's will, and from governments which pretend to or seek the authority of some absolute law independent of will, is law-making by conventional rules and customary practices, empirically established, which tend to preserve in vigour a vital inheritance of rights and amenities in the necessary conduct of government.

That these devices are not simply the most efficient contrivance for a desired result, although the general aim is to allow a regulated competition for a regulated exercise of power, is shown by the specificity of the regulating rules: what is practised with eminent success in one constitution is not likely to be borrowed with advantage. For example, the disadvantages of presidential government in the United States, which are real and may be crippling, cannot possibly be remedied by taking over what has proved most effective in British parliamentary practice (Question Time, for example, could hardly replace the inquisitions of Congressional committees).[43] The American constitution has been described as a frozen model of the British constitution at the time of George III.[44] What is true, of course, is that with borrowings at that time from that model it has followed a different course of development in other political and geographical circumstances. Relying heavily on the character, calibre, and methods of the President, the people have proved the adaptability of their form of government in the responses of successive chief executives to the challenge of events. Although capable of improvement, under pressure of new needs and technical changes, presidential government stands or falls as a system with its own genius and resources, and its own grass roots. In general, the same may be said of other democratic systems that have worked reasonably well for some generations. And those systems which have not yet established themselves as viable, in which politics jump from crisis to crisis and the name of politician is an insult, would not necessarily do well to copy devices that worked smoothly elsewhere. For, again, Britain which enjoys an enviable success in these things has to offer the world as its peculiar excellence only the possibility of a delicate maintenance of party solidarity in a two-party system, with scrupulous regard of its leaders for the mandate and an always clear formulation of real election issues. Apart from the world's slow stain by which all standards are tarnished and suffer erosion, at any moment events may explode or issues may blow up which demolish such unsure foundations. Every democratic people must work to preserve and improve the devices of their own system, and not be dazzled and distracted by any gleam of success elsewhere. A language may borrow words, but not syntax.

Constitutions, however, on the whole tell the story of old unhappy far-off things; the battle has passed over, and what really interests most people most are the programmes for which the parties seek a mandate. Nevertheless, even programmes have their season; and out of season the factious and factitious come into their own and give politicians their bad name: or perhaps more frequently, and worse, political methods encourage or require by bargain or tacit understanding an avoidance of real questions which are controversial, resulting usually in the serious, sometimes calamitous, aggravation of problems by neglect, or drift into a crisis of the regime. And when the programme does matter supremely to many people, the democratic constitution may be under severe strain, since the stakes may be high and division run deep; or if there is a common programme the sacredness of procedures may seem ritualism, the trivial formality of the law. In all circumstances, the constitution is in constant jeopardy; it is fragile; and in modern times it is exposed to the climate of ceaseless social change. With all this, it is not merely a political expedient, a device, for it is the ethos of a society, the morals of a people, their manner of living together, and therefore, as Aristotle said, the first thing in which they are to be educated.

4. THE REIGN OF PLENTY

The idea of playing the game of politics according to rules is all right so long as some have not too much to lose by playing and others too much to gain by not playing. So long as social thinking continued in political terms and on constitutional lines, this condition was assumed to obtain. Hobbes, Locke, Hume, Burke and Bentham all laboured to demonstrate the equal public interest in avoiding the appalling evils of anarchy or of misgovernment. The mutuality of society, represented in the idea of the contract, was an identity of interests in upholding institutions which prevented anarchy or prevented misgovernment.

This was the thinking of men who had property to protect and augment (or, rather, of men whose interests were bound up with those of a class of men who actually owned considerable property) and therefore had a common interest in protecting it and maintaining the legitimate ways of augmenting it. It was hardly a way of thinking which could equally arouse a sense of common interest and public spirit in the proletariat, the men who had no property and small hope of gaining any, who had only their labour to sell and a leonine bargain to expect. Maintenance of this order of things could not always seem to their certain advantage. And if the rules of the political game allowed, and therefore encouraged, them to build up power of their own, could the owners of private property be expected to surrender to numbers, to continue to play according to the rules?

When Marx in 1848[45] looked at society and at history from the point of view of the propertyless many, he did not see any general interest in providing and maintaining conventional rules for regulation of the access to and exercise of political power; he saw coming a ruthless struggle of irreconcilable class enemies; he saw the few able to do injustice without having to suffer it. There could be no common interest in maintaining this state of affairs. It was in the interests as well as in the power of the owners of industrial property to exploit the labour of the people they employed, and they could not be expected to let political freedom go so far as to let the workers escape from the bondage on which this large interest of the capitalist industrial system was directly founded. Whatever shifts of power the rules of democratic government theoretically allowed, and even facilitated, could be in fact, or in effect, only shifts within the dominant class: government by force might give way to government by fraud, but never to government by the people for the people.

Marx's view could not have had its profound and far-reaching influence if there had been nothing new in it. There always had been rich and poor, debtors and creditors, independents and dependents, men who took advantage of their privileged position to use the less fortunate as means to their ends (who in another light might appear as able and energetic men deserving the service of or their success in organizing the labour of the ruck of average, complaining mankind, individually helpless). History had ever been the ample and gorgeous annals of the rich. Marx was not commenting on that, nor taking up the cause of the downtrodden. He made what was claimed to be a scientific contribution. He did not denounce exploitation, he measured it (in the labour theory of surplus value). The capitalist system was founded on it, and eventually it must ruin the system: the goods produced would not be sold, the goods needed would not be bought. Meanwhile, in the short term, capitalists survived at each other's expense, ownership passing into fewer hands, misery increasing with the exploitation of colonies in the search for markets and raw materials, turning the rivalry of capitalists into the rivalry of nations, a world scramble for the spoils of imperialism.

The contradiction is poverty in plenty. By the division and organization of labour and by technological inventions and applications, the economic machine had become capable of producing abundance. At the same time, in the hands of private owners driven by profit-making it could not produce and put into the hands of the workers the plenty their labour made possible: because it denied them purchasing power by exploitation (without which there could not be profits), because it produced (attracted by profits) luxuries before basic needs were met, because it was restrictive (when profits were not forthcoming). In sum, the economic machine could not produce plenty in the hands of private owners, and would become increasingly restrictive. In the hands of the proletariat, whose only interest was in the production of plenty and of first things first, it could not fail to yield abundance for all.

Marx thus reproduced in economic terms the naive assumptions of political theory (sinister interests alien to the general interest) which he scorned.[46] Just as in the political theory the overwhelming majority were presumed to be equally interested in the constitutional order, so in this economic theory the masses who are not owners of the means of production are uncorrupted by special interests and have an identical interest in the production of plenty for all. Society is to be regenerated through them, by their expropriation of the expropriators, as formerly, for the radicals, by getting rid of kings and oligarchs, by democracy.

Marx's thinking drew on German philosophy, British political economy, and French socialism. In the grand manner of the age, it was a comprehensive historical and scientific synthesis, explaining the whole of the past, predicting with precision the future, and providing the guide to action and the answer to every question. In a detailed comparison with Comte, marks might be fairly evenly divided between these prophets of sociology over most of the course (after all, the law of the three stages may be as true and as useful as the materialist dialectic) until they come to their prognosis, when Marx runs far ahead, for even in 1848 the Dictatorship of the Proletariat was seriously historical and the Church of Humanity was not. Even in his day Marx dominated and steered the *avant-garde* of the international working class movement.

As a critique of classical economic theory and of liberal political theory, exposing actualities and tendencies, marxism would have been penetrating and valuable to the analyst; but the theory was peculiarly inseparable from action, the scientific precision of the analysis formulated at the same time the strategy of working-class politics and the laws of social development. If economic exploitation of labour could be measured and shown to result inevitably in the stultification of technological progress and the breakdown of capitalism, the working-class had their marching orders and could be organized for victory, since only they could deliver society from the impasse, end the political struggle and start the administration of the production and distribution of plenty. Man alienated from himself in a long pilgrimage, enslaved and tortured by his own creations, gods, kings, machines, would at last be restored to himself and enjoy his own powers in an age of universal reconciliation, fulfilment, and plenty. This pilgrim's progress was not allegorical but sober history, not utopian thinking but scientific socialism. The working-class party would not be another political party, one other organized sectional interest in the democratic state, competing for votes in the constitutional game. The communist party would be a different kind of party, would select its own members, claim their total allegiance, condition them, and when in power would fill not merely ministerial posts but not less carefully every key position in every organization throughout the country, for this once-for-all transformation of human society and human being. At this point-of-no-return, beyond politics, the painful record is closed and the history worthy to be called human begins.

5. SHOUTS OF APPETITE

When Marx and Engels wrote the *Communist Manifesto* in the nascent phase of capitalist expansion and with Guizot's example of the theory and practice of representative government before them, their powerful statement was a revelation and a gospel. But gospels are revealed only to obscure men inhabiting an underworld of eager and expectant sects. In the fulness of time the gospel may or not become an orthodox creed and the obscure sect an agent of manifest destiny. The spread of Communism has succeeded the spread of Christianity, and promises, or threatens, to cover the globe. The disillusionment of intellectuals with the God that Failed is beside the point. The point is that there is in the world a demonstrated alternative method of promoting rapidly the industrial and political development of a backward people, a method sponsored by an exponent whose great power achieved by these means is greatly admired or greatly feared.

This situation has had baleful effects, strengthening the hands of reaction, forcing the world into political polarity, raising the ultimate question, Who shall kill whom? This is a harsh climate which does not favour the democratic virtues and values necessary to the viability and vigour of parliamentary party regimes. Doubts and fears of the possibilities of democratic government are encouraged. The people and/or politicians are liable to be insulted or are jostled and edged near the abyss of scorn.

Of course, on the other side of the iron curtain there are doubts and fears and strains and stresses, too. The claim to scientific accuracy of Marx's economic analysis, once the strength of the party, is now an encumbering superstition. The party dictatorship produced its own forms of corruption. Police surveillance as the basis of power proved demoralizing, and broke down. But the inevitable jockeying for power and quest for a basis of support brings new anxieties and strains. The New Class is no more immune than the Rule of Saints from human failings: that is all one knows, and all one needs to know. It is not possible to study the USSR from the outside, to follow the shifts of power, the failures of incentives and deterrents, the fluctuations of hope and fear, aspiration and disenchantment. One can know that there as everywhere there are human changes, and that in the closed society the future is still open, that if the USSR is not utopia, neither is it *1984*. Noting that, we return to the anxieties in our own case.

Popular feeling is shocked by the apparent incongruity of the party game with the appalling seriousness of contemporary problems. Journalists run between exploiting the sport and personalities of the game and issuing a serious call from its vanities and inanities to the duties of public life. All such popular feeling of frustration may be considered as surface movements, but there are deeper currents of anxiety with their source in reflective judgements upon democracy in our time. Consider three examples; drawn from the Italian historian, Guglielmo Ferrero, the late Lord Percy of Newcastle, and Walter Lippmann.

The argument of Ferrero in *The Principles of Power* (1942) is that if mankind is to escape from revolutionary violence and its sequel of horrors in government by force and fear relieved by national wars, the first test of government is not efficiency but legitimacy, that is to say, consent. The old prescriptive rights and traditional sanctions (heredity, aristocracy, Bible and Church, splendour and veneration) have gone or withered, and the only possible modern basis of legitimacy and consent in western industrial societies is the popular vote. But this principle of legitimacy is not in itself something absolutely rational and just which solves the problem of government once for all; it has good and bad possibilities, and is simply the basis of a workable solution: from it must be deduced 'rules for a rational ethics of authority that will transform the former mystical veneration of government into a widespread knowledge and sentiment of the respective duties of government and subjects'. The old principle of primogeniture had secured legitimacy at the cost of risking the freaks of heredity and of denying organized opposition. Free universal suffrage, which is the present necessary condition for a legitimate government, risks the inertness or the irresponsibility of the masses. Ferrero quotes the Abbé Siéyès, theoretician of the Third Estate in the National Assembly, to show the drift of radical thinking:

'The government in England is the subject of a constant struggle between the Ministry and the aristocracy of the Opposition. The Nation and the King seem almost to play the part of simple spectators . . . if the People . . . wished to take a hand by means of real Representatives, does one honestly believe that the importance today given to the *balance* of powers would not disappear with the system which alone necessitates it?'

Here is the republican assumption that the people if they take the government into their own hands through representative institutions have nothing to limit their sovereignty, *de facto* or *de jure*: there is no opposition and no other obstacle to the writing of rational legislation giving effect to the general will. If this assumption, says Ferrero, leads in practice to a suppression or neglect of minority interests by the majority, the basis of democratic legitimacy is destroyed by a resort to force proscribed by the democratic principle. The right of opposition to elected majorities is the democratic principle.

'In the respect and by the respect for reciprocal limits, the government and the opposition become the two jointly liable instruments of the unique general will and amalgamate their dualism. . . . The most precious fruit of this union is the attachment of the masses to the institutions of democracy.'

'If all the people are not agreed both on the principle of legitimacy and on the great moral and religious principles of life, the right of opposition becomes a struggle to the death.' Democracy is not simply a model set of political devices which has been invented and may be exported, like a steam-engine: it is historical, and, in a given society, its conventions may be used to wage cold war or to bring about national collaboration.

'The socialist party has always had a right wing, which has tried to make the masses collaborate in democratic government, eradicating as far as possible the revolutionary spirit of the programme. But the programme remains, and is in contradiction with the aims of legitimate democracy. The latter tries to administer the collective interests of society together and harmoniously; socialism wishes to destroy the existing society and replace it with a more just and happier society. This forces the issue and raises fears, passions, struggle.'

Ferrero concludes that the democratic principle thus understood is the sovereign political obligation.

'Loyalty to the principle is a sacred promise made by each to all and by all to each: all are equally bound to respect and uphold it, no one has the right to judge it from a personal standpoint, to think himself free to accept or refuse it.'

This requires, he very well recognizes, a good deal of give and take, and is not itself a simple solution.

G

'Two things complementary to each other are needed: that those who rule know that they must make untiring efforts to minimize as far as possible the faults and disadvantages of the formula, and that in view of these efforts, all classes realize that they have the duty to tolerate the inevitable faults and disadvantages of the government to the extreme limits of human patience before destroying the system and, in pursuit of the myth of non-existent perfection, delivering themselves into the hands of revolutionary government. Above all, both governments and subjects must realize that, principles of legitimacy being human, limited, and conventional, they must be applied in loyalty and good faith for what they are, and not with deception in the intent to use them as instruments of domination and obtain results contrary to their nature.'

Lord Percy, in *The Heresy of Democracy* (1954), far from thinking that the democratic principle promises to solve the problem of legitimacy, suggests the opposite.

'The chief problem of civilized government has always been to regulate, not so much the exercise of political power, as the succession to such power. Democracy, in effect, abandons the problem; it not only refuses to protect itself against usurpation but invites it and, indeed, relies upon it to solve all major issues of government.'

What this surprising statement means, presumably, is that democracy leaves wide open to the demagogue the way to power, for, Lord Percy goes on, 'the most "available" party-nominee occupies the throne of the people's Chief Delegate until the coming of the fairy prince'. What the masses want is the satisfaction of their appetites by the State, since democracy means that they can confer total power on their own nominee. The laws and devices which oppose, or seem to oppose, or limit, the exercise of the sovereign will of the people can have no legitimacy. This is the doctrine of the Democratic State which, Lord Percy argues, was created by the French Revolution and was, and is, generically different from the older type of parliamentary 'democracy'. The failure to recognize its essentially totalist character, he says, was the crucial mistake of the peace-makers in 1919; and their failure still cripples liberal statesmanship in the British Commonwealth and in the United States. What is required, he thinks, to save Western Europe from the democratic superstition is a philosophy of Dualism, which is the ancient inheritance of civilization, not merely the dualism of government and opposition (a modern recent parliamentary development), but the dualism of the secular state and its province and the permanent moral and religious interests and ends of human existence which the State is not competent to satisfy. The philosophy of total democracy and the pattern of its law-making, justice, political organization, and the use of executive power are based solely on natural appetites and material wants, and for the satisfaction of these sovereign irresistible power is concentrated in the State, and can deliver the goods; but at the cost of destroying everything else, and ultimately itself.

'A government conceived, first and last, as an organ of power cannot decentralize; it cannot nurse life nor encourage growth. It can find its justification only in war; the national unity to which it sacrifices every other social purpose is the potential unity of a nation in arms.'

The true function of government is to make room for, and to protect and promote, a 'holy communion' of Christians separated from the world of politics, or, at the least, men and women who have other than economic and political interests and ends. What is most needed, therefore, is a government of law which creates a stable environment of mutuality, of reliable liberties and obligations, in which individuals can live and move and have their being on their own responsibility. The multiplication of legislation can destroy the very notion of law. And the sovereign power of the people to sweep away or to set aside established law is a demoralizing threat to the dignity of personal life. When law in this sense is replaced by administration which, with the power and authority of the sovereign people and modern science and technique, promises to achieve all purposes at the price of obedience, that is the end of the Christian conception of man—and of much else. In the historical experience of Western civilization, the freedom of the individual in society has been regarded as the essential means, not only of a good life, but to the perfection of humanity; freedom, that is, within the framework of a defined moral order which the individual knows and accepts. When the State, instead of limiting itself to the maintenance of that order, itself claims to be the means of a good life and of the perfection of humanity, and offers to incorporate the conscience and will of the individual in its corporate power, government makes claims which all men who have not forgotten what they are must resist and protest against.

'if men are to be governed by their own consent, they must be offered a government which proceeds on intelligible principles towards definable purposes. And these principles and purposes must be religious in the sense that they must be based upon a coherent view of what man is, of what constitutes for him a "good life", and of the means by which it can be obtained . . . of such must be the principles and purposes of any political philosophy which seeks to govern men in the future without repeating the crimes and blunders of the past.'

Walter Lippmann's argument in *The Public Philosophy* (1955), like the other two, is an appeal to history and morality. His analysis selects as the special danger the encroachment on the executive of mass opinion, which time and again on crucial issues, he contends, has in this century, since the first world war, constrained governments to act against their better judgement. The prime condition of democratic government's being other than catastrophic is that the two functions of executive responsibility and popular control shall be maintained separate and in balance:[47] the government must govern, offering leadership, initiative, decision, and action; the electors must be represented, consulted, informed, and must give or withhold consent. The executive is not merely an agent to accomplish the will of the people; it stands for the long-term public interest of the historic community; and it has information and abilities which separate it from the people, whose demands are only one factor in a total situation. Democracy itself will sink into ineptitude and anarchy, and be abandoned by the people in favour of absolute authority, unless government takes and insists on the responsibility of governing.

Just as the liberal philosophy, deriving from the Stoics and Roman jurists, required the ruler to be himself subject to the law and forbade him to make laws inconsistent with 'natural law', that is to say, the moral law as understood by right reason, so it still requires the sovereign people to be subject to established law and to legislate only in accordance with the moral law. This public philosophy brought free institutions into existence, and they cannot be maintained without respect for it.

Unfortunately, Mr Lippmann argues, this philosophy is out of fashion, that is, intellectual recognition of an objective moral order. Nothing is believed if it cannot be seen and touched. The voice of the people is the voice of God; the elector is always right if he is in a majority; there is no higher authority than the popular sovereignty exercised in the right to vote, and no stronger sanction than numerical superiority. Appetites, since they can be gratified, no longer have to be restrained. Man does not have to acquire a second, disciplined, nature. Perfection does not have to be postponed, or enjoyed only partially and ideally: it can be brought in by collective power, and enjoyed whole here and now. Such ideas, concludes Mr Lippmann, have destroyed the whole content of traditional politics and education, and with it the experience which gives civilized peoples their maturity and human worth.

'That is the central and critical condition of Western society: that the democracies are ceasing to receive the traditions of civility in which the good society, the liberal, the democratic way of life at its best, originated and developed. They are cut off from the public philosophy and the political arts which are needed to govern the liberal democratic society. . . . In Toynbee's terrible phrase, they are proletarians who are "in" but are not "of" the society they dominate.'

For good measure, on this theme I throw in also Sir Thomas Taylor's Riddell Lectures *The Discipline of Virtue* (1954),[48] in which he argues that the sovereignty of parliament, that is, of an elected majority, can be restrained only by certain widespread permanent convictions.

'First, we shall put the liberty of Christian worship and teaching, for apart from that all other liberties are, or will soon be, illusions. Second, the right of free association, giving significance and meaning to the civic life of the ordinary man. Third, the development of a system of natural rights flowing from the Christian doctrine that man is a creature of God infinitely precious in His sight and that this life is a time of training and preparation for the life to come. Fourth, the rule of law to buttress and support the rights of men. These are some at least of the cardinal safeguards against the encroachment of the State, merging into the despotism of a secular Utopia.'

All these representative arguments are prompted by the fear that democracy means that the masses will lay hold of the State as the direct agent of their will, an instrument of unlimited power to satisfy unlimited appetites; and that this delusive idea is the lure to loot, plundering policies and programmes; that democratic government is a modern spoils system. Against this tendency and danger, it is proposed to rely on: (1) loyal use of democratic institutions, with scrupulous respect for opposition and minority interests; (2) separation of the executive as responsible not merely to party and majority but specially to the historical nation and to conscience, professional and moral; (3) respect for the limits of political government and regard for the needs and ends of citizens as persons and as Christians; (4) education of the nation in these principles.

Is this fear that democracy will end in an explosion of mass appetites well founded? Is an insidious erosion from irresponsible materialism a more serious danger? Are the proposed safeguards adequate? Are the fears expressed only fears of further losses on the part of still-entrenched privilege, and are the proposed safeguards pathetic attempts to thwart democracy? The theory and practice of communism are plain to see. In theory, it does promise unlimited abundance for the easy gratification of all appetites, once the economic machine is firmly and finally in the hands of the proletariat; and in practice it does institute the dictatorship of the party in order to achieve this consummation. Further, the dictatorship has the power to try to ensure by direct coercion, if necessary, that the productive efficiency which delivers the goods is maintained. In western societies, where the issue of political democracy is in question, the economic consequences of mass demands may remain obscure until the foundations of democracy have been destroyed and communist or fascist dictatorship offers the only alternative to the miseries of anarchy. Indeed, if only material appetites of the masses exert the pull or pressure of power, there is no longer any point in democracy, no objection to a dictatorship which will deliver the goods. Hence the insistence of objectors on religious interests and moral ends.

One test of the relevance and significance of all this argument from the conservative side about present drifts and the future of democracy is to consider what left-wing writers who are not communists have to say. Of these, the late Harold Laski is perhaps the most useful for the purpose, since of all contemporaries he was most evidently heir to the *philosophes*, steeped in the radical tradition, a liberal and humanitarian caught in the dilemmas of the social revolution. The difficulty of using his ideas as a test (although it may make them more appropriate) is that they fluctuate between liberalism and marxism, or, better, amongst liberty, equality, and fraternity.

If there is a pole which draws Laski's thinking and steadily reduces its oscillations, it is equality: he upholds and justifies the demand for equality, in the rigorous sense of economic and social equality. The passion for equality is, he thinks, a constant in human nature. Each man presses for the sacrifice of uniqueness for the sake of identity; those who are excluded from privilege want only to destroy privilege. The fundamental principle of democracy, in his view, is 'the assertion that men and women have an equal claim upon the common good'—not legitimacy. Liberty and equality are not even separate, but are 'different facets of the same ideal'. Only in one classless society can the ideal of equality be realized, and only when equality is attained can liberty be given a positive meaning for the masses, and true democracy established. Therefore, in practice democracy must mean a constant drive towards the establishment of greater equality of income and property. The theoretical limit is that each man shall receive an identical return for his labour, an equal share in the social product; exceptions to this rule in the form of differences in reward can be allowed only if it is rationally demonstrated that such differences result in an increase in the total product and that those who are discriminated against benefit equally with those who are given a larger reward.

The dilemma is that movement towards this never-to-be-renounced ideal of social justice tends to destroy political democracy, in so far as in the last resort the powerful groups whose economic interests are threatened will save them by smashing democratic institutions. Much of Laski's thinking is coloured by this fear that the only political possibilities are revolutionary socialism or fascism. Socialism requires unchallengeable state power to establish a classless society and economic equality; and in carrying out this programme a socialist government cannot be scrupulously considerate of the opposition and minority interests. The programme threatens to destroy the continuity which is required by cabinet government in a parliamentary democracy.[49] Political democracy can function only when the differences of interest and policy in a society are relatively insignificant; that is to say, it will function best when the classless, equal, homogeneous society has been created. Political democracy cannot be used to create the equal society, that is the dilemma. For not to build an equal society is to abandon democracy.

The conservative fear that democracy may mean the mounting demands of mass appetites released from religious and social discipline and destroying all other values seems, then, to be justified by Laski's fear that these demands will be resisted, unless and until the popular party takes possession of the unchallengeable power of the state. And the conservative demand that political and economic interests shall be qualified by, if not subordinated to, moral and religious ends is matched by Laski's insistence that achievement of equality in these interests is the indispensable basis of the good life. Political democracy in the modern phase is caught up in this kind of conflict, or obscured in this kind of confusion.

Exclusive interest in the programme is in any case draining the life-blood of political democracy. Freedom now means to the masses the world over economic security upon the basis of expanding welfare offered and guaranteed by the government. This modern demand for a political order which will guarantee the individual a rising standard of living expresses a decisive change in men's expectations, due to the spectacular achievements of technology. Modern governments will have to justify themselves by the satisfaction of these expectations. No one should any longer expect them to be inspired by Whig principles nor restrained by fear of heresy.

6. THE ULTIMATE QUESTION

The conservative voices[50] which propose moral or religious or philosophical barriers to the popular will expressed in an electoral majority offer a counsel of despair. At the outset of modern government, Madison (in Number X of *The Federalist*) noted that if the majority have the interest and the opportunity to carry into effect schemes repugnant to the interests of minorities or the well-being of the nation, 'we well know, that neither moral nor religious motives can be relied on as an adequate control'. He relied on constitutional devices. Even when the nettle of faction (rooted mainly, as Madison recognized, in different and unequal property interests) is grasped, when faction is institutionalized and controlled as party government, is the control likely to prove adequate in the long run? Is it not likely that in the long run the popular party will gain a settled and overwhelming majority, and gradually bring about that solution which Madison put aside as impracticable, 'giving to every citizen the same opinions, the same passions, the same interests'? What will the coming permanent majority want, in that case? Liberty? Religion? Culture? Empire? Or consumer goods? An American standard of life, an increasing volume of available consumer goods: is not just this the world over what the masses will want and will demand as soon as it comes into sight? The masses have become historical, not because mobs make revolutions, but because their age-old drudgery organized as productive labour and their dumb resignation organized as decisive votes have made their numbers count, first as useful, then as necessary. The reign of plenty by the division and organization of labour and the applications of science and the machine requires a mass market. Does it matter whether the method of organization is capitalist or communist? By contrast with the *ancien régime* they are barely distinguishable. Is there any other destination than the marxist utopia, the reign of plenty, with the conflicts of politics superseded by the business of administration? Will this be the definitive solution of the social problem, the consummation of man? Or will it be the demoralization of mankind, as Nietzsche feared, 'green meadow gregariousness and bovine mediocrity', the assimilation of mankind one to another, a wearing down of all differences under lateral pressure, since only the masses are catered for, a grinding reduction to the smoothness and likeness and infinitude of sand, a sum of insignificance, a prospect of nonentity?

This ultimate form of democratic government, founded on the permanent consent of an overwhelming majority, has no precedent and therefore no name. Tocqueville, observing the tendencies of democracy in America in the first half of the nineteenth century, tried to picture it thus:

'The first thing that strikes the observation is an innumerable multitude of men all equal and alike, incessantly endeavouring to procure the petty and paltry pleasures with which they glut their lives. Each of them, living apart, is as a stranger to the fate of all the rest—his children and his private friends constitute to him the whole of mankind; as for the rest of his fellow-citizens, he is close to them, but he sees them not—he touches them, but he feels them not; he exists but in himself and for himself alone; and if his kindred still remain to him, he may be said at any rate to have lost his country. Above this race of men stands an immense and tutelary power, which takes upon itself alone to secure their gratifications, and to watch over their fate. That power is absolute, minute, regular, provident, and mild. It would be like the authority of a parent, if, like that authority, its object was to prepare men for manhood; but it seeks, on the contrary, to keep them in perpetual childhood: it is well content that people should rejoice, provided they think of nothing but rejoicing. For their happiness such a government willingly labours, but it chooses to be the sole agent and the only arbiter of that happiness: it provides for their security, foresees and supplies their necessities, facilitates their pleasures, manages their principal concerns, directs their industry, regulates the descent of property, and subdivides their inheritances—what remains, but to spare them all the care of thinking and all the trouble of living?'*

If this glimpse of the social scene under a settled regime reposing on the consent of the masses bounds the prospect in the direction of

* World's Classics ed., p. 579.

the sovereignty of the people, what is in view under the aspect of the sovereignty of the nation?

Mass fears may be as strong and compulsive as mass appetites; the desire for consumer goods may even give way to a demand for nuclear weapons. The sovereignty of the people may solve the problem of government in a certain way, perhaps definitively, but the sovereignty of the nation solves nothing. It does not even continue to raise the ultimate political question, Who shall kill whom? For a mushroom cloud hangs in the sky a more ultimate question mark which preys upon all human endeavour.

NOTES: CHAPTER II

1. *'the earliest exposition of the Whig theory':*
   'Freedom in Christianity', p. 37 in *The History of Freedom*, ed. Figgis and Laurence (London, 1909).
2. *St Thomas had laid down:*
   on valid law, *Summa Theologica*, 1a-2ae, xc 1-4; on war, 2a-2ae, xl 1; on property, 2a-2ae, lxvi 2.
3. *the reign of God through . . . conscience:*
   see Acton's 'Beginning of the Modern State', pp. 31-4, in *Lectures on Modern History*, ed. Figgis and Laurence (London, 1906).
4. *so that duty may be done:*
   'The Study of History' in *Lectures on Modern History*, p. 10: 'the equal claim of every man to be unhindered by man in the fulfilment of duty to God' is 'a doctrine . . . which is the secret essence of the Rights of Man, and the indestructible soul of Revolution'.
5. *absoluteness and paramountcy of the moral law:*
   'All human laws are, properly speaking, only declaratory; they may alter the mode and application, but have no power over the substance of original justice' (quoted by Kirk, op. cit., p. 41, from Burke's 'Tracts on the Property Laws'). For Original Justice, see St Thomas, *Disputations*, iv 'De Malo', 1.
6. *representative government:*
   Guizot's lectures of 1820-22, which he revised in 1851 after his retirement from politics, were published in translation in 1852 in Bohn's Standard Library.
7. *Modern society . . . industrial organization:*
   the reorganization of traditional political society for industrial work under the administrative leadership of technocrats was the principal idea of Saint-Simon, Comte's master: 'Tout par l'industrie, tout pour elle.' See *Doctrine de Saint-Simon*, ed. C. Bouglé et Elie Halévy (Paris, 1924). The prescience of Saint-Simon is brought out in a modern analysis which still has force, James Burnham's *The Managerial Revolution* (New York, 1941).
8. *it was not merely so:*
   see J. R. Tanner's *English Constitutional Conflicts of the Seventeenth Century* (London, 1928) for the complex issues and the occasions of cleavage.
9. *Colbert pronounced the blessed words 'laisser faire':*
   quoted by Acton, *Lectures on Modern History*, p. 326, note 38.

10. *obstructive:*

because it obscured the need for analysis and for machinery to identify and maintain the general interest, and because it occasioned a prejudice against parties.

11. *its authority in its generality:*

it is of the first importance for historical thinking to recognize that at this time number did not stand for the triumph of the masses, the ascendancy of the common, but for the ascendancy of the universal, the disinterested, whether in the thinking of Hume or Rousseau or Kant or Madison or Bentham or of others, and conceived by these in very different ways. It may be that Burke was more realistic (and advanced) in opposing property to number as principle to passion, responsibility to irresponsibility, but he missed the point of his time, the need and search for a general interest that did not prevail. Disinterestedness is not merely a fine quality of feeling, it is mainly a product of social organization. 'The individual scientist is not objective even in physics, it is the jury of his fellow-scientist that conditions the objectivity of science' (Karl Popper in *The Poverty of Historicism*, p. 155, London, 1958). The conditions on which the public interest will be maintained are not yet fully understood, but the opposition of number to property was a necessary first step in exploring the ground. The general interest for eighteenth century political thinkers was expressed and safeguarded by the common sense of numerous individuals (the majority) in so far as they reflected for themselves and were not corrupted by a faction nor influenced by contagion. This is equally true of, say, Hume, Rousseau, and Madison, although the methods they propose for securing the independence of the voter so that disinterested opinion prevails are very different. Take Hume. 'Cardinal de Retz says that all numerous assemblies, however composed, are mere mob, and swayed in their debates by the least motive. This we find confirmed by daily experience. When an absurdity strikes a member, he conveys it to his neighbour, and so on, till the whole be infected. Separate this great body, and though every member be only of middling sense, it is not probable that anything but reason can prevail over the whole. Influence and example being removed, good sense will always get the better of bad among a number of people' (Essay XVI 'Idea of a Perfect Commonwealth').

Comte, some hundred years later, sees in the republican myth of the French Revolution the triumph of 'le sentiment social', the concentration of all the powers of man upon the common welfare; he thought this was the indispensable foundation of the necessary reorganization of society, but was not itself that reorganization (*General View of Positivism*, pp. 52, 86).

12. *'Republicans listen . . .:*

Histoire politique de la Révolution Française, Aulard, p. 428.

13. *Number X of The Federalist:*

edited by Max Beloff, Oxford, 1948. Hamilton also deals with this question in Number IX. cp. also Hamilton's speech on the Constitution in *Debates of the New York Convention*.

14. *Condorcet's emphasis was in point:*

Talmon, op. cit., p. 26-7, makes a perverse mis-reading of Condorcet in refusing to see this point, and, again, in refusing to see that political empiricism, at this time, is not to be opposed to universal principles, nature and reason, since at that time these concepts served as an appeal to human experience against the establishments of authority and tradition. A true empiricism is possible only with the elimination of teleology from nature and 'faculty' from reason, and this was not to be expected of Condorcet, with full critical awareness. At this time, the ideas of 'reason and nature' were useful and necessary to give confidence to the venture into new possibilities of social experience, because the actual experience of 'the dependence of man on man and class on class' belied the mutuality and consent which many had learned to *feel* as the essence of society, and which *were* essential to a shift of morality from a religious to a social basis. This is of capital importance, and not to grasp it is totally to misunderstand the intellectual and moral impulse of the Enlightenment. The ideas of 'reason and nature' became doctrinaire only in so far as they remained immune to the test and correction of the social experience they initiated. (It was one of Comte's merits that he holds on to this.) On p. 44, Mr Talmon does seem to grasp it, but he lets go to hold more firmly to his thesis. It is indeed legitimate to affiliate totalitarian democracy to Rousseau, but Rousseau's own theoretical and spiritual affinity is with utopian theocracy, a regime with quite other pretensions, and with tendencies to liberal constitutional democracy.

15. *Condorcet's project was revised:*
Aulard would seem not to be right in thinking that the difference between the two versions was merely factious and factitious (p. 292). On the other hand, Talmon's account (pp. 78-122) is fully comprehensible to a mind made up in 1950-51.

16. *Jaurès has argued:*
Histoire Socialiste, tome iv, 'La Convention' II, pp. 1769-71. Again, Talmon's account (pp. 111ff) although accurate is misleading.

17. *Thucydides shows Pericles:*
see J. H. Finley's *Thucydides* (London, 1947), pp. 127, 154 (with references) for an exposition of this theme.

18. *Machiavelli:*
for an exploration of the liberalism of Machiavelli, and a parallel with Montesquieu, see J. H. Whitfield s *Machiavelli* (Oxford, 1947); p. 97 for the use of *virtu* and its connexion with *virtus* and *virtutes*. For a harsher view that connects him not only with seventeenth century absolutism but also with Utilitarianism, with Hegel and German and Italian nationalism, and identifies him as a 'constant and contemporary influence', see Acton's 'Introduction to Il Principe' in *History of Freedom*, esp. pp. 223-5, 231.

19. *Hobbes:*
for the connexion of Hobbes with Thucydides, and for a clear account of the shift in him from the medieval to a utilitarian idea of natural law, see Perez Zagorin's *A History of Political Thought in the English Revolution* (London, 1954), pp. 166-85.

20. *the nationalism was in the minds of statesmen:*
Eric Robson's *The American Revolution* (London, 1955), pp. 39, 90, 162. The book is an extremely stimulating view of the period by a young historian of the Namier school.

21. *refusing to save the Union:*
for a discussion of the issues and opinions and personalities in the civil war as of present significance, see Myers' *Are Men Equal?*, pp. 68-110. For

another view of the sequel to the civil war, King, *The Conservative Mind*, pp. 295-8.

22. *the arousal of a people:*
for this phase in the Revolution, see Aulard's *Christianity and the French Revolution* (tr. Lady Frazer, London, 1927).

23. *an early legal-minded king:*
and it is Edward I of England who is quoted in the article *Représentants* in Diderot's *Encyclopédie*, putting in his mouth the Romano-canonical maxim: there is no more equitable rule than that things which interest all should be approved by all, and that common dangers should be repelled by common efforts. How devices of expediency became regular and necessary means of administration, and customs became rights, and forms were respected as principles, is usefully traced in George L. Haskin's *The Growth of Representative Government* (Oxford, 1948).

24. *their ineptitude: . . . in the handling of Parliament:*
Williams M. Mitchell, in *The Rise of the Revolutionary Party in the House of Commons 1603-1629* (New York, 1957), tries to discover by an analysis of procedure 'the period in which the direction of the business of the House passed into the hands of the House itself and into the hands of the generality of members and out of the hands of a small, powerful, court-controlled group' (p. 36). He traces the increase in the use and importance of committees, including the committee of the whole House, and concludes that in the parliaments of 1626 and 1628 nothing could be clearer than that the members opposed to the crown and zealous for the liberty of the subject were running the committees.

25. *The Long Parliament:*
see Tanner op. cit., pp. 91-109.

26. *infinite political discussion:*
the most comprehensive account is by Zagorin op. cit.

27. *failed to . . . manage his parliaments:*
the argument of H. R. Trevor-Roper, 'Oliver Cromwell and his Parliaments', in *Essays presented to Sir Lewis Namier*, ed. Povey and Taylor (London, 1956).
For a more positive view of Cromwell and of his contribution to the development of parliamentary democracy, and for the idea of sovereignty at this time, see Maurice Ashley's *The Greatness of Oliver Cromwell* (London, 1958).

28. *the dominant Anglican:*
Godfrey Davies, *Essays on the later Stuarts* (San Marino, California, 1958) p. 51.

29. *to control the game of politics:*
The political struggle was thus concentrated not merely in parliament but mainly in the House of Commons; because if the checks on the Commons which constitutionally lay with the Lords and the Crown were freely used they would force ultimate issues and threaten to destroy the constitution; therefore the interests of the Crown and of the peers had to be strongly enough represented within the Commons not to be exerted against the Commons. Burke's constitutional balance and moral harmony were essentially achieved within the House of Commons, which greatly facilitated democratic constitutional development.
For the intrigues and issues which brought William to England, see

Lucile Pinkham's *William III and the Respectable Revolution* (Camb., Mass., 1954).

Lord Acton, who had an unusual nose for historical guilt, accepted the Whig interpretation of history which took first shape in the period of organized Whig Opposition (1762-82) and summarized it in a couple of pages (*Lectures on Modern History*, pp. 231, 276). If modern historians find less reason for enthusiasm, it is at least admitted that the English Revolution saved the country from an English version of the French monarchy and kept the road open to parliamentary development (see J. H. Plumb's *Sir Robert Walpole*, vol. i, chap. 2, London, 1956).

Reluctantly, even conservative-minded grandees were driven to see the subservience to France which the Stuart idea of monarchy involved, and were alienated from it and brought nearer to those who stood for control of the king's servants and policies by Parliament, representing propertied interests. This can be profitably studied in the case of the Marquis of Halifax, one of the best political minds of the time. See H. C. Foxcroft's *A Character of the Trimmer* (Cambridge, 1946): for James's own idea of his sovereignty, p. 217; for notes of speeches defining the role of Parliament in relations with William III, pp. 318, 321. 'He clearly foresaw the enormous powers, for good or evil, which inhere in political organization, as contrasted with mere numerical superiority' (p. 338). The radical turn given to the triumph of the Whig ideas is exemplified in Richard Price: 'Imbued with the ideas of Locke and generations of English Whigs, he believed that the sovereignty of the people had become a principle of the British constitution through the Glorious Revolution and the Hanoverian Succession. Therefore, he insisted that each portion of the Empire ought to be allowed to govern itself in strictly local concerns. Price did not aim merely at arguing abstract political ideas through his writings, although some of his critics accused him of it. Rather he wished to assert principles which he believed to be embodied in the British constitution and the basis of government in all British areas' (J. P. Agnew's *Richard Price and the American Revolution;* Urbana, Illinois, 1949).

30. *the attempt was vain:*
see C. S. Emden's *The People and the Constitution* (sec. ed., Oxford, 1956), p. 105. Burke's laud of the Whig Junto of 1708 in *Thoughts on the Present Discontents* (177) is worth remark here.

31. *Opposition:*
a new view of the politics of the eighteenth century has of course emerged from the scholarship initiated by Sir Lewis Namier in *The Structure of Politics at the Accession of George III* (sec. ed., London, 1957). Of general interest are: J. H. Plumb's *Sir Robert Walpole* and his *The First Four Georges*, R. Pares's *King George III and the Politicians* (1953), Sir Lewis's Romanes Lecture 'Monarchy and the Party System' (reprinted in *Personalities and Powers*, 1955), and Eric Robson's *The American Revolution*.

For the basis of Opposition in the country, see Lucy Sutherland's essay 'The City of London in Eighteenth Century Politics' (in *Essays Presented to Sir Lewis Namier*) and S. Maccoby's *English Radicalism*, vol. i 'The Origins' 1762-85 (London, 1955).

For a succinct statement of the older view, see Lord Acton's 'The Hanoverian Settlement' in *Lectures in Modern History*, pp. 264, 275-6.

For the constitutional influence of the Press, A. Aspinall's essay 'The Reporting and Publication of the House of Commons Debates 1771-1834' in *Essays Presented to Sir Lewis Namier*, and his *Politics and the Press*.

For a vivid account of Walpole and Townshend in opposition, setting a precedent and a pattern, see Plumb, *The First Four Georges*, pp. 5of.

32. *competition to get into Parliament:*
chap. I of *The Structure of Politics at the Accession of George III*, esp. p. 16.

33. *made this parliamentary game safe:*
cp. p. 103 below.

34. *longer than used to be thought:*
because the Whig interpretation of history took Burke's *Thoughts* not as a political pamphlet in the Rockingham interest but as contemporary history and political philosophy, 'the most instructive . . . political treatise in our language' (George Otto Trevelyan in *The Early History of Charles James Fox*, p. 144). Sir George declares: 'Burke's great pamphlet on the Discontents showed with marvellous clearness . . . that the patriots of 1769, when they protected Wilkes in his rights, were in truth defending the commonwealth against an attack upon its liberties more covert and less direct, but quite as determined, as that which was planned by Strafford and repelled by the Long Parliament' (p. 208).

For the modern view, see Pares, *King George III and the Politicians*, and Plumb, *The First Four Georges*, pp. 123ff; also, Robson, *The American Revolution*, pp. 25, 62, 149ff. But also Emden, *The People and the Constitution*, pp. 51, 109-10, 136.

35. *Hume is . . . afraid of party:*
Essay VIII 'Of Parties in General' and XIV 'Of the Coalition of Parties'. On the connexion of party and civil war, there is an interesting passage in Foxcroft, *A Character of the Trimmer* (p. 123): 'He told me it was to be feared some unhappy differences might arise in the nation from the disputes about the succession; and in case it should come to a war, it might be convenient to form something of a party in one's thoughts. He told me that he knew very well there was but one other and myself that had any considerable interest in my neighbourhood; asked me my opinion how their inclination stood . . . and he did agree with me that the loyal interest was not only much more numerous, but consisted of more wealthy and active men; and that those who were so busy in Parliament against the Court, were men of little power or esteem in their country'—Halifax to Reresby, 1680.

36. *The first modern . . . party issue:*
Emden, *The People and the Constitution*, p. III and chaps. v and vi for the conditions and growth of party organization and opinions on party. Also Wallas, *The Life of Francis Place*, pp. 322, 326.

37. *Voting measures the force of public opinion:*
The People and the Constitution, p. 73.

38. *men, rather than . . . measures:*
The People and the Constitution, pp. 238-44.

Burke, who strongly disapproved of pledges, referred to 'the cant of not men, but measures' (the reference was to Chatham) used to dissolve or to disparage 'connexion', that is, party, but it was on reform measures that effective party organization was first formed (Maccoby, op. cit., and Graham Wallas). Bentham says of the aphorism: It is the opposer-general's justification, this way or in reverse (not measures, but men) according to whether you are opposing party or bill, or else justifying support of your party or opposition to ministers against your own sincere opinion. The point, however, is that men are good or bad as ministers in virtue of their measures (*The Book of Fallacies*).

39. *Fox pointed out:*
in the House of Commons, May 26, 1797. *Selected Speeches on the Constitution*, ed. C. S. Emden (World's Classics, 1939), vol. ii, pp. 134-6. Also Betty Kemp's essay 'The Stewardship of the Chiltern Hundreds' in *Essays Presented to Sir Lewis Namier*.

40. *monopoly of the time of the House:*
'the new rules of 1862 . . . constitute the real watershed between the ancient parliamentary regime and modern practice' ('The Changes in Parliamentary Procedure, 1880-82' by Edwards Hughes, in *Essays Presented to Sir Lewis Namier*).

41. *absolute representation:*
The People and the Constitution, pp. 70-1. See also Elie Halévy's *History of the English People* (Penguin ed. vol. i, 241-2): the House of Commons as 'the legal country' independent of public opinion was a fiction of the constitution expressly contradicted by the practice of dissolution, adopted by George III and his ministers towards the close of the eighteenth century, and this practice therefore marked a democratic development of parliamentary government.

42. *in so far as the mandate principle is respected:*
for this whole view of the mandate and of the constitutional basis of popular control, see *The People and the Constitution*, *passim*, but esp. pp. 197-316.

43. *For example:*
Dean Acheson in *A Citizen Looks at Congress* (London, 1957) begins with an examination of an early thesis of Woodrow Wilson on the assumption that 'The most striking contrast in modern politics is . . . between Congressional and Parliamentary governments' (p. 31) and that American practice can be improved by studying the British mechanics of parliamentary government. Mr Acheson shows that this is a mistaken approach; especially on the inappropriateness of British party organization to the American scene (pp. 30-4).

44. *a frozen model:*
Eric Robson op. cit., chap.x.

45. *in 1848:*
the Communist Manifesto was published in February 1848, some three months after Marx and Engels had been authorized by a Congress of the Communist League to draft a complete programme, theoretical and practical.

46. *Marx . . . reproduced:*
there is the same pattern of argument in Marx and, say, St Just: the general interest which consists in constitutional liberty and equality [economic plenty] will be spontaneously upheld by the public spirit of the great majority if and when the great privileged interests which stand in the way of constitutional liberty and equality [the production of economic plenty] are removed.

Basically, this is the simple truth that the conditions of thriving activities and basic satisfactions tend, in so far as they are understood, to be protected by those who are enjoying them. This is a truth which can be observed in a small community, say, a school. On the historical scale, the conditions of thriving activities and basic satisfactions can never be easy to understand. Nevertheless, the simple abstract truth is the heart of the radical faith. So long as this faith is open-eyed it does not commit the radical to hopeless utopian courses.

47. *executive responsibility and popular control shall be . . . separate:*
cp. Kirk, *The Conservative Mind*, p. 287.

48. *For good measure:*
a better choice might be Richard Law's *Return from Utopia* (London, 1950) which reaffirms with a renewed and profound conviction the conservative's union of politics and religion and his insistence on the distinction, even opposition, between parliamentary or constitutional government and democracy: 'our political institutions have been developed over long centuries, not to express the people's will . . . but simply to check the pretensions of the executive power' (pp. 182-3).

Worthier far to stand as champion for the host of modern theocracy is Bertrand de Jouvenel, whose 'explorations' in *Sovereignty* (tr. J. F. Huntington, Cambridge, 1957) were unfortunately encountered too late to be dealt with in these pages. Suffice it to say that if I had read this book sooner I should have referred to it at many points in the writing of my own, but should have seen no reason to modify, save by further explanation, what I have written.

49. *the continuity which is required by cabinet government:*
Laski in *The Crisis (1931) and After* quotes A. J. Balfour: 'Let the political parties be reduced to two, but let the chasm dividing them be as profound that a change of Administration would in fact be a revolution disguised under a constitutional procedure. Does not this illustration show how delicate is the political machinery whose smooth working we usually take as a matter of course? Is there any ground for expecting that our Cabinet system, admirably fitted to adjust political action to the ordinary oscillations of public opinion, could deal with these violent situations? Could it long survive that shock of revolutionary and counter-revolutionary violence? I know not. The experiment has never been tried. Our alternating Cabinets, though belonging to different parties, have never differed about the foundations of society. And it is evident that our whole political machinery presupposes a people so fundamentally at one that they can afford to bicker; and so sure of their moderation that they are not dangerously disturbed by the never-ending din of political conflict.'
Cp. p. 87 above.

50. *the conservative voices:*
those quoted in this section join those who inspired the opening of Chapter 1 above, and the theocrats of earlier days. Theocrats, evident or disguised, want to stabilize and tranquilize society on the basis of impersonal law: for them the aim of politics is to make law prevail over will, a law that does not have its source in will. The conservative ideal is thus bound up with a religious view of man and society, for only a religious view would *substitute* law for will, duty for interest—and this can be done only notionally or hypocritically. When in practice government becomes a set of expediences and devices, the religious conservative idealizes the checks on the power of the Executive as hindrances to man's hindrances to the fulfilment of duty to God, if not as hindrances to social perdition by plans and programmes for or by the unregenerate people. ('In western democracies the notion of the rule of law predominates over

H

the idea of the sovereignty of the people, vastly so in practice and to a less extent in theory. So long as this continues to be the case, the Christian and theological origins of our democracy will continue to be plain to the eye of the careful observer'—Casserley, *The Bent World*, p. 74.) Marx also substituted law for will in politics, but this law was itself a law of material development that blessed and promised the gratification of appetites, a secular religion. The difference between utopian theocracy and totalitarian democracy is also plain to the eye of the careful observer. We shall never see Plato's state nor Rousseau's, but the marxian state is with us, and marches on to its ends or its end. The moral is pointed by Mill in his Diary for April 8, 1854, referred to in chap. 1 above, note 42.

CHAPTER III

The Perfectibility of the Species

ARGUMENT

EIGHTEENTH CENTURY *philosophers discovered that human behaviour is socially conditioned, and on their assumptions about human nature they invented social systems in accordance with nature. Nineteenth century philosophers discovered that both social systems and human behaviour, in spite of the illusions of other philosophers, are the work of laws of development beyond human control. Twentieth century philosophers are not happy about inventing social systems nor large-scale social theories of any kind. There is enough to do to find out what is in fact going on in some fairly specialized section of the vast social field. But if twentieth century philosophers did want to invent a social system suited to human nature and in control of human behaviour, they know far more about human behaviour and its conditioning than the eighteenth century did; and since then political change has raised the mass of people in the scale of political decision, and mass interests and mass pleasures dominate the social scene today. That is to say, the job could now be done as never before. Therefore it is not extravagant to suppose that sooner or later it may be done. When Aldous Huxley wrote* Brave New World *he drew current trends to a conclusion. For an animal that seeks pleasure and avoids pain, this is Utopia. It is even respectable, for in a commonplace way it promises to do for the masses something that high religion has offered to the chosen few.*

All the same, the intellectual is revolted. But what is his case? Anyhow, his regrets and his fears, and his powers to express them, inject into the upper atmosphere a vapour of alarm and despondency too volatile to sink into the lungs of those engaged on the floor. His voice will not be listened to even if what is in question is the ruin of the human species in order to perfect it.

I. RESEARCH UNLIMITED

Often the pious or sententious language of the past makes one feel uncomfortable. The language of Condorcet's dream might affect one

as the US proposal for a Disarmament Commission affected Mr
Vyshinsky, might make one 'laugh all night':

'Finally, we see the rise of a new doctrine which was to deal the
final blow to the already tottering structure of prejudice—the
doctrine of the indefinite perfectibility of the human race of which
Turgot, Price, and Priestley were the first and most brilliant apostles.'

The philosopher who said 'knowledge, liberty, virtue, and respect
for the natural rights of man are the only real goods we possess' was
not the prophet of our age. The bright face of equality in which he
saw the human future had a dark side plainly visible to Tocqueville;
but that vision of eventless domesticity, the senility of the human
race, was also a dream, a bad dream if you like, but perhaps sweeter
than reality. Mankind is not very likely to sink into a state of permanent quiescence, and there are worse possibilities. Historical man,
driven by his own passions and tormented by his own deeds, but also
the victim of events, situations, and systems he can neither escape
nor control, is still in need of the social salvation he has been deceived into thinking will come. He knows now that it will not come.
Teleology is no more true than theology.

Are we not still, and now hopelessly, in the predicament from
which Comte sought and thought to rescue us? The revolutionary
principles cannot found any new order. Nor can the old regime be
brought back. But at this time of day can we set off hopefully to find
in history the principles for the permanent foundation of modern
society? The social science on which Comte relied is devoted to
trying to find out what is in fact going on. Its specialists are busy on
their investigations, measuring, for example, the effects of social
class on the response to educational opportunity. Who knows
enough to predict the social future in all its complexity? Who knows
enough to undertake to elaborate general methods of control? Such
tasks are postponed, that is to say, abandoned.

Quite rightly abandoned, no doubt, in the view of contemporary
philosophers. After all, science, at its best, can provide the means
only if the ends are given; and the end of theology and of teleogy
means that the ends are not given. The language of Plato and
Aristotle, with the problems it set and the answers they found, is
even more obsolete than the language of the Bible.[1] If one wants a
formal definition of man, there is nothing better than Aristotle's
formula 'rational-animal', which derives all the specific attributes of
man from the defining essence of the differentia, rationality. Good
enough, if the working purpose of the definition is to mark man's

distinction of himself from other animals. But if one thinks of the essence of rationality as this formal ordering of ideas, and therefore of man's perfection as consisting in a perfect ordering of ideas, corresponding to a perfect formal structure in the universe, with perfect conformity to that order, then, this is a tragic mistake with a progeny of mischief as the stars of the heaven and as the sand which is upon the sea shore. Then one asks, What is justice? instead of investigating our use of the word 'justice'; or, What is good in itself, or the chief end of action? instead of comparing 'goods'. Much worse, one exalts abstract knowledge over experience, contemplation over action, intellect over the passions, and substitutes the order of ideas for the order of nature and language for reality. Then it is possible to body forth the perfection of the species in an elaborate definition of justice which is the whole of the *Republic*, and Plato can show that perfection to consist in the appropriate excellence of the several functional classes in the State in due subordination and co-ordination, corresponding perfectly to the excellence of the equivalent parts and their order in the human psyche.

Unfortunately or fortunately, no species is perfectible unless it has a built-in pattern of this kind. One cannot sensibly speak of a 'perfect cow' or a 'perfect dog', for breeders have been able to have different ideas, and have explored and exploited a variety of possibilities, for use and enjoyment, and certainly not excluding fad and fancy. Anthropological studies show a similar variety produced by different methods but on the same principles. If the objection is made that these are merely differences in physical type, which do not preclude excellences, virtues, ideals, as the goal of a common perfection, the answer must be that in fact the patterns of culture are different and that in what are assumed to be advanced cultures different ideals subsist. If Christ is the divine exemplar of what human beings are intended to be, if the saint devoted to the imitation of Christ is the type of human perfection, however much a challenge to most ordinary ways of living, this pattern of perfection is not the only one possible, and is certainly not built-in: it becomes a pattern only by choice, and the rejection of alternatives.[2]

Reason, then, in science and philosophy, fails to provide us with ends or with a common human ideal in terms of which man is perfectible. That does not help to mitigate the conflict of nation with nation, class with class, race with race, creed with creed, man with man. The world goes on, certainly, in spite of mutual destructiveness. But also the mutual destructiveness goes on. Nuclear weapons have heightened the consequences dramatically, and done more than anything in history to bring us to our senses. But that has not yet brought any dramatic change in our goings on. Whether the appalling possibility of all-out global war will sober statesmanship short of catastrophe and induce a creative act or will become too familiar to prevent the irretrievable blunder sooner or later, or what will happen, is the gigantic question mark which overhangs all our thinking and doing, and makes this generation the most fateful in the history of mankind. Quantity of destructiveness has changed its quality, and has therefore changed the calculations which go to the making of decisions for or against the courses and policies which risk a resort to force. History, if not reason, has now made out with blinding plainness and compelling force the case for organized international security and world order as a common end for all mankind. On the other side, is massed all the non-reason and unreason which historians and psychologists have taught us to add to the definition of man: the natural and necessary aggressiveness which is not always manageable, and the fears which are not always unreasonable, so easily and frequently linked with other impulses and likely to be found in conjunction with situations and occasions which detonate a reckless explosion. The fact that in the present world situation there is a question at all silences all that can be said. Those who are thinking hear only the uneasy silence in which the answer is awaited.

2. THE LATEST MODEL

There is one possibility of coping firmly and finally with the human situation which should be given full and fair consideration. *Brave New World*, on acquaintance and in the light of alternatives, may begin to look less like a bad joke and more like the one secular hope left to mind at the end of its tether.[3] The failure of hopes founded on the liberal sciences of politics and economics and of those founded on sociological laws of history does not exhaust the resources of science for the control of society. If the utopias have turned into nightmares, they are at least closer to us, and may lose some of their terrors by familiarity, and perhaps disclose advantages. If the brave new world is brought into existence, it is at least possible to maintain it, precisely because it consists in a deliberate elimination of all the sources of trouble; it institutes thereby a stabilization of human affairs. On these terms, men can deal with man. Look at it again: it is not merely a satirical fantasy, mocking a civilization absorbed in a culture of gadgets; it is an instructive demonstration of the conditions on which human beings can at last take their affairs in hand and put an end to their torments. If theology and teleology have failed, technology may avail.

Orwell's wicked alternative model, *Nineteen Eighty-four*, quite the most hideous book in print, is a violent wind that blows up from the left and drives us towards this haven. It bears no scents from blessed isles.

Huxley's story, which more or less amused him when he wrote it, and to which he reacted more positively in a Foreword which he wrote to a reprint fifteen years yater, can be taken as a serious project. In this Foreword, Huxley saw four alternatives as the shape of things to come in 1946: we may blow ourselves to smithereens; we may choose to decentralize and to apply science to producing a race of free individuals; we may get a number of national militarized totalitarianisms, having as their root the terror of the atomic bomb and as their consequence the destruction of civilization, or, if the warfare is limited, the perpetuation of militarism — Orwell's picture; or else one supra-national totalitarianism, called into existence by the social chaos resulting from rapid technological progress in general and the atomic revolution in particular, and developing, under the need for efficiency and stability, into the welfare-tyranny of Utopia. Ruling out the first and third, not as impossible but as unattractive, we are left with Huxley's own choice, the decentralized free civilization (which he had not formulated as an ideal when he wrote the story), and his Brave New World. Obviously, Huxley's choice could be attained only by widespread deliberate and sustained purpose. Equally, Brave New World could exist only as the creation of a deliberate, bold, resourceful, and sustained social art. Neither is something we shall drift into. The others might be. The last sentence of the Foreword is: 'You pays your money and you takes your choice.'

Of these two choices (if drift is not choice), Huxley's plainly calls for a more mature, widespread, and unlikely decision than the other. It is unlikely because it is against the grain of things, whereas the other, as he says, is 'called into existence by the social chaos resulting from rapid technological progress . . . and developing under the need for efficiency and stability. . . .' The impact of his fable resulted from the suggestion appealing to our fear that this is indeed the kind of world which the future will turn into, because we are being carried in that direction by the rapid current of uncontrollable social change. Therefore, although Brave New World is unthinkable without extremely bold, far-reaching, irreversible decisions, nevertheless, it is a world which can be brought into existence in spite of ourselves, simply because the situation we are drifting into and not choosing may sooner or later be so out of control and menacing that it forces us to take or consent to the necessary decisions which would establish Brave New World, accepted as the attainable alternative which offers stability happily combined with security for accustomed values and a familiar and desired way of life.

Thus, the fantasy whose author set out lightly to flutter fears by exposing the drift of contemporary hopes may end as the one serious instructive model for the relief of man's estate. There are conditions of secular salvation, on which men can enjoy social stability, perfect adjustment one to another and of each to his environment and his lot, a final deliverance from the endless strife and anxiety, a clean-up once for ever of all the dirt and misery, the sin and malaise, the crankiness and cunning, the violence and brutality which have stained and fevered and poisoned the lives of men and women down the ages. The idea of Herbert Spencer that in the fulness of time the process of social evolution would bring about a perfect adjustment of man to his environment cannot be relied on, unless it means that inevitable events will compel men finally to stabilize their environment and the conditions of their existence or else succumb to them.

Social philosophies have been founded upon assumptions about man's essence or about his behaviour or upon assumed cosmic or historical laws. If, however, man is a conditioned animal, an indefinitely conditionable animal, there is no ground for these assumptions, no fixed point on which to found the construction; expectations will continue to be falsified by events unless and until the social scientist gives up trying to explain and predict starting from 'natures', a study of natural determinism, and sets out to determine a definitive man in a definitive environment: the social philosophers have only *interpreted* man in various ways; the point however is to *change* him. Rather, the point is to fix him, and his environment. Left to himself, man is not going to become more perfect, whatever that may be understood to mean. What is likely is that the unintended, unforeseeable consequences of what he does will make his problems more and more intractable, until they overwhelm him. The ideas of the eighteenth century humanists, of nineteenth century historical prophets, and of contemporary conservative reactionaries are, alike, useless historical relics. The true rationalist and radical will look at the problem realistically in the light of the alternatives. Was it happiness that was supposed to be the chief end of human action? Pleasure can be maximized and pain minimized, troubles and anxieties eliminated, security and stability established, if the requisite means are adopted which science has furnished. This is Huxley. Otherwise, there is Orwell. Or there is the mess that is likely to be made by a global explosion of superweapons. On secular assumptions, can there be anything else? Unless the kingdom of God is coming anyway, these are the things that are coming anyway. There is something to choose among them, and at this stage the choice is ours. Man as a species is perfectable on Huxley's conditions. His world has adolescent appeal, it is a world made safe for pleasures of the most usual kind, it is the greatest happiness of the greatest number as far as human calculation of pleasures and pains can ever hope to produce it, and, in so far as enlightenment and emancipation meant getting away from the superstition of traditional ideas and ideals and from the inhibitions of tabus, it is an enlightened and emancipated world. Thus, although it does not follow the expectations of the early radicals, it makes sense in the terms of their thinking. It is certainly not what they saw in the glow of their ardent striving, but it may well be the daylight aspect of their dream. None of these things could be said of Orwell's horror, the awful shadow of inescapable darkness which will swallow up the generation that refuses the light of *Brave New World*.

Man, then, can create himself and his environment in perfect and stable adjustment, for the sake of pleasure and ease, if he is rationalist and radical enough. Why should the scruples and whines of disgruntled intellectuals, hopelessly maladjusted to modern civilization anyway, stand in the way of this perfect catering for mass satisfactions as a permanent way of life? Of course, if the Christians are right, if there is a divine order, it cannot be done, or it cannot be done with impunity. Of course, if they were right it would not be necessary. The strength of their position, as the defence of conservatism in the profoundest sense, is stronger than they think even when they proclaim it; but the weakness of their position on the other side, the side of its credibility, still more, its intelligibility, is far weaker than they think even when they admit its vulnerability. The half-dismantled keep is not a defence on which to rely. *Brave New World* that to begin with looked like fantasy or nightmare, may, on reflection, come to look like temptation, and then, with familiarity, like the inescapable truth about human life in the mass, which will grow more tolerable and even more desirable as our prejudices fade with the dead hopes of other things.

Of course *Brave New World* remains an essay in rationalism and radicalism bolder than anything previously conceived, and its breach with the ideas of 1789 is at least as wide as its separation from the Christian-conservative tradition. Such a break in continuity cannot be easy. It will require resolute and ruthless decisions. They would be unthinkable if it were not that more terrifying alternatives press hard, and will press harder. The science is available to carry through the job. What is in question is the nerve. On this point, a few reflections suggest a convincing answer. What has been done in totalitarian States by dictators and their accomplices and tools is evidence enough, if history had not been sufficient, that men have the nerve to take such steps as these. Indeed, the main point of contemporary satires is precisely to focus a searchlight on this fact. If we are conditionable, before steps are taken to introduce the drastic conditioning of *Brave New World* we shall get used to the idea, we shall be influenced by propaganda filled with its immense attractions by comparison with the probable alternatives. We are used to science fiction and to apocalyptic visions. We have got used to strange things in the visual arts. In a generation or two, in major respects *Brave New World* is likely to seem more familiar and more acceptable than many dominant features of our still old-fashioned world.[4] After all, Huxley made his point by showing the full and final outcome of the kind of world with which we were becoming increasingly familiar.

The species is perfectible in a definite and definitive sense, then, if we are rational and radical enough for a major decision: the mechanical means are available; the incentives are strong enough to have a chance to prevail over the inertia and the resistances; the special opposition which Christianity puts in the way is not more likely to prove effective in this case than in so many other cases which history records. However, I am not arguing that we should take this decision. I am saying that this alternative demands serious consideration, that it is better than some others, that a good deal that would be objected to it is likely to be mere prejudice, that it is a rationalist-radical solution which seems more feasible than earlier hopes for the emancipation and enlightenment of the masses. Christian objections are obvious and insuperable, although they may be swept aside. Humanist objections may seem just as obvious, and even more impotent; but they are not so obviously insuperable. If this kind of decision is ever taken, under pressure from the masses or with the support of the masses, it will be undertaken by leaders who are not Christians and who have convinced themselves that no better alternative is open to mankind.

3. ABOLITIONS OF MAN

An author who aspires to write in the radical tradition leaves the foregoing pages with some feeling of shame. He may try to restore his self-esteem by murmuring, 'We are all terrorists nowadays', but that only shows the sorry pass to which we have all come. Having exchanged the fear of God for the fear of man, and of human existence itself, we are more strung up than ever, and every writer falls to the temptation to play on our nerves. Those who do not still crave the excitements of terrorism are sated with horrors and immune to the beastliness of intellectuals, both equally evil states. The rationalist, whose respected predecessors made it their prime business to debunk religious terrorism, knows that it is his business today to dispel the fear of human existence and to restore man's confidence in himself — for which simple debunking does not suffice.

To have indulged even in the mild terrorism of the foregoing pages might be inexcusable if it were not as a matter of fact necessary to do our political thinking nowadays with the kind of concept elaborated in *Brave New World*.[5] It is closer to the facts and the possibilities than the *Republic*; it is *Leviathan* or *The Fable of the Bees* brought up to date. It is necessary now to take *Brave New World* more seriously than Huxley himself at first intended, for the old-fashioned forms both of radicalism and of conservatism begin to look as primitive and pathetic as Comte thought they were, a vain childish striving on the one hand and a clinging to nurse on the other. Since what most ordinary people ordinarily want can be specified and provided and since most of the most objectionable features of human existence can be removed or mitigated, why not set out to do it?

To decide for or against *Brave New World* in a rational way, one would have to bring together all the relevant information. This would include (i) the detailed steps necessary to establish *Brave New World*, (ii) the probable consequences of taking these steps, positive and negative, (iii) the consequences of rejecting *Brave New World*, (iv) the motives involved (a) in choosing *Brave New World*, (b) in rejecting *Brave New World*, (v) the alternatives, together with similar information in respect of each of them. Since an exhaustive examination of the question in this way would be a large-scale undertaking, and the exigencies of modern publishing and the tastes of modern readers forbid big books, and for fear of making heavy weather of an argument that too few will take seriously, I shall confine my consideration to one of the consequences of *Brave New World*.

The most striking aspect of a society brought under definitive control, as depicted by both Huxley and Orwell, is the reduction of the dimensions of human existence. Time and space are tampered with in a radical way. There is no remembered past, and the future, being a repetition of the present, has no significance. All indepen-

dent reality is screened, so that no unchecked influence filters
through. History and science are brought to an end, and thus the
twin sources of comparison, and therefore of criticism and change,
dry up. In *Nineteen Eighty-four* the records are continuously faked
to confirm current policy; in *Brave New World* history is furtive,
obscene or ridiculous: in both, science is employed on maintaining
the situation and is definitively cut off from all new fields of application. With the stoppage of history and science by the emptying of
time and space, their inner correlatives, independent thought and individual sensibility, have no use or meaning. The direct conditioning designed to eliminate them only hastens this adaptation.

In Sartre's play *Huis Clos* the future only is removed; the past is
too well remembered, and there remains the independent outer
reality of other people's minds: together, this constitutes hell. In
Brave New World these sources of suffering are removed: there is
nothing to redeem, nothing to achieve; the power of creation has
been brought to an end, and with it the misery of human existence.

The operation is evidently drastic, mutilating, but it is also
evidently useful, since it does away with the sources of trouble. It
may become necessary. After all, it has always been the rule, even
when the world was much simpler and man was not faced with the
terrifying problems of today. What does a primitive society do but
interpose between the individual and the world a detailed pattern
of culture which suffices and in terms of which he lives? What do
the disciplines of some of the great historical religions offer but
escape from or transcendence of the temporal conditions of human
existence, by doing away with history and the independent world?
These have catered only for the very few who were capable of the
necessary renunciations and who desired union with undifferentiated Absolute Being; the multitude followed afar off, with
reverence for the saints who enjoyed for them vicarious blessedness.
Brave New World caters for the many, and meets their capacities
and suits their tastes. It is perhaps fitting that a world which has
achieved science and democracy should put them to a final use
sanctioned by age-old wisdom. It is the one way of dealing with that
historical source of all our troubles so hated by so many of our conservative and religious thinkers, the Renaissance, that high point of
blazing intensity in the consciousness of past, present, and future in
their vital interdependence and creative integrity.

C. S. Lewis gave to his Riddell Lectures of 1943 the title *The
Abolition of Man*. His thesis was that 'Man's conquest of himself
means simply the rule of the Conditioners over the conditioned
human material, the world of post-humanity which, some know-

ingly and some unknowingly, nearly all men in all nations are at present labouring to produce'. This process, in his view was the result of the abandonment of allegiance to the *Tao*, absolute law, absolute values, absolute truth, which kept men sane and safe, their surrender to arbitrary will in themselves and in others. When the tourist ceases to experience the waterfall as 'sublime' and has his private sensibilities about it, civilization is on the edge of the cultural slide into the abolition of man.

Unfortunately, independent thought and individual sensibility, bound up as they are with the temporal-spatial character of experience, cannot be stabilized under the mild regime of absolute truth, law, and the rest without also starting the slide into abolition. Professor Lewis's homoeopathy is the fashionable, though old-fashioned, treatment: fixing of the environment and reduction of spatio-temporal reality by the imposition of absolutes cures man of the dangerous forms of independent thought and individual sensibility and saves him from abolition by inducing enfeeblement. Of course quasi-abolition may be necessary if anything quasi-human is to survive. That is the modern question, the new view of the old notion of the perfectibility of the species. The modern world is the result of a movement against Mr Lewis's conditions for the survival of man, and the question is whether that movement will or can lead to the realization of man in and through independent thought and individual sensibility, the creation of personal experience, on the fully spatio-temporal conditions of human existence, or whether man will have to retreat into conditions which stabilize society at the cost of tampering with the natural conditions of human existence.[6]

Are there, indeed, any 'natural', 'cosmic' conditions of human existence, not created by society, and if so why give them an absolute value? If there are precedents for tampering with these conditions, set by the historical religions which denied the reality of the world of history and science, is that not good enough? If man could be abolished or reduced to good purpose by thinking reality away, by ancient techniques, he can be abolished or reduced to even better purpose by keeping reality away, by modern techniques. The superiority of really abolishing reality instead of interpreting it away is that it can be done for all, and once for all.

The reality which is created in *Brave New World* in place of the realities of history and of the objective world is just as real. Indeed, it becomes the only reality. It is only now, in thought, that we are able to compare them. Once, following a decision, *Brave New World* is established, there will be no other possibility even in imagination.

The solution has the beauty of finality: the species is perfected because alternatives are all extinguished. If this choice is really open to us, this is the most fateful generation in the history of mankind. In any case, we know that it is and are terrified by what man is and the responsibility he bears.

Apart from historical attempts of ancient religions and absolute philosophies to escape from the conditions of human existence, there are the everyday attempts of ordinary people to escape in one way or another from these conditions. In so far as we live in and by comfortable opinions to which we have no title and which separate us from independent reality, what in all this normal existence is different in principle from *Brave New World*? As for history, the mood used to be contempt for the past, pride in the present, and expectations of everything from the future, and we have come to extol the past, hate the present, and dread the future.[7] In such ways, history and science are thrown away, and, refusing to learn, we can have no reasonable hopes. Better have the need to learn and the meaning of hope removed with history and science, in exchange for the regular gratification of ordinary desires.

Christianity because it is historical in a unique sense tries to make the best of both worlds, the world of history and nature and the world of eternity. At the time of the coronation of Elizabeth II, a leader-writer in *The Times* asked what the ceremony would be like if it were deprived of its religious character. He concluded that a secular celebration might do justice to the past and the future, and that 'Only the present, which to the purely secular mind is a fleeting moment of experience, devoid of significance until it finds its place in the pattern of history, would get less than its due'. The argument goes on to say that secular faiths can all too easily get heroic sacrifices from peoples, but the consecration of the present, daily duty done, the regard for an eternal and eternally relevant standard of right, is a contribution of Christianity.

There is, it must be admitted, some theoretical excuse for this notion that there is no secular ground for the possession of the present. The triad of moments in the dialectic, the perpetually renewed emptiness of consciousness in Sartre's analysis, these are ideas which encourage the thought that a secular philosophy can find no anchorage in the present. But no fantasy in the head can steal the heart out of the body of humanism. Temporal experience is three-dimensional. Otherwise, experience is ephemeral and unreal, destroyed if any one of these dimensions is suppressed. Without the past, there is no eye, no light, no mind; without the present, there is no life; without the future, there is no completion, or no renewal.

The future shows most clearly that the moments as they fly are not homogeneous units; they are charged and differentiated and placed, forming the structure of something which has a beginning, a middle, and an end. The present is never merely a 'becoming' because the past and the future are always given with it, but always given differently.

By contrast, the moments of a Christian life are equivalent, structureless, equally detached, equally significant, equally insufficient, equally instances of 'the one action'.[8]

> And right action is freedom
> From past and future also.

This would make nonsense of secular experience, which is unthinkable and unreal apart from its three-dimensional temporality.

The inner life of the Christian and of the humanist are thus extremely different, yet both are rooted in the temporal character of human existence. Man is a thinking reed for the christian Pascal and for the humanist Russell;[9] and he is so because of these conditions. His dignity is judged superior to that of the Universe which threatens to overwhelm him. But now, at this moment in time, he is invited to transform himself, by transforming his conditions, into something simpler, standard, which will survive longer, or which enjoys a better chance. The symbol for this safe future is something we have seen: the memorial parade of little wooden crosses.

When Comte took freedom of thought (with its origin in Protestantism) as chief of the ideas of 1789, necessary then but ultimately destructive, the principle of all unsettlement, the root of absurdity, he knew what he was saying.[10] He also knew that intellectual authority was the only appropriate control over thought, and he believed it would be sufficient. It has not been sufficient. Nor has political authority, with all the will and the power. You cannot finally suppress freedom of thought by bans, but if you can remove the past and the world of independent nature and all contemporary differences, all sources of comparison, you do not have to. The troublesome mind of man is at an end.

4. THE CHOICE

We who still in some measure have the mind of man to use and misuse and disuse can still survey his position in the cosmos, his emergence out of a still inapprehensible past, his still tragic history, tragic because of standards, of possibilities, because of the past and the future, because of mind and nature; we can in a glance take in something of all this, enough for comparison with the dimensionless existence which will never be clouded by any recollection of it if we decide that ease and sensual gratifications and security and the standard of living and perfect adjustment are the better part of human achievement. This comparison now is the choice, the ground of choice: there is no way of proving a right or wrong here. The choice itself is extreme: with little or no hesitation we divide, turn our backs to the right or to the left, taking on the one hand to perfectly carefree, unbroken, dimensionless joy, and on the other awakening with physical sobbing passion to truth and tragic, comic, messy temporal existence.

Nothing could be more dramatic, more simple, more just, if this were a properly personal choice each one of us had to make on his pilgrimage. The view of human destiny as pilgrim's progress in meeting temptations and making decisions is a view seen through the eyes of deity. We are involved in collective mankind, and stand to suffer for the temptations we have resisted and the decisions we have not made, or, the obverse, we decide not for ourselves alone but for all mankind, as Sartre says. If there is offered us at this time a definitive choice for all mankind of the kind we are considering, we need hardly speculate about the outcome: it is natural and inevitable that the many will make one choice and the few the other. If one calls them the masses and the *élite*, one should not think that this is a difference of social class, for it is not the uneducated masses who have thought that a good education is 'that which leads to all kinds of pleasures, without danger, and without inconvenience'. *Brave New World* was the study of the sophisticated before it became the spontaneous preference of the naive. That the masses will prevail is the meaning of modern history, and the meaning of the despair of modern intellectuals. But there is no poetic justice in this to appease the bad conscience of those whom the Lord has allowed so long to do injustice without having to suffer it, for the masses are not the age-long victims, they are merely the many, and the *élite* are not the privileged masters, they are merely the few. This might seem like the nemesis which Burke prophesied would follow the abandonment of property for numbers as the basis of political authority. But this is not simply the result of political democracy, it is a result of the machine. There was no escape.

A final reflection in the consideration of this choice: this possibility to end all possibilities is offered not only to the most fateful generation of all history but also to the most privileged. We are privileged not indeed because we have fateful decisions to make, but because we have at our disposal not only unexampled techniques, but also unexampled sources of wisdom. This generation is fateful because if we cannot tackle and resolve human problems sufficiently well, with enough encouragement and promise, they never will be dealt with successfully without a drastic reduction of the dimensions of human existence. This generation is privileged because we are in a position to look back on all the promises of salvation from which in turn men have hoped everything: the great religious promises, the moral prescriptions, the scientific programme, the political and educational dreams, the economic machine, all these in their day have promised everything, and this does not mean they have delivered nothing. They have all been proved, positively and negatively. We are in a position today to make an evaluation of human experience that will at least be sufficient for our needs. If we are capable of learning, we shall not perish for lack of understanding and vision. The past and the future which are the prime sources of trouble are still the only sources of hope and of faith.

NOTES: CHAPTER III

1. *more obsolete than the language of the Bible:*
   cp. Reinhold Niebuhr's *The Self and the Dramas of History*, esp. Part II.
2. *if the saint . . . is the type of human perfection:*
   it seems to be assumed by most Christian critics of eighteenth century philosophers that in 'perfectibility' they had in mind something like 'the kingdom of heaven'. In this connexion, two distinctions are needed. (1) In the view of Hume, 'men of sense' everywhere despised 'monkish virtues' that 'serve no manner of purpose; neither advance a man's fortune in the world, nor render him a more valuable member of society; neither qualify him for the entertainment of company, nor increase his power of self-enjoyment'. A society of enlightened, useful, and agreeable persons, a community of responsible free and equal persons, was the ideal; education and constitutional government were the methods of attainment to be employed, not repentance and conversion. (2) The perfectibility, however, was not primarily the individual moral perfection of all future men, but, rather the cumulative learning from experience which perpetually increased cultural resources available for human advancement. Condorcet contrasts the primitive or animal perfectibility of the individual with the transmissible progress of the race (*The Progress of the Human Mind*, pp. 5-6).
3. *Brave New World:*
   This book, one of the classics of our time, was a *jeu d'esprit* when its author wrote it in 1932, a philosophical fable when he revisited it in 1946 to write a Foreword to the Penguin edition, and a work of sociological science when he paid a second return visit in 1959. In *Brave New World Revisited*, Mr Huxley is able to say, 'I told you so' by simply saying *The Organization Man, The Hidden Persuaders, Battle for the Mind, The Next Hundred Years, The Power Elite*, all published in the US, 'the pro-

I

phetic image of the rest of the urban-industrial world as it will be a few years from now'. Taking respectful note of *Nineteen Eighty-four* (1949), Mr Huxley thinks we are turning from that alternative and moving up to *Brave New World*, mainly because it is easier and safer to enslave men by persuasion and pleasure than by fear and punishment; the lure of the sun proverbially prevails with the traveller over the violence of the wind.

4. *in a generation or two . . . more acceptable:*
a friend who teaches sociology in an American university reports that his students when directed without comment to read *Brave New World* found it a genuine Utopia. To a question about the attitude of the savage, the answer was, 'Maladjusted'. This happened twice with different students. However, when it got round that this was not the official view of the satire, the pattern of response changed to conformity with usual expectations.

5. *the kind of concept elaborated in Brave New World:*
in which society is organized wholly and solely as a catering establishment for mass appetites.

6. *The modern world is the result . . . and the question is:*
religious conservative and liberal thinkers insistently challenge the faith of the eighteenth century humanists and their heirs (e.g., chap. i, sect. i and chap. ii, sect. v, above); their own faith is not less open to challenge, but it is the common destruction of both religious and humanist faiths that brings to life Brave New World as a visible alternative.

7. *dread the future:*
'. . . if we compare the impact of the future upon us in this technical age with the sense of the future as we find it in a simpler society possessing far less technical equipment, we shall see at once that in many important respects we are more and not less worried by a sense of foreboding, of unknowable and imponderable hazards and uncertainties waiting for us round the corner in the blinding darkness of the not-yet' (Casserley, *The Bent World*, p. 95). For this reason, 'security' has become 'the supreme universal god', security from depressions, from unemployment, from progress (Drucker, *The End of Economic Man*, p.71).

8. *'the one action':*
'The Dry Salvages'. Cp. 'Burnt Norton'. T. S. Eliot's *Four Quartets* (1944).

9. *Pascal and . . . Russell:*
Pensées No. 348; 'A Free Man's Worship' (1902), reprinted in *Mysticism and Logic* (London, 1917).

10. *Comte:*
Système de politique positive, iii, pp. 550-2.

CHAPTER IV

The Pursuit of
Rational Ends by Rational Means

ARGUMENT

IF ONE turns at last from the ambitious social philosophies of simpler times and from extravagant fears and fantasies of our own time to sober studies of our social complexities, it is reasonable to think that the way to gain proper social control over what is going on is to learn what it is and to learn to do it more purposefully and efficaciously, unless the case requires, in some affairs, that we stop doing what we are doing and try some other course instead.

The classical ideal of social control was bound up with the notion of a complete and permanent set of laws. This notion of permanence and perfection which inspired constitutional thinking is not useful for the purpose of regulating social change made irresistible and incessant by industrial development and radical politics. As a matter of fact, the kind of law which has regulated (and initiated) social change in England for the last hundred years has been in effect social planning. A plan, if it is adequately informed to start with, not only achieves something of what is planned, but also creates an experience from which those associated in the plan may learn more of what they want and how to get it. In social plans, there is not a single-minded purpose but a manifold design, an initial reconciliation of interests and desires in a compound intention, which may be revised in the light of what happens when effect is given to it. In this way, to discern the form of actual social process and to perfect its practice by that standard, forgetting all that belonged to the irrelevant aim at a perfect set of laws, is to exercise the most intelligent, democratic, and creative social control possible. This concept is exemplified in the political process in the cycle legislation—administration—evaluation.

The Education Act of 1944 exemplifies one phase of this process. Education is in itself a powerful means of social control, but it is mainly a means of reproducing society in its own image and not of changing society into likeness to some social ideal. Nevertheless, in addition to the need to recruit and train the experts on whom modern society increasingly depends there is the need to provide for *the general education of the great majority as citizens and human beings; and here education, as the discipline which enables a child to make the most of what he has in and open to him, comes into its own, its universality, and is not merely the mould of an existing order. This universal task of education is made socially urgent by the effects of social selection in modern society, the need to prevent a dangerous division into dynamic and static types, active and inert citizens, an élite of responsible experts and a mass of beneficiaries, successful top people and a residue of failures.*

The most vivid example of devastating social change out of control has been in land use and the visible destruction of community. The work of reclamation, preservation, prevention, and development has been taken in hand and presents, on the whole, an encouraging example of creative social control. In this field, the restored self-planning small community is heavily starred by some idealists; but preoccupation with the interesting possibilities of this development shuts out many other attractive alternatives.

Finally, the general interest need not mean an impossible harmony of interests nor a reduction to standardized mass appetites, with government as public caterer. The actual public interest, which includes national security as well as social security and economic viability as well as civil liberties, imposes stern requirements, disputed in detail but not in principle, and, chastened by these requirements, the struggle for power and the struggle for goods goes on, regulated by the party system, collective bargaining, and the tradition of free institutions, not without risk but also not without stability and direction.

Such a survey if it gets above the chill hollows of despondency and the mists of confusion is not a view of a promised land, for it is only a view of what we are doing and have been doing, and it suggests only that to do better is not, in the main, to do otherwise, but, again, to discern and perfect the form of what is going on and to perfect practice by that standard.

However, these practical ends and means cannot do everything to satisfy the citizen's personal wants, and he must learn for himself in his own case the character of a happy life.

I. METHOD OF SOCIAL CONTROL

The demoralizing fears that are abroad in the political democracies are roused by two opposite kinds of evil. To the old dismay that 'things are in the saddle and ride mankind' has been added the conviction that this unnatural state of affairs has passed beyond hope

of any recovery of control: war, population increase, economic dis-
locations, the results of scientific progress, have become as fatal
as natural calamities, and they are more disastrous. There is the
opposite fear, that successful organization, concentrated in or symbolized by the State, will stifle all that is distinctively human and
makes life dear to men; or, in another form, that the tastes and
ideals, and ultimately the existence, of the cultivated few will be
sacrificed to satisfy the common appetites of the masses. These in
modern form are the ancient fears of the evils of anarchy and of
misgovernment. In spite of the growth of experience and the confidence of theorists, they have not been allayed, they have been aggravated. This failure of reasonable expectations deepens the depression.
Underlying all is the irony that the removal or massive reduction by
human intelligence of natural evils has led to a massive increase in
the evils that follow human actions, that the evil for which human
beings are responsible is the type of evil least amenable to control
by human intelligence, that the instruments of control or amelioration (science, government, military defence, mass production) are
themselves out of control and threaten catastrophe. The demoralizing consequences of these acute and not unjustified fears have been
widespread: apathy, despair, anger, destructiveness, revival of the
occult, discredit of man.

Is it really true that human intelligence cannot tackle with reasonable hopefulness the evils caused by human actions? The question,
it has been assumed, turns on the extent to which the social art can
be guided by a reliable political science.[1] Attempts to construct
such a science have followed two general lines.

(1) There have been the attempts to formulate the laws of history,
to predict the future on the basis of a total explanation of the past,
and thus to indicate the scope and limits of efficacious political
action. This method, based on an early inadequate understanding of
science, had some use in the nineteenth century when large scale
social transformations were going on in the advanced industrialized
countries, and, in the fluidity and confusion of change, indications
were needed of the direction of development. The predictions
proved unreliable, but they were not unfounded. Now that the
shape of things that were then to come has emerged plainly into
sight there is not the same need for that kind of general guidance,
anyhow; for what the issues are is clear enough, and if we wanted to
know what decisions will be taken and what the outcome will be
we should have to consult the occult sciences. This seems to put
us back in primitive times as far as our major interests are concerned.
The outcome of the paramount issue of security cannot be pre-

dicted. This fateful issue clouds the sky and weighs on us with an oppression which will be ended only with decisions or the lack of decisions which we fear will be to the lasting detriment of the nation with whose fate our own lot is bound up, or to the detriment of all mankind. The academic revival of interest in augury is symbolic. The psychological needs which augury used to meet when inscrutable imminent events concealed men's fates cannot be met in an enlightened way by reliable scientific general predictions.

(2) The most useful political science has been furnished by descriptive analysis of institutions as they exist and work, together with sample surveys and statistical studies of all manner of social phenomena.[2] Studies of this kind have superseded the kind of political thinking that was preoccupied with theories about the State and about political obligation. This is not merely a change in intellectual fashion, nor a return of the prodigal to the sober empiricism of his English home after a spendthrift spell amid foreign seductions; it is, rather, that the days of constitution-making and of radical political questions and first principles are with us the days before yesterday. Nowadays we are naturally more interested in investigating the ways in which our going concerns actually work, since there are now so many of them, long established and growing in complications. Talk about liberty, equality, human rights, popular sovereignty, and the claims of the State will, perhaps, never be meaningless, because little or nothing is likely to be established once for ever in this world, but the battle does pass over, and today, apart from our being mainly engaged on the international front and in finding out how to manage a managed economy, any effective thinking about human rights and the like needs to be informed about what is going on, and that requires elaborate special investigations: the simple assumptions of old-time abstract thinking on these questions are disestablished for ever. The question is not human equality, for example, but how much equality we can and want to afford, with what priorities.

Descriptions of the working of parliament, of the civil service, of the political parties, of the various kinds of committee, of lobbies and pressure groups, of the Supreme Court, of the International Court abound at different levels and for many purposes. Very few writers today in western countries, especially of advanced textbooks, are much concerned to explain or theorize about the institutions they describe. Some are concerned to make their description a basis for informed criticism and proposals for reform. Most institutions are already a stabilization and rationalization, and thereby a controlled development, of primitive practice or spontaneous behaviour. Reflective analysis of the spontaneous motion which goes to swipe a ball or to shout down an argument results in the inhibition of certain wasteful or ineffective movements and the encouragement and stabilization of the effective ones for the purpose in hand, producing the batsman's style or the formal rules of procedure for public discussion; and this rationalization can be refined, elaborated, and perfected, improving performance and achievement.[3] These are examples of techniques which have a universal validity and scope, as do others similarly produced, like the methods of scientific inquiry or committee procedures. Such procedures and techniques enter into the constitution and conduct of institutions, but most institutions, although they include such finished rationalizations of behaviour, remain in their complex totality, because of historical development and adaptation to circumstances, advanced forms of primitive practice or spontaneous behaviour, which reflective analysis can help to modify for the more effective achievement of contemporary purposes.[4]

This critique of institutions in order to methodize their success and eliminate their failure is a wholly different form of rationalization from the production of a rational plan to be substituted for the institutional practice, as technically more efficient. For example, a national wages policy can be devised on equitable principles equitably applied, and such a rational determination of wages would solve a heap of dangerous and intractable problems, and be intellectually and morally more satisfying than the hazards, inequities, and anomalies involved in collective bargaining. This is not practical politics, of course, and it is not practical politics because collective bargaining, itself a rationalization of *laissez-faire* economic behaviour, is a going concern, a system of incentives and deterrents, of hopes and fears, not merely a system of principles.[5] Therefore any rationalization of wages policy must look at existing practice in the context of new factors and interests involved, and propose practicable and acceptable modifications for the efficient achievement of defined purposes.

Methods of social control, all this means, are in actual institutions and procedures, and not in theories or plans; but institutions and procedures become methods of social control only in so far as they are understood, perfected, and used as such, in so far, that is to say, as they approximate to mastered techniques perfecting behaviour for a specified purpose. Or, in the case of a failure or serious imperfection of an institution or procedure, because of changed circumstances, methodical control requires that the behaviour shall be analysed, halted, re-designed, and institutionalized on the new pattern. Both these operations are difficult enough in the simple case of the person who wants to succeed and knows what he is trying to do: in the case of society, the complexity and confusion of interests and wills would make methodical control seem to be out of the question. History shows that the case is not so hopeless. Was it possible, for example, to control the class struggle and the social changes which would develop out of it? Not by institutionalizing the direct indivisible sovereignty of the people. Not by institutionalizing public opinion in the Church of Humanity. Not even by forcing the issue and instituting the Dictatorship of the Proletariat to preside over the liquidation of class interests.[6] Not, that is to say, by a theory or plan of control that assumed some end or purpose or law for society and would institute the means to achieve it. Rather, success in western societies came by institutionalizing in party politics the actual conflict of interests and opinions. After the widening of the franchise, following radical agitation informed by radical theory, the appeal to the people as the basis of support for government encouraged and required party organization, and the rules, conventions, and procedures by which people and politicians learned to regulate party politics created a controlled system of control. Similarly, a market economy was developed under *laissez-faire* as a controlled system of control, interpreted by political economists, regulated by financial institutions, and worked by business men. The adequacy of these, and other, established systems of control is in question now. Can the descriptive analyses of their working which are being made be used to show how they could be modified to make them efficient in the control of social change in present circumstances? Control by whom in whose interests?

The question is not a stumper, for it is not highly relevant. The rationalist is justified in saying, 'Tell me what you want, and I will tell you how to get it'. Social rationalism, however, does not necessarily imply a naïve assumption of common interest, nor a crude imposition of dominant interest, nor even an assumption about the 'purpose' of society. The *laissez-faire* economy together with political democracy constituted a determination of legitimate expectations with a corresponding distribution of satisfactions in response to personal efforts, an elaborate self-regulating method of social control. There was in this an element of common interest, of dominant interest, and of assumption about the purpose of society, and so long as these elements were cemented in prevailing public opinion, and so long as the self-regulating mechanism remained not violently disturbed by the social changes induced, the system held together and worked tolerably well.[7] The overhaul of theory and practice now required would not be worth undertaking if the system has served its turn and is now obsolete, that is to say, if liberal institutions (i) cannot be made efficient methods of social control, (ii) have no distinctive value, (iii) are not widely valued, (iv) are unable to compete with totalitarian institutions. If the crudest interests of the masses predominate, if programmes supersede principles, parties, and procedures, if the common and gross ends of mankind become so important or so desirable and attainable that everything is subordinated to organization to obtain them, liberal methods of social control have no future. These are questions which only history can answer. All that present thought and discussion can attempt is to recover or discover the vision of a dynamic society under liberal control — our society. Eighteenth-century humanists thought that man could re-make himself and fulfil the laws of his nature, if he re-made the laws and system of education of his country. Nineteenth-century prophets, supported by many more today, thought that the industrial revolution had destroyed community and personality. Contemporaries tell us that party politics are futile, or else that the coming triumph of one party threatens to sweep away all standards and that liberty and responsibility will fall under the drums and tramplings of one conquest. Here are sensitive areas of major hope or fear which are worth exploring to see what possibilities are left for liberal forms of control, how efficient they are likely to be, and what they are likely to be worth.

2. CREATIVE LAW

If a comparison is made between modern concepts of knowledge and of law and the classical concepts,[8] the most striking difference is in the abandonment of the classical ideal of a final slim system of truths or of laws to be handed down to the latest posterity. Remains of this euclidean utopianism are all around, for it was still dominant in the nineteenth century. Notions of evolution or of development did not displace it, since the completion of the system (and with it the stabilization of society) was only postponed: these notions, indeed, on the philosophical side sprang from and demanded the classical ideals of knowledge and of law.[9] Confusion, unnecessary mental distress, and uncertainty of control have been occasioned by the continuance of these concepts, in various forms, when they have long been at variance with practice.

Consider, for example, the modern classical liberal conception of law, from Locke to Lippmann.[10] The law is the same for all (like the rules of the road); it is enforced equally and its remedies are equally available (the government's prime duty is to provide by lawful means public order and security and cheap, prompt, incorruptible, and efficient administration of the law, which primarily protects property and regulates contracts); the law is minimal, the least that is necessary to enable everyone to plan and follow his own courses with reliance on the predictable behaviour of his neighbour in ordinary social and business relations; the law enables the citizen to get rid of the government if it fails to serve the public interest by maintaining law and order in this sense.

This liberal idea of law was 'emancipated'; it was emancipated from the notion of law as divine, revealed in innate ideas or immemorial customs; although Locke retained the notion of 'natural law' and Mr Lippmann wants to revive it.[11] Society constituted by a limited set of rules which provide secure conditions on which everyone may pursue his own interests, by contrast with the supposed 'state of nature' in which the law of the jungle obtains, or with tyrannies which compel the sacrifice of the general interest to 'sinister' interests, is a rational human institution, a decision based on an understanding of how men behave without rules and how they might behave with rules devised for mutual convenience. In this sense society is a plan, or, rather, constitutional law is a plan, and liberal thinking about constitutional law was thinking about a planned society, and was the prelude to a new type of law making.

It is a commonplace that after the Reform Act of 1832 the business of the House began to change more than the character of the Members. Instead of merely supporting or opposing the Ministry in carrying on the King's business of executive government, the House was increasingly occupied with social legislation, 'a sudden and vast expansion of Parliamentary duty',[12] in Gladstone's words, resulting in 1882 in a change in the rules of Parliamentary procedure which gave the government a practical monopoly of the time and attention of parliament for its programme of legislation. Seen from the standpoint of a popular leader, the political situation was described dramatically by Joseph Chamberlain in 1885. Preoccupation with the franchise had for long years crowded out crucial problems, he said: 'the great problem of our civilization is unsolved'; it was, 'fair shares'. 'Now that we have a government of the people by the people, we will go on to make it the government for the people.'[13] G. M. Young has described the new radical conception of politics: 'To raise, by agitation, a powerful head of opinion; through the Caucus to embody it in a solid well-drilled party; to cast it into legislative form, and then by means of the closure to force it swiftly through the Commons; these, to certain masterful and aggressive spirits, were the tactics proper to modern politics.'[14] He goes on to say that this threat in the 1880's of which Chamberlain's 'unauthorized programme' was the type came to nothing by reason of circumstances, the British constitution, the preoccupation of the Radicals with many questions, and the lack of an inflamed public opinion on any particular domestic question. 'The Unauthorized Programme of 1885 was, to some serious minds, a portent of revolution. But a great deal of it was carried out by Conservatives who hardly remembered that it had ever been a programme at all.' In other words, the ordinary business of Parliament became, had indeed become before Chamberlain made his announcement, the enactment of legislation of a new type: social planning. The great social transformations which in our time have been carried out by successive Five Year Plans in the USSR, and now in China and India, were carried out in England in the nineteenth century not only by private enterprise but also by state planning, which set up new authorities and multiplied the duties and added to the powers of central and local government.

This planning type of legislation was in character and content and in the method of producing it greatly different from the 'liberal' notion of law as a sufficient system of regulative or restraining rules which create stable conditions for the free activities of self-dependent persons. If the great revolution has been the shift from a society based on status to a society based on contract, and if the social contract is the constitutional model and the law of contract the model for civil legislation, the planning type of legislation must seem retrogressive, objectionable, and its promoters and authors enemies of the public; and this, indeed, has been the view of liberals, held with more or less vigour. This was the theme of Dicey's famous examination of the influence of opinion upon law in the nineteenth century, which encouraged Sir Roland Wilson's less known forthright re-statement of the liberal view of law, *The Province of the State* (1911).

The planning tendency was not socialism, not due to the influence of doctrinaire socialist thinking. It proceeded piecemeal under the pressure of claims, needs, events, powerfully reinforced later by the overriding need for emergency powers of government control during two world wars, and between them by the need for energetic action to deal with an unprecedented slump in the markets of capitalist economies. These events set liberals like Keynes, Beveridge, Salter, Mannheim to attempt to reconcile free institutions and liberal values with the new responsibilities of government and the need for social security.[15] Professor Hayek was nearly alone in persisting with warnings of the extreme danger of allowing one toe to stray from the footpath through the wicket gate of individualism.[16] In principle, he insisted, an economic government plan is necessarily enslaving and destructive. It is necessarily enslaving because, in so far as it is effective, it imposes an initiative which disallows every other. It is necessarily destructive because it not only does destroy every other initiative but also because the initiative it imposes must, by comparison with the initiatives it destroys, be abstract, arbitrary, ill-informed, and therefore ultimately abortive, unless driven to a remnant of its ends by high-handed violence. In the general field of bureaucratic control, to set up tribunals to provide remedies for outraged rights was merely mockery. There could be no compromise.

Hayek was answered by anticipation by another great liberal, Salvador de Madariaga, who wrote in his book *Disarmament* (1929):

'At any given time the world presents a certain network of facts recognized as law. Frontiers are defined, obligations and rights laid down, zones of influence recognized, debts acknowledged, limitations of sovereignty accepted, occupations of territory admitted, in fine, a system is established which constitutes, so to say, a zero of history, a starting-point, not for history which has none, but for our own thoughts. Then, life flows on and every day something happens, some change takes place which gradually makes the world of facts and forces move away from the world of law. This nation grows weaker; that nation stronger; this territory, once uninhabited, grows to be an important centre of population; new national feelings appear where careless and self-ignorant masses were once herded together by a foreign power; the nation yesterday subjected grows stronger than its subjecter; economic and financial currents are reversed. Between the static set of laws and the dynamic set of forces there appears thus a set of conflicts. At every point in the world disruptive forces begin to act. This may be said to be the normal state of the world considered as a whole.'

A set of conflicts between a static set of laws and a dynamic set of forces is an equally valid description of the situation under municipal law. The liberal wants maximum permanence and minimal regulation in the laws so that he may freely do his own planning with a reliable basis for his calculations; but his initiatives are bound to produce far reaching changes, which destroy the assumptions of his euclidean utopianism. A legal code to be revised 'once in a hundred years' (Bentham), lawyers' law, is not the kind of law which as a matter of fact in the nineteenth century and since has regulated social change in England. Social and administrative legislation in this period has been empirical planning: bills drafted after patient consultation and negotiation with the interests affected, and subject to drastic amendment in draft.[17] The Local Government Act of 1888 was said to have been the outcome of at least ten years labour. Every administrative change has been experimental. Trial legislation through permissive powers or local experiments often preceded a general Act, rules were tried out and revised, consolidation was postponed until the new law had been assimilated and established, flexibility was preserved by keeping the body of the Act to general principles. All this is abundantly exemplified in legislation on public health, education, factories, poor law.

What happened in that period was 'the building up piecemeal of an administrative machine of great complexity, which stands in as constant need of repair, renewal, reconstruction, and adaptation to new requirements as the plant of a modern factory'. Sir Courtney Ilbert who described in these words the process of social legislation in this country supplemented his long experience in drafting parliamentary bills with a period of office as legal member of the Viceroy of India's Council. In this office he was legislating as an expert, not drafting legislation for interests which had already determined the content of the proposed law. He describes the difference. 'The Indian legislator has much more difficulty in discovering how his proposed law will operate, or whether it will operate at all. The difference is, in fact, between legislation by experts, with the minute but incomplete knowledge that experts possess, and legislation by a popular assembly.' What a popular assembly does is 'to avert revolution, by making laws which adapt the political, administrative, and economic arrangements of the country to the requirements of the time'. One way he adopted in India of consulting opinion affected by a proposed law was to publish it in draft before its introduction into the Council.

As a matter of fact, then, the great bulk of modern legislation is in the form of statutes which are social plans, rather than rules of the type of the Highway Code. These statutes less than any other type of legislation have the tendency to set up a set of conflicts between a static set of laws and a dynamic set of forces, because their ideal is not permanence but revision; they themselves are and remain dynamic, in the sense of promoting change and being subject to change. The ideal of 'liberal' law is that it shall be the same for all, its prohibitions and requirements equally enforced and its remedies equally available, and shall be reliable also in the sense of the law of the Medes and Persians. The ideal of the plan is that it shall continuously inform and be informed by the activities it controls.

3. THE CONCEPT OF INFORMED SOCIAL PLANNING

Public planning is a particular form of planning in general, of which private enterprise planning or planning in personal life are other particular forms. The plan initiates a course of action which produces events experienced by the agent, in the light of which he modifies the plan; so that, in a sequence of phases, the plan is continuously initiating action or being modified by the results of action; and this modification is not merely a more efficacious employment of means to an originally intended end (a continuous adjustment on the 'feedback' principle), but also a modification of the end in view, a revision of intention, a recasting of desires, a development in understanding. One learns from the experience of others in so far as one is learning from one's own, and one learns best from one's own in so far as one has created it, just as in study one learns best in the pursuit of an inquiry which one has originated or made one's own, rather than in the passive receipt of teaching

The first principle of planning in general, then, is this phased continuity in which the experience created by the action initiated is used to modify the plan for the initiation of a further course of action, in an indefinitely prolonged sequence of refinements in controlled realization and transformation of an original intention.

The second principle is that the plan shall be initially informed. It is not an arbitrary intention founded on wishes. It is a settled resolution consistent with other established purposes and grounded in practicability. As in study, one has to learn what questions it is profitable to ask, so in the management of personal or of social life one has to learn what plans it is profitable to work out.

Planned activity is thus a sustained interplay of thought and action originating in an informed intention renewed and revised in a succession of phases. Planning which is inadequately informed at the outset and which remains inadequately informed by the experience it creates is planning to little or no purpose.[18]

In the public field of social action the plan is of course heavily complicated at all stages, but these two general principles of initial information and subsequent revision (in fact, merely the phasing of the operation of living and learning by experience) are valid and sufficient. In this case, the initial information is not merely knowledge (the role of experts), it includes also wills, the opinions and interests of parties. The initial policy, to be embodied in a plan or a

statute, is an outcome of consultations and negotiations with representatives of all those interests which will be affected by such a plan
and of all those who will be required to participate in carrying it out.
This concentration and sifting of relevant information at the outset is carried on by means of advisory committees, pressure groups,
lobbying, commissions and committees of inquiry, negotiations,
discussions in the Press and on the floor of the House and in committee on a Bill, deputations, conferences, exchange of letters and
memoranda, and the like. That modern society is so closely and
highly organized in all activities and interests, so often complained
of as an oppression and a threat, is a condition without which public
plans could not be adequately informed and revised, and would
therefore be as destructive as Professor Hayek thinks they must be.[19]
That is to say, these 'oppressive' collectivities are in form the necessary basis of sensitive, creative public planning which stimulates
and employs maximum participation. And public plans have been
with us a long time, on the statute-book and otherwise, as the necessary form of social control. Thinking about responsible freedom
or creative social control or humane values has no relevance unless
it is related to 'organization' and 'plan' as necessary basic forms. The
difference between an authoritarian and a representative form of
organization is well understood. The equally vital difference between an authoritarian and an 'informed' form of plan is not so well
understood.

Of course, there has to be an authority competent to take and to
seek the relevant information, to make decisions, to formulate the
plan, and to exert whatever coercion may be required to get the plan
going and to make it work; and in legislative planning this authority
can be only the government.[20] But authority, although necessary,
does not make the plan. If it does, experience shows, the plan is
likely to be still-born, a dead letter. There is no doubt that much
state planning in the USSR has been mere genuflexion before an idol,
and not effective because not informed.[21] But this kind of ineffective-
ness is older than doctrinaire ideas about state planning. 'It is characteristic of the haste, prejudice, and industrial ignorance with which
the Parliamentary majority acted that its Combination Act of 1799
had, even by its own standards of right and wrong, to be largely
amended in the following year when workmen's petitions gave Opposition the requisite information and opportunity.'* The major
plan that encounters considerable resentment and resistance will
be publicly defeated or will provoke sabotage or will induce wide-

* S Maccoby, *English Radicalism, 1786-1832*, p. 132. See also A. Aspinall, *The
Early English Trade Unions* (1949), chap. ii.

spread evasion, apathy, and malaise.[22] In so far as this is true, there are not two forms of planning, authoritarian and liberal, but only effective or ineffective planning. However, it would be absurd to deny effectiveness to ruthless coercive planning in some circumstances. What is true is that where democratic institutions and habits obtain, public plans *can* be highly 'informed' and *must* be if they are to work What is important is that plans which are highly informed are highly creative.

'Information' in this connexion, it must be repeated, embraces far more than technical knowledge; it is a taking account of all interests affected, of beliefs and aspirations, of rights and habits, of prejudices and privileges; and they are taken account of by the official initiators of the plan not merely by anticipation but mainly by dealing concretely with claims and representations.[23] By the time a legislative plan becomes an Act of Parliament it is a practicable project because account has been taken of the relevant and represented interests and opinions. In a major case, it will be an act of statesmanship as well as an Act of Parliament, it will be a compromise that really does initiate a new phase of national collaboration in some field, whatever anomalies persist, whatever patchwork disfigures the rational face of the new arrangements. Of such a kind was the Education Act of 1944, in which the various categories of teachers, of administrative authorities, of experts, of churches, had their say, which reconciled old conflicts, consolidated previous reforms, ventured into bold undertakings, and initiated in a national endeavour of the highest importance a comprehensive informed programme, to supersede a state of affairs of which the Minister opined there was only one thing to be said, that it was 'bloody bad'.

The plan is not only informed, it also informs. It is publicly discussed in the course of its formulation, and when at last it is given to the administrative departments and to the public[24] as a decisive formulation, it is given with an explanation of its terms and requirements and the reasons for them, so that all those who are affected by it, and especially those who have to help to work it out, see what is being attempted and why, and what means are proposed. Much of this may be devolved by the Act upon government departments or local authorities or other public bodies, who have their own established techniques and arrangements for consultation and collaboration with interests affected, so that in day to day practice there may be a continuous responsiveness to actual needs.[25]

That public planning in various forms controls most of our social life is demonstrable and past argument, and that it will expand beyond its present limits is rather feared than doubted. That necessary planning need not encroach on established freedoms has been argued by leading liberals, most of whom have conceded that liberty in the modern state requires a proper element of planning. That planning, including public planning, is in form creative is not so widely appreciated. Not until this perception is widely enjoyed will there be reasonable grounds for a recovery of social confidence and eagerness.

Public planning of all types is in form socially creative in the following senses. (1) In bringing to a focus on a project the diversity of relevant interests and opinions in the country, the plan brings them into reflective consciousness and discussion and eventually combines them dynamically in the social project. The experience of the project in its working out results in revised opinions and purposes, and eventually in a revised project. However crude the plan, however much a compromise, it is the highest form of social consciousness and action in respect to a given activity of which a given people in given circumstances is capable, and it creates the most formative experience for the development of a social intention in clarity and unity. The dynamic set of forces is not moving away from a static set of laws in which they were once reconciled, for the diverse interests and opinions are combined in an agreed plan which proposes over a period to alter the existing situation in a significant way; these opinions and interests are therefore also hopes and fears vested in the project which they have helped to initiate and which they are engaged in working out; when the time comes, revision may mean consolidation of purpose, with some rectification and development, or it may mean the raising of issues which split the collective purpose, in any case it means a course informed by a uniquely relevant experience deliberately created; and if this is repeated in a succession of revised initiatives, it is an ever firmer appropriation of ends and an ever finer adjustment of means, with a heightening of social consciousness, whether in integration into a common purpose or in definition of divisions.

(2) A social plan is not only a controlled development in social relation of existing purposes and interests, it is also a development of knowledge. Of course a plan is not a piece of research nor an experiment designed to test an hypothesis,[26] but it is normally in part an application of current knowledge in a definite programme, and this is a test of assumptions and an exploration of the conditions on which accepted knowledge is valid and useful. Clinical practice is not research, but it makes a vital contribution to the understand-

K

ing and usefulness of established knowledge, and even to its extension. The analogy is not exact, but there is usually in social planning
an element of applied knowledge[27] which gains greatly from the
experience of practice, for example, economic or educational theory
may partly inform a plan and be usefully reviewed in the light of
the results. There is also knowledge gained of the practicability of
policies and of the efficacy of means empoyed. Apart from these
public aspects of knowledge, there is the private knowledge gained
by participants of their own motives and ends. All this development
of knowledge, which cumulatively may be of decisive importance
for social control, is conditioned by the plan and the experience
it determines, and takes effect only in so far as that experience
issues in a revised plan.

Social planning is 'scientific' in the sense that relevant knowledge
is used to inform the plan, but not in the sense that the plan is a
rational blueprint, for the greater part of the 'information' which
goes to the making of the plan is probably contributed by the interests and opinions affected. A national wages policy, for example,
is not a suitable social plan in the present climate of opinion, however 'scientific'. On the other hand, the social plan is more scientific
than science in this context, in the sense that it applies appropriately
to the case the same general principle which informs science. Science
is built up by the technique of creating the precise experience from
which can be learned the answer to what is in question. Social planning in successive phases creates continuously the precise experience
from which interested parties can learn what they want and what
they can have and how they can get it. This would hardly be possible
unless they were at the same time to some extent already enjoying
it. And in the constant revision of means and ends which planning
involves the technical questions prompt the moral questions and
moral interests promote technical conscientiousness.

(3) Finally, public planning is in form socially creative because
it mobilizes the energies of men, sustains social vitality. Here it
will be compared, on the one hand, with the release of energies
under *laissez-faire*, and, on the other, with the appeal to the
instincts of the herd.[28] *Laissez-faire* encouraged the enterprise of
some of the most able and energetic individuals. It has been found
necessary to take measures to encourage group feeling if an all-out
effort is to be sustained by a whole people, as during war. The point
of an informed planned effort is that it enlists rather than inhibits
private initiative, that it finds scope for outstanding ability, energy,
ambition, and that, at the same time, because it is creative in opening
up new opportunity and increasing practicability of purpose, it

stimulates the interest and evokes the capacity of the great majority of those whom it affects. The combination of enjoyed personal scope with social responsibility and the experience of collective creative power engenders the public spirit which sustains the conditions and promotes the success of the planned effort. This is an emotional reinforcement of the technical and moral learning from experience which the plan formally induces.

The 'informed' plan is democratic in form, its technique requires the fullest consultation and participation and that the competent decision making and enforcing authority be the most comprehensively representative body available. That is to say, the 'informed plan' is impossible in a society without democratic institutions and conventions, and at the same time it is the necessary complement of democratic political institutions. It is the form of social collaboration, even when there are wide diversities and deep divisions, for it starts no closer than these diversities and divisions allow and it induces the experience most conducive to an enlightenment of purposes and closer integration. It is the form of social control over social change, since it initiates controlled change in major sectors of social operations.

Of course, new law is not confined to legislation of the planning type. Rules and procedures regulating free activities of individuals and of corporations, established rights and duties, provisions for appeals and remedies, are as necessary a prerequisite of 'informed planning' as democratic institutions are. It can take place only in a liberal political democracy. On the other hand, 'informed planning' is not confined to social legislation; it is appropriate to other forms of public initiative and to private industrial enterprise.[29]

In the latter case, the competent policy-making authority is not representative in the sense of democratically elected, but there is every reason why policies and decisions should be informed by the interests affected (as well as by relevant data) and the interests in turn frankly informed of reasons for policies and decisions, so that the leadership makes itself representative and interpretative, and not merely authoritative, and secures participation. 'The pattern of management', which embodies sifted, analysed, and generalized experience, and seeks to institutionalize successful practice (itself, therefore, an 'informed plan' to be continuously revised in the light of the experienced it institutes), both separates and integrates the functions, operations, and phases of the productive or other industrial or commercial process, in order to maintain and raise efficiency and in order to have under control an instrument of *adaptive* economic behaviour instead of the institutionalized practice of *established* technical and social skills (Elton Mayo). This controlled instrument of adaptive economic activity is not only enabled to maintain its complex of interests in a context of challenging and threatening changes, its own normal programme initiates a succession of such changes. 'The pattern of management' will include perfectly rationalized components on the time-and-motion-study model and personal but proved methods of adapting the requirements of profit-seeking enterprise and machine industry to the tempers and temperaments of living people, in order to be able to enlist and sustain in a reliable way the spontaneous tendencies to cooperation which are found to be normal. The organized attempt by means of standard organized management systematically to combine adaptive efficiency with the humanization of industry is a necessary element in the discipline of a welfare society, an important component in the method of social control.

Not only business management but also public administration is a planning process. There could hardly be a more explicit recognition of the three-phased cycle of 'informed planning' as the essential process of administration than the following statement in a recent work.

'In one sense planning is inseparable from administration. The object of administration might be roughly defined as the deliberate and rational organization of resources to attain a defined objective, and planning is an essential part of any cycle of administrative action. The organization is given a task; it collects relevant data; it hazards forecasts (with some estimate of their reliability) about factors outside its control; it puts forward a scheme for using the available resources in the available time to secure the defined objective — or it recommends that the objective is unattainable. The preparation of such a scheme is 'planning': the preparation of the plan passes into the execution of the plan, and execution is accompanied by continuous observation of success or failure. These observations themselves become part of the data for a new plan (or a decision to abandon the enterprise), so that the process of planning is continuous, even though marked off into stages by plans formally made and approved at turning points in the action.'*

If the concept 'informed planning' be understood to mean this three-phased cycle of operations, informed initiative-performance-
_____
* *Central Administration in Britain*, by W. J. M. MacKenzie and J. W. Grove, p. 355.

reformed initiative (or inform-perform-reform), the condition on which democracy is genuine sustained social collaboration and participation and not merely occasional voting at general or local elections is that every kind of social activity shall be initiated and controlled in this way. In the major social activities, the informed plan stimulates, informs, co-ordinates, and enlarges the independent initiatives of which it is itself formed, and creates for its participants an experience from which they may continuously learn and in the light of which they will want in due course to revise and renew their purpose. Persistence in planning of this kind is the self-education and self-creation of a society, an increasing vision of and command over its destiny. This ideal surpasses the older democratic ideal of unanimity achieved in debate, 'the sense of the meeting' in which the opinions of all were compounded and the opinion of each trancended,[30] for it adds to the dialectic stirring, sifting, and settling of juxtaposition in debate the necessary dimension of time in which the experience created by the resultant resolution works its own unique transformation. Social creativity in this kind must ever, of course, be more diffuse than personal creative achievement, but, for its participants and beneficiaries, it has promises and satisfactions of its own, and, in terms of power, it may embody the pure technique of the highest human activity with sovereign majesty.

To this argument that planning is in form creative, and therefore that social planning is so, two apparently sufficient objections are likely to be raised: (1) that the argument depends so entirely on ideal assumptions that it contributes nothing significant to practical politics or to the problem of social control; (2) that you can plan effectively only the means to a given end, so that social planning requires either a common social purpose which, except in wartime, is usually to seek or else the imposition of an end by a ruling clique.

(1) The ideal assumptions are (i) that the interests affected by a proposed plan are consulted and represented in the making of it, (ii) that they are therefore either party to it or have made plain their objections to it, and that in either case they are prepared to co-operate loyally in giving effect to whatever is in the outcome duly and constitutionally decided, (iii) that the plan is in the same way in due course revised by all the parties in the light of what has been learned in practice. That is to say, the ideal assumptions are no more unrealistic[31] than the assumptions on which democratic procedures are founded, and practised more or less faithfully every day. In fact, the argument has not been: this is what we ought to do if we want to institute social control of social behaviour and social change.

The argument has been, rather: this, as a matter of fact, is what we have, increasingly, been doing since the middle of the last century; we are accustomed to doing it and we do it somehow inevitably; but by looking carefully at what it is we have been doing we can discern its form, and being conscious of the valid form of what we are doing we can do it to better purpose, with less public folly and more public spirit, less groping, grasping, and letting go and more perception of what we are about, less muddle and more progress. In the field of human endeavour, this is the way to institute control and achieve perfection. In inquiry, in argument, in the arts, in games, form, derived from analysis of successful practice, is the instrument and standard of control. In saying that planning is in form creative, one is claiming, of course, more than control, but only on the reasonable assumption that human activities are creative if they are so controlled that they develop and prosper. Planning is in form creative because it not only creates the most appropriate experience from which the minds concerned can learn but also the state of mind most apt and able to learn. Of course it does this only in so far as the plan really is informed and informs, in so far, that is to say, as it really engages the participants and continues to inspire and direct what they do, is and continues to be their embodied thinking in control. This is an ideal, but it is an idealization of what is in fact going on, and it can be realized with closer approximation by attention to the form of planning, its phasing, its continuity, the fulness of the information which goes to its making and its successive revisions and of the information which is given out with the initiation and the revisions of the plan. Public awareness of the form of this social technique, leading to an acquired mastery of this only method of creative social control, would be the most solid and permanent ground of confidence on which to construct social essays in exploration and invention; instead of lagging along, living and partly living under a regime which some like and some lump, creating bureaucracy by supineness and evasions, stubbornly dense with obsolescent ideas and ideals; perhaps even stupid enough to think it is necessary to burn down houses to enjoy roast pork.

(2) The form of social planning requires at the outset the establishment of the most workable compromise in the existing diversity of interests and ends. Unity is not imposed; the end proposed is some social change which has some motivation and promises some benefit and which can be made acceptable enough, however reluctantly, to the interests affected. This flat and feeble statement represents the nadir of social planning. It is the job of statemanship to achieve a 'sense of the meeting' form of compromise as the initiative of a

plan, a new social enthusiasm and vision born out of the discussion and thinking occasioned by the proposed plan; or else, according to the possibilities of the situation and the issues involved, a party with a powerful conviction and widespread support in the country and sound technical information may, without infringing or endangering democratic consent and co-operation, plan its purpose, with due consideration for the protests and representations of its opponents, short of frustrating the purpose. In no other way is any radical change possible; and radical changes have been wrought during the last hundred years in both these ways. But major social change is not necessary every day, and is not necessarily the most creative social change. Planned public initiatives are, or may be, going on every day in every field of public interest, and these, cumulatively and by addition, can be as decisive as the spectacular though peaceful social revolutions, and perhaps even more productive. The same need for statesmanship or vigorous and intelligent (not necessarily political) party initiative combined with democratic respect for affected interests holds of these lesser or unofficial initiatives. It is comparatively easy to learn to succeed in doing what one is resolved to do, the political job is to get done what not everybody wants, or else to induce all or enough people to want to do something or to see it done or not to resist having it done. The plan is an initiative, however it comes about, a head of pressure, whatever its source, which encounters resistances and limits; but in so far as it induces some change in the light of which everybody will think again, it bears the promise of greater unity, clarity, and urgency of purpose; and it does so because this is not a limited experiment but a continuous and endless process.[32]

All human activities are usefully subject to appropriate planning. The State can demand certain results from scientists or artists and forbid certain enterprises and prescribe certain opinions and proscribe others. This of course is not planning but dictation. The conditions of effective thinking, of fruitful research, of creative art, of efficient production can be studied and publicly promoted; and this may occasion mistakes and political differences, but public promotion of the public conditions of these activities, as distinct from the private and personal initiative proper to them, is the form of creative social control over these creative activities, and none other is tolerable, since any other defeats the purpose of planning to promote these activities.

The public character of the plan is itself a criterion of appropriateness in social planning. A plan in itself is neutral, and may have good or bad results. A smash and grab raid may be beautifully planned;

the Suez folly may have been technically perfect (it wasn't). Such plans are not fully public. In as far as a public plan is fully public, in the sense that it is fully informed by the affected interests, it is in the circumstances necessary and constructive, even though it may be short-sighted and have unhappy consequences. This strange doctrine is true only because real life is like that. We are under an obligation to consider the advice of others and to learn from past experience, but having duly done so we can only act in the light of that, and learn by the results whatever they may be. This moral responsibility and this fatefulness inhere in collective action as well as in personal conduct.

Social planning has had a bad name not only because it is confused with State dictation but also because it is so easily and so usually badly carried out. The half-baked plan or a lack of priorities may be as bad as the imposed plan, perhaps worse. Pressure of parliamentary business does not give time for the adequate working out of controversial and technical questions in a complicated piece of planning legislation in which the whole country is involved. Perhaps in such a case the floor of the House should be kept clear for principles and the detailed provisions should be devolved upon bodies outside. Whatever the proper remedy, the point is of the first importance, that to get social control by an informed plan, instead of bureaucratic rule, devolution may be necessary, so that general principles may be thoroughtly hammered out and agreed in the House, and so that the House may remain the nation's vigilant watch on the Executive.

Resources in money, men, and materials are always limited and never justify an attempt to carry out at the same time all that may be demanded or desirable. For political reasons, the attempt is likely all the same to be made. The inevitable result is a dilution of skills, a debasement of standards, maimed schemes, a bewildered and exasperated public. Then nothing is made a success,[33] the last state is worse than the first, social planning falls into disrepute, government and administration becomes rulers versus the people, the conditions of responsibility are dangerously impaired: strife, anarchy, and dictatorship may not be far off. Priorities are required, and require genuine national decisions.

4. CONCEPT OF THE POLITICAL CYCLE

Thus the concept 'informed planning' as the three-phased cycle inform-perform-reform is a general form applicable to all social activities, and furnishes the clue to a method of perfecting them. In social legislation, public administration, and business management, as the main theatres of social initiative and control, this is a clue worth strictly following. The concept is equally applicable to the institutions themselves which embody past experience and perpetuate patterns of successful practice and to the operations which they initiate and control or the policies which they form and carry out: both (the institutions and their programmes) can be continuously corrected and developed by learning. This does not happen as a matter of course; it requires due separation and a thorough working through of the phases; that is to say, clear comprehension of the process, in the first place, and systematic attention to it, in the second place.

None of the three major social operations mentioned above is self-contained. In particular, social legislation, in its preparation and enactment, is only the initial phase of its particular cycle. Public administration (which also has its own cycle) is the second phase of the legislative cycle. It is useful to think formally of the political process as a three-phased cycle, legislation-administration-evaluation,[34] a particular instance of the general formula, inform-perform-reform. The main agents in the political cycle are, in respect of each phase, parliament, the public administration, and non-governmental organizations and research institutes. In any major legislation everybody is more or less involved, individually or in associations, but the stream of tendency and influence is eventually focused in each phase through the main agents. The due separation and thorough working through of the three phases is the method of intelligent democratic control of the political process. The phases of preparation and evaluation are essentially political, in the sense that the interests affected have their proper say and due influence, and policy is neither determined nor re-shaped merely by administrative considerations, research findings, nor executive fiat.

The function of the public administration in this cycle is of course to plan, organize, and enforce the resolved policy which represents the national will. By seeing that what has been resolved is in fact done, the administration also provides the assurance that social experience is self-determined, is the result of the decisions taken. Otherwise, there would be improvisation without notation, and no means of nor meaning in revision. Unless *post hoc* can reliably be counted as *propter hoc* there is no useful comparison of what happens with what was expected; there is no necessary relation between the social policy and the social experience, and it is not possible for anyone to begin to learn with assurance what he wants

and how to get it: politics remain primitive, incoherent, uncontrollable. The slow spiral of political progress is in the discipline of
separating, integrating, and faithfully working through the three
phases of the political cycle. Sound administration is an assurance
that social experience is the result of the policy jointly determined,
and equally an assurance that a policy jointly determined will be
carried out. Without this assurance, social policy cannot be tested
and its amendment is not worth while: there is no instrument of
control to be employed.

The diffuseness of the political process at best, even in a society
in which all activities and interests are highly organized, gives
special importance to an adequate separation, integration, and working through of the three phases in the case of the political cycle.[35] The
phase of evaluation and revision is liable to be most diffuse.[36] The
collection of data by interested associations and the promotion and
use of specific research and the eventual sifting and routing of this
relevant material, along with the representations of interested parties,
to the site of legislative revision are not operations which could be
truthfully described as complete nor as systematic. Something does
happen on these lines, but this is not usually a phase which is as
adequately worked through and integrated into the cycle as it might
be; which means, of course, that two of the three phases, at least,
are usually deficient. This deficiency modern societies are competent
to remedy.

The concept of political process as a three-phased cycle initiated
by legislation stands in equally strong contrast with the *laissez-faire*
and the totalitarian concepts. The *laissez-faire* concept came into
existence in justified protest against obstructive and irrelevant im-
positions and interventions of the State in the sphere of trade and
industry. The concept developed on the positive side as the notion
of autonomous activities guaranteed by a State which provided only
security of life, property, and contract, and therefore the reliability
of economic laws.[37] On these assumptions, administration was
almost entirely judicial: there was no purposive political cycle,
there was only the inevitable business cycle. The concept still lingers,
but its utopian character is now manifest. Although enthusiasts for
its euclidean virtues may allege that it is not disproved because
never tried, they are not politically ever likely to be able to try it,
and if their grievance is to be kept alive it must be nursed in a home
for lost causes.

The most conspicuous feature of totalitarian societies for a generation past has been the succession of state plans, but this was not an

original ideological feature of marxist communism;[38] planning was forced on the bolsheviks as social legislation was forced on Victorian liberals by the exigencies of the situation. The machinery which has enabled society to endow its citizens with basic conditions of welfare and with increasing practicability of purpose (which is the substance of freedom) has been set up and set in motion and is kept moving by legislation of a planning type, in the East as in the West. In a society which is inevitably changing, though not changing inevitably, the changes are likely to bring chaos and anarchy unless they are themselves brought about by a public initiative. That is not the last word, however, for the difference between the public initiative in a totalitarian context and a public initiative in a political democracy has an importance even greater than we are accustomed to assume it has.

Totalitarian planning absorbs the political phases into the administrative phase. The State may not wither away, but the political phases dwindle to a vestigial remnant.[39] There probably is the three-phased cycle inform-perform-reform, but the information which goes to the making and the revision of the initiative is limited to the calculations of the chief executive (with the necessary extent of expert assistance). The whole process is simplified to an administrative or a business management cycle, and of course admits of humanization and liberalization in the same way. Forgetting for a moment the shocking indignity of it all,[40] one may suppose that this drastic simplification at least serves efficiency (speed, flexibility, economy of means), and that political liberty in the West is a luxury only to be afforded out of ample means, and perhaps only so long as the advanced industrial powers can maintain an undisputed lead. However, the reduction of the political cycle to an administrative or management cycle is only efficient and enviable if the purpose in hand is as simple and unquestionable as an assigned organizational task. For the multiple, variable, and imponderable purposes and satisfactions of a total civilized society not at war, the reduction of the political cycle is monstrously inefficient, the simplification is a drastic impoverishment. The political phases, through organizational freedom, are occupied with the production of alternatives for comparison and choice, which in the context of experimentation provided by the political cycle spreads the social conditions of growth in maturity of judgement and purpose, and fertilizes and cultivates the soil of originality and creative achievement. Anyhow, the shocking indignity of political servitude (of whatever stripe) is not to be forgotten for a moment. Rousseau is soberly and simply and for ever right: 'When a man renounces[41] liberty he renounces his essential manhood . . . There is no compensation possible for such complete renunciation'.

As a fact of the democratic order, the political cycle cannot be opposed to any party ideology or programme as such, for it provides certain facilities and limits for them all and has, as it were, nothing of its own to promote. Nevertheless, it does stand as a concept in opposition to any doctrinaire political theory and also to the usual presuppositions of conservatism. That it is in this way opposed to doctrinaire theory, that is to say, theory not properly grounded in nor subject to experience, is sufficiently obvious. Less apparent is its inconsistency with theoretical conservatism.

The philosophical conservative[42] is usually imaginatively dominated by his impression of the profound complexity and resourcefulness of the world order; he would trust Nature (or God) rather than man. For the rational mind to reduce all things to its own measures, and for men to treat all things as raw material to be shaped into means for their short-term and short-sighted purposes, seem to the conservative to be brash and blasphemous ways of taking and tackling what everybody must know is an independent and ancient world, a mysterious and eternal order: this form of self-confidence is an invitation to disaster. He prefers the intuitive to the rational, as nearer to the inscrutable source of wisdom; and he feels that immemorial customs, traditional and unquestioned ways and beliefs, and established institutions are the proved and trustworthy guides and controls in human affairs, more original and subtle and more adequately adaptive than innovating designs and rational plans can reasonably be expected to be.

Now this conception does stand in contrast with the concept of the political cycle, in which people do initiate the social changes they want, and afterwards evaluate them. It is as much opposed as the *laissez-faire* concept, although on different grounds and for different ends. Again, there is no question of a practical choice. However noble and attractive the conservative ideal, it is not in the modern world a valid and viable way of social life, however tragic that may be. The changes forced on modern societies can neither be avoided nor adequately met by reliance on spontaneous adaptations. Moreover, even in terms of experience (and for the conservative experience is fundamental), the failure to take and revise an informed initiative is a failure to make the most of experience, to penetrate, possess, and develop it, to accept and explore its possibilities, a refusal of the happy union of mind with nature, in which the spontaneous is fertilized by the rational and the rational made generative and regenerative by union with the spontaneous.

In any case, although it may be said that in the assumptions of the concept of informed social planning (and therefore of the political cycle) there is an implied critique of the assumptions of at least some forms of conservative theory, there can be, it must be repeated, nothing in the concept of the political cycle which bears against particular policies, proposals, or criticisms which spring from conservative sources. What is not admissible in the concept of the political cycle (and in the democratic order) is the idea that conservatism (or socialism) is in any way morally or politically (if possible, still less logically, of course) obligatory.

The political cycle is not to be identified with the democratic cycle of party government,[43] and the point is to distinguish them. The party in office carries out its programme and goes to the country, and the party returned does likewise; and the electorate learn by trial and error in this rough and ready manner what men and what measures they prefer of the alternatives offered. This is as necessary and important a factor in the political cycle (legislation-administration-evaluation) as in the democratic process; but they are not identical, because (1) legislation rough-hewn in the electoral programme is shaped in the statute[44] by more than party interests, and because (2) the period of administration, study, and assessment before revision is due has no necessary connexion with the electoral cycle. The more or less crude conduct and showmanship of party politics may obscure the real political process of achieving an informed statute and learning from its experienced results. In an adult society[45] the main function of the parties would be to educate the public in this evaluation of administered statutes, not of course without the bias of partisan interests, but with a serious effort to relate the familiar results and those brought to light by research to the intentions and expectations of the original statute, when the time was due for a revision of the statute, so that in framing the new initiative more people would know more certainly what they wanted and what they might hope to get. The interests most closely affected learn this for themselves in respect of a given piece of legislation, perhaps without and perhaps in spite of a lead from the parties. The point is that although the formula of the political cycle (legislation-administration-evaluation) is an abstraction that cannot be applied in a democratic order apart from the party electoral cycle, it represents a continuous political process by which organized interests can and do learn for themselves what they want, what they can hope to get, and how they can expect to get it.

The all-important point under stress here is this: that the political cycle is a living-and-learning process more comprehensive and closer to actual interests and established facts than the electoral cycle, and that unless and until political parties, organized interests, public administration, research bodies, business management, the Press and other publicity channels, all participate coherently in the political cycle and find their focus in its phases, there will not be the degree of social self-determination which makes democracy important and which for the credit of humanity there ought to be.

This ought-to-be suggests, finally, that for simple citizens and organized interests to learn more perfectly what they want, what they may hope to get, and how they can expect to get it may not be perfect enough: ought not citizens to be taught what they ought to want, and is a society viable until its citizens have learned this and unless they behave as they are taught? This is the dangerous idea from which it is the mission of radicals to save society.[46] (When conservatives also wish to preserve society from this disaster, bless them too.) Crude appetites, agreed, is not stuff of which to make the Good Society. But to *substitute* law for wills or a general will for empirical wills, except through the process of the political cycle, is political fanaticism, an appalling evil to pile on top of the unavoidable burdens and inherent difficulties of social existence. The political cycle is social discipline enough, in that the empirical will is checked and challenged; people and interests are forced to think again, to make comparisons, to see results, to ask questions, and to answer questions. The transformation to be wrought by this induced detachment and reflection is modest in its requirement, from the strictly social point of view. Much that is not admirable remains legitimate, and although law is no substitute for will, neither is will a tolerable substitute for law. But there is no serious problem here on the negative side; experience shows that a democracy can maintain law and order. On the positive side, what can be expected from a more systematic social attention to the phases of the political cycle surpasses in practice the outcome of less realistic hopes, even if it is no more than that more people learn what they truly want and can hope to get.

Conservative nostalgia for an established order with settled forms of behaviour and unquestioned expectations attached to undisputed status has been made acute by the disastrous alternatives which seem to enclose modern man in a dilemma: the anarchy of *laissez-faire* individualism or the oppression of totalitarian collectivism. Escape from the dilemma is dreamed of in invocations of the irrecoverable past or in rather precious idealizations of community. But there is no necessary dilemma, for the citizens of societies in which the dilemma is posed have only to become clearly aware of the rules of the democratic order and follow them more intelligently and strictly, since this *is* an established order, and moreover, if the political cycle is not rooted in an eternal order, it is so for all practical human purposes, since to create the experience from which it is most profitable to learn and to go on to learn from it is the highest form of activity in which human beings can engage. Regular and regulated participation by all in the creation and evaluation of the social experiences they most need is not a precious idealization of community, and is a natural reconciliation of individual aspirations and the requirements of collective power.

This analysis has not ventured below the obvious, but society often suffers from neglect of the obvious, and to pick out the features of the familiar, like opening a window, may help to save a deteriorating situation.

5. LIBERAL EDUCATION

Education, being a society's method of self-reproduction, is a primary and powerful means of social control. Being a method of self-reproduction, it is not a primary means of social change. Education is necessarily conservative: you educate for a society and cannot successfully educate against society, nor attempt to do so without grave risks. Even if the schools were not officially committed to meeting the requirements of society as it is, the family, the institutions, the manners, morals, and opinions which prevailed in society would prevail over the schools. When Rousseau, who with the eighteenth-century philosophers believed in the power of law and education to make all things new, set out to show how his ideas might be applied in practice, he had to begin by subtracting his Emile from society. Insulated like Robinson Crusoe, deliberately, he could be made self-dependent, educated for himself and for mankind, but systematically estranged from his fellows. Rousseau could save himself from absurdity by holding up his other belief on which his faith in education depended, that the opinions, manners, and morals of a people, their whole behaviour, followed from their laws.

Plato's philosophy might be viewed indifferently as a theory of education, a theory of ethics, or a theory of politics, that is, of the State; because education for citizenship was at the same time education for manhood, since the nature of man and the nature of society

enjoyed a natural and happy correspondence, and therefore education for society could do no violence to the ideal of personal happiness and self-fulfilment, and vice versa.

A philosopher who has this confidence, or a traditional authoritarian society, or a society with a pressing particular purpose in
education (as, for example, to create a homogeneous people out
of disparate immigrant elements), has little difficulty in making the
schools an instrument of control. On the other hand, a society which
is sorely conscious of a divided inheritance, which values freedom,
and which faces change, is not in the happiest position to reproduce
itself confidently through its schools. Nevertheless, the Education
Act of 1944, a fabric of compromises, informed by studies and inquiries
as well as by negotiations and discussions, as such social legislation
ought to be, was a brave attempt to formulate a long-term national
plan.

The compromises reconciled, amongst other interests, the Anglicans and Dissenters, though not the Catholics, the public and private
schools and the public system, the elementary and the secondary
teachers. At the same time, the Act formulated a comprehensive
social philosophy of education: there was to be free primary, secondary, and further education for all, suited to the abilities and aptitudes of the child, and on a footing of social equality. Nothing could
be more socially generous nor educationally fitting.

Nobody could have expected this vision to be translated abruptly
into social accomplishment. Shortage of money and materials, and
therefore of buildings and equipment, of suitable and suitably
trained staff, old methods and standards and habits of mind (dearer
to parents than to teachers), these and other handicaps and obstructions put immediate limits to the changes initiated by the Act.
Parents whose children were selected at 11 plus for education in the
new modern type of secondary school resented the stigma of failure
and feared the blight of prospects, for which they were no longer
able to compensate by buying a cheap place in a grammar school.
The middle classes struggled to maintain the differential by buying
places in private schools and public schools. Conservatives concentrated from the first on 'saving' the grammar schools. Thus the
national plan for education was bedevilled at the outset with political party issues and threatened to become a front in the cold war of
the class struggle. In spite of this, the actual remarkable accomplishment in school building, in establishing a staircase of educational opportunity, in developing the content of and enthusiasm for the new
type of secondary education, in laying the foundations of a complete
public system and thinking out its rationale, in raising the public

will for education and expectations from it, is dissolving stereotypes and preparing for experimentation and phases of significant change.[47] Perhaps in no other social activity is there as much continuous discussion of what is going on,[48] with the attempt to measure and assess achievement and falling short, in order to redirect efforts to better purpose; the discussion is by teachers and administrators, by political parties, by trade unions, churches, and other interested associations, and by writers in the Press; it represents diverse interests in education and is concerned both with administrative problems and with the content and methods and objects of education.

The awakening to the power of education is world wide.[49] The decision of the rulers of China to embark on the formidable task of replacing the ideographs with an alphabet is a spectacular example, as impressive as the sputnik. The Western powers have felt driven to rally themselves for a new drive and a new deal in education. This means, of course, immense national efforts to improve and spread scientific and technological literacy in order to take part in the strenuous and fierce international competition in every field of technical endeavour. (It has been suggested that the Ministry of Education has taken the pre-eminent place of the British Navy.) There can be no doubt of the effectiveness of education geared in this way to a national purpose and policy. History provides enough examples. The success of the American high schools in making people good to get along with, socially easy and pleasant, will do for a reminder; and the success of the British public schools in continuing in and out of season to issue their particular products is another. The examples are also a reminder that this is a success of a society through its schools and not all their own work.

If education has been put on the national agenda in a big way here and everywhere, then, it is because (even beyond national rivalries) the survival and progress of civilization (as well as its destruction) depend upon the production of an adequate supply of highly trained scientists and technicians; and because education can deliver the goods. These business considerations are paramount (and such considerations always have framed any educational system) because we no longer have any choice but to depend increasingly on the development and application of this body of knowledge and skills. Existing and prospective levels of population can no more survive and improve their conditions of life without the services of these highly trained specialists than they can without the food and raw materials with which only these experts can provide them.[50]

L

This being so, the educator and the social thinker who want education to be a reliable and powerful instrument of social control and social creation and not merely a necessary contribution to industrial survival and expansion should not be frightened by the tide of national interest in and expectations of education as flowing too violently from the wrong quarter to be anything other than a menace, for many currents have contributed to the present head of water, which is capable of floating many types of craft serving for many uses, pleasures, and destinations.

The balance between specialized and general education and the content, methods, and aims of general education make the central problem.[51] Special training and academic specialization are the dynamic elements in the system, the source of rapid change; they have their own momentum and because they serve imperative national needs in the competition for life and influence they are assured of adequate attention. It is widely recognized that these progressive elements require compensation by permanent elements which will give stability and universality to the system. This basic general education, if there is to be a common citizenship, has to serve the needs not only of specialists of all kinds but also of those who do not specialize, whose further education, when it becomes available, is limited to part-time attendance in county colleges.

Some have suggsted that it is enough, and best, if the specialists are induced to reflect on their specialism, stimulated by courses in its history and philosophy. Others want courses for scientists in the humanities and for humanists in general science or the history of science. At earlier stages, the common core curriculum is the thing, with English, Social Studies, General Science, the Arts, and of course physical and moral education.

There is merit in all these suggestions. But the problem is trivialized if it is treated by playing permutations and combinations with an inherited culture and a traditional curriculum, without looking first at the society now in the making to discern the reshaping it will get as a result of the sifting and training of native talent, with diminishing regard for old economic distinctions and social traditions. And the problem is hopeless if half the answer is not found in the changes in the theory and practice of education which have already taken place.

The least disputable part of education takes place in the nursery, infant, and primary schools. These have been the 'progressive' schools of the public system.[52] Their education is modern, that is to say it is a loving recovery of the spontaneous education which used to take place in the old villages of Europe. This immemorial education has been institutionalized, that is, taken to pieces, understood in the light of modern child psychology, and put together again, reinforced by knowledge and with some improvements in practice, and some loss. The child who used to grow up with brothers and sisters and neighbours, familiar with and learning domestic crafts and village trades, cradled in traditional songs, games, and stories, participating in a folk culture and in the church calendar, does this still today at school perhaps with less vigour and reality, but more carefree and with more variety.

The school has to meet the home and the local community more than half way in creating the suitable environment for the maturation of the child, but it is not alone. The educational efforts in the school are complemented and reinforced by other mass social services: housing, clinics, insurance, advisory help, youth service, and the like. This immense social effort is not relieving parents of their responsibilities; on the contrary, it is, physically, morally, and technically, enabling them to understand and fulfil their duties. The trained workers in these services are propagating good practice and insisting on a reasonably high standard of performance. The process tends to be doubly cumulative: the experience gained in the practice of these services improves the training given to the professional workers in them, and therefore the skill and efficacy of their service; the more parents are enabled to bring up their children intelligently, the better parents their children will be. A welfare society is indeed a partnership, 'a partnership in every virtue and in all perfection'.

What the child needs in order to mature properly at his own pace and become a self-dependent and dependable adult is fairly well established.[53] He cannot be stabilized and socialized unless he is enabled to become competent in enjoyed activities. He is not educated but besotted or turned into a lout and a hooligan by being driven at studies or activities for which he has no aptitude nor capacity. He does thrive on and may be educated by what is enjoyed, and participation in enjoyed activities does tend to evoke a spontaneous public spirit, a morale which vigorously upholds the light authority which is recognized as the source and the force of the rules which regulate what everybody really wants though contrary impulses frequently get the better of him. This type of order and discipline, with its appropriate techniques, incentives, and restraints, leading on to the moral order of a free society,[54] is as different from *laissez-faire* as from the authoritarian methods of a patriarchal society. The child cannot be educated if he is master; the opportunity of education is wasted, and he is ruined. The teacher who understands the child's current goals, his dependence and independence, the phase and rate of his maturation and the materials and activities apt to stimulate and develop him, is in a position to educate him, without repression and without falling victim to him. This, no doubt, is asking a great deal; but the process of education does not admit of administrative problems nor of the limitations of adults. By concentrating on essentials and interesting the child in his own education, the job can be done.

General education, whatever it is, does not do the work of a finishing school: it does not turn out well-informed persons with formed taste and several accomplishments. Whatever else it is, its prime virtue is that it is rudimentary. Unless it conserves and enlarges origins and swells the springs of vitality, education is fatal. Inquisitive ignorance, fresh sensibilities, aspiration and admiration, creativity are the indispensables, and it is the inexorable requirements of established imperatives and standards set by superior achievement and by social traditions which have to come to terms with them, somehow, if education means anything worth bothering about. General education is rudimentary in the sense that it is concerned with elementary encouragement and equipment, but the grammars, groundings, and grindings are useless unless they are in fact consummated in use: worse than useless, for they make a wickedly wanton sacrifice of the child, since there is now no excuse for thinking that the mind is improved by what is done for no other purpose than exercise.

General education, then, is general in the sense that it is education of universal aptitudes and attitudes, to find out, to try out, to make up one's mind, to exercise skill, to enjoy, to bear responsibility, to make comparisons, to resolve difficulties and remedy failures, and the like; but it is general also in the sense that education in these experiences and these techniques is particularly applied to individual needs, possibilities, and prospects in a way that leads to the child's discovery and exploration of himself and the alternatives open to him because it makes him conscious master within his capacities of the universality of these experiences, techniques, relations; he learns that he can use them for himself and that they will carry him as far as he cares to go: his participation in his own education leads to his undertaking responsibly and knowledgeably the management of his own life.

The point of the argument is that we know enough and can perhaps reach enough agreement to design, practise, and improve a general education which will be considerably different from any older notion of liberal education, now mostly misleading; and that more than half of what can be done is being demonstrated already in many primary and some secondary schools. What results can be reasonably expected eventually from such a plan of general education; shall we get a homogeneous educated democracy, a classless society? This was out of the question on any older plan of liberal education, and what an educated democracy may eventually mean on any modern plan of general education is only dimly discernible. Probably too much can be made of the present difference between families which have their own traditions, standards, and resources and those which depend largely on public services, down to the 'problem families' which have to be taught the elements of decent living. Probably the social processes will go on which have raised the lower standards and required a public basis for the development of professional services of all kinds.[55] The public services, not least the public system of education, will improve, and there will be general assimilation in habits of dependence upon them. At the same time, the struggle to maintain differentials, of income and social class, will go on. And the staircase of educational opportunity and social mobility has by no means yet been built so wide that it is equally accessible to ability from whatever quarter. Worth is still by poverty depressed, and may not rise even slowly.[56] Change, the direction of change, and the slowness of change in the transformation of the class picture are as certain as such things can be.

The differentiation symbolized by the selection at eleven plus is permanent and inescapable and ultimately more significant than the class distinctions which are in dissolution. The comprehensive school may meet many of the educational and social objections to the tripartite system, it may provide a diversity and a standard of educational resources which cannot otherwise be afforded, it may be the needed school of common citizenship: it may in fact supersede the tripartite system. What it cannot do is to hold together the destinies and styles of life of those who pursue higher studies beyond the school and those who do not. The social implications of this differentiation ought to be faced. The comprehensive school, whatever its merits, is a glib, even dishonest, treatment of this particular problem.

Seen in extremes, the difference is between a dynamic type of personality and a passive type. The dynamic type[57] is intellectually well-endowed, eager to qualify for responsibility, out to plan, work for, and manage a career. The passive type lives from day to day, taking what comes rather than tackling the business of determining what shall come. The difference is already evident in habits and outlook at the middle or later secondary stage, because the dynamic type has to sow for a later harvest, to live laborious days, to abstain from and postpone spending time on enjoyment. The other is able to live more fully in the present. In the sequel, with the increasing arduousness of the climb to key positions and the bondage of responsibility to be endured there, with the shorter working week and improvements in the securities and amenities of the worker's lot, and with the focus of his education from start to finish on the enjoyment of leisure, it may seem that the workers in their relatively passive, day to day, condition of life are the real beneficiaries of industrial civilization at last. This conclusion would gratify many in the century of the common man. But it is not true. The abstentions and sacrifices of the dynamic few (who are increasingly many), their characters and qualifications, the cares imposed by their responsibilities, will exact proportionate remuneration; they enjoy not only the exercise of their powers, the pride of position, and the prize of achievement, but also the practicability of purpose which comes with the disposal of financial means. They also are in the fullest sense, and pre-eminently, beneficiaries of our industrial civilization, with its abounding opportunities for the employment and reward of trained abilities.

In short, there is no class of slaves in an advanced industrial civilization: all are equally and differentially beneficiaries. The sifting and training of abilities raises social endeavour to a higher power, to the increase of human possibilities for all. This happy picture does not please everybody. The workers are organized to take care of themselves, the specialists can exact their price—or emigrate; if their scale and style of life is different from schooldays to cremation, now and in any future society, should anybody be worried? Most of the objectors do not count, but there is at least one question worth serious thought: will this building of society on sales the world over, this scramble for consumer goods and a rising standard of living, this materialism, not rot morals and culture? A short and true answer might be that spoils have ever been sought and seized wherever there has been the power to do it,[58] and what is enjoyed today is more fairly proportioned to productive effort than ever before; and that the Barbarians, the Philistines, and the Populace were all excellent people, and all sadly lacking in culture. But mere excuse, or shining by comparison with the shabbier side of the past is no answer to the doubts of these who question the likelihood that social change will be controlled to advantage, that, in particular, the results of how we teach will teach us how to teach.

General education will be successful in so far as it enables young people of all kinds to choose and use, to select and perfect, among the variety offered or open to their individual scope and hope. The choice is a choice of occupation, a choice of mate, a choice of life, the planning of homes and holidays and families. The standard of life, concretely, is liberty, practicability of purpose, the alternatives open. Education, concretely, is the rousing and raising of one's powers, active and responsive, so that one is enabled to discern and cultivate one's scope, exploring possibilities, framing alternatives, making decisions, settling acceptances, raising refusals, learning from experience and knowing what one is doing. There is here the educational answer to the rising standard of living, for general education applies to all sorts and conditions of children.

Does this not go back on what was said earlier, that schools are powerless to educate society? Are not uncultured homes and the corrupting influence of commercial advertising and the mass media too much for the rudimentary business of general education? Part of the answer is to distinguish more closely what can and what cannot be hopefully attempted in the schools; the other part is to make some discriminations in regard to the mass media

What cannot be hopefully attempted, obviously, is the education of a child for a society that does not exist, or which he will not actually live in. He can perfectly well be educated to make the most of his own possibilities and of those which are offered him by his contemporary world. Of course in the case of a badly handicapped child or in the case of bad times this is a bad look-out, but it would be perverse to let bad cases colour our whole outlook. Normally, a child can be enabled to stand on his own feet, to find what he is interested in and can become reasonably good at, and to establish himself in a group, and thus to become educable and sociable. If he is not disabled from the beginning and is not dulled for life by being driven to drudge at the three R's and the like, if he is encouraged to do what he would and can do and enabled to do what he has to do, there is no reason why he should not be awakened to what is in him and what is open to him. This being so, he has founded within him a basis of self-dependence from which to have and live a life of his own, and he can be encouraged and enabled to go about it. If the springs of action are fed, if the sparks of living are kindled, he can in due course be left to himself, having been well started and knowing what he is up to. Being self-dependent, interested in his own pattern of good living, he is also dependable, interested without undue envy in the pattern of others, and upholding the general order in which these particular patterns are found. He is not an object of contempt, modern cannon fodder, the standardized consumer of standardized goods, a product of mass education in conformity, formed under social pressures and unable to stand up without the support of social pressures, because he has been awakened to the interesting possibilities of a life of his own through the experiences and techniques which put in his hands a choice of life.

What can in this way be usefully attempted in school is directed to use and enjoyment of what is available in the world we live in, and is therefore not automatically frustrated by the influences which prevail in society at large, particularly the cultural influence of the mass media. Contemporary culture,[59] as distinct from inherited culture, deals with contemporary events, problems, experiences, experiments, achievements, possibilities, in a contemporary manner. The mass media take part in this handling of contemporary life, not in an exemplary way, nor in a wholly contemptible way. There is relevance, there is excellence, there is point and pungency; these media purvey useful and enjoyable things, no doubt along with much rubbish and something pernicious. The argument here is not that it is all good enough to get on with or that it is not so bad that it matters very much; the argument is that here is the common stuff of common contemporary life handled in a way that has common contemporary appeal, in a way that is useful or enjoyable to most people: all told, it influences significantly people's interpretation of life, their sentiments, attitudes, imagination, conduct, their response and their action. This of course is just what the truly cultivated person complains of, that the mass media are diabolically influential, that they pervade every place and storm every soul, and that they vulgarize or trivialize everything they touch; that the popular Press mocks political democracy by treating the news as entertainment, that the staple of the screen is sex and violence, one half of mankind at the other's throat with woman sprawling between, that juvenile delinquency is flattered, that the nude and the rude have put the accomplished art of the old music hall out of business, in a word, that Gresham's law prevails in the cultural market. The denunciation is often too sweeping, but there is enought in it true and sad enough to sober the reflections of anyone who cares what he says on the subject.

Perhaps one may justifiably hope that popular culture has sunk to the nadir, and that left to nature and happy chance the tendency will improve. But here we are talking of social control, in particular, of control through education, of what can be done by policies and techniques to work with nature and make happy chances virtually certain.

If the public is inert, if individual lives are baseless, similar, imitative, effortless, and envious, the mass media will correspond to this condition, cater to the cravings of the crowd, corrupt the corrupt, and mould the moulded. The assumption of my argument has been that general education discovers to the individual the interest and possibilities of his own way of life, and furnishes him with the techniques of management. The vitality is in the young, it can be furnished and not quenched, and it is more interesting and exhilarating to stand on one's own feet and follow one's bent, if one is shown how, than to drift with the crowd and lean for support. General education on these lines is working with nature, a not impossible task, and is working against prevailing social influences only to a limited extent. There is in what the mass media provide a good deal to the purpose of individuals living their own real lives in a personal way; and by their selection of this they mould the mass media in the long run more than they are moulded. Educators if they know and do their job are stronger than the mass media, which can spoil only the spoiled, and none but they can redeem popular culture by enabling their pupils to use it with discrimination for their own purposes, and to become critically aware of its absurdities and of its false values.

This reassurance is valid on two conditions. The first is that it is not pretended that general education can do away with envy, prevent the flight from freedom into conformity, stop jealous social pressure against differences, save people making a hash of their lives. It can do a very great deal about these things, without removing their possibility. The great deal it can do is to provide knowledgeably and deliberately the most favourable conditions for individual success, without which there is only an odd chance; and in giving the individual his best chance, education gives society its best chance.

The second condition on which one may feel reasonable reassurance at the prospects of social control by education is that it is not assumed that there is or can ever be, or even ought to be, one culture universally valid and shared. If culture is real, it springs from, and in turn influences, experience; it is relevant, meaningful, only if it is available at one's own level, although there may be at every stage a ladder of ascent. The difference between the dynamic and passive personality is only a difference of degree, otherwise the conception of general education put forward here would be hopelessly mistaken, but it amounts at the extremes to a difference of type, and certainly to a different style of life and pattern of living. Similarly, there are differences in the depth, compexity, and subtlety of experience which are the basis of cultural differences. These differences are inescapable and permanent. What is inborn and what bred in is no matter for argument without knowledge, but it is evident enough that originality springs from no man knows where and that taste may be a standard product of an established class. With the erosion of established class edges if not the breakdown of class structure, which follows social mobility from selection by genuine equality of opportunity, accompanied by an equally genuine personal emancipation by general education, there will be the greatest diversity in styles of life, patterns of living, and interpretations of the world that has ever been seen.

The prospect on this assumption disposes of the fear of Tocqueville that the lateral pressures of political equality will reduce all to uniformity. It does not necessarily appease Nietzsche's horror of mediocrity. Still less will Mr C. S. Lewis be disposed to discern in this prospect any escape from the slide into moral and cultural anarchy, the abolition of man by relativity. Are there no absolute standards which judge all men and all things and divide for ever the true and the false, the right and the wrong, the high and the low? The words have a quaint sound which might make one suspect that there is something archaic in the way of putting it. Here, anyhow, only the political part of the argument is relevant.

Cultural diversity in the sense of a choice from the variety available and diversity in the use that is made of it, that is, in styles of life and patterns of living and interpretations of the world, does not entail moral and social anarchy if there is a common attachment to common institutions and common acceptance of the full mutuality and toleration which is the moral basis of society; and general education means education in and for both this diversity and this unity.[60] A society in which culture is thus personal and authentic and in which there are many groupings of like-mindedness has a tough and flexible stability that cannot be rivalled.

Of course there is a superior culture, in the sense of one that that is serious, highly cultivated, refined, informed by and informing a many-sided and profound experience. Of course this culture is the work and the resource of a minority. It never has been a class product, and it is not going to be a class preserve. The commercial market is too rough and ready a method of selection for its survival; it has depended on patronage, it will depend on subsidies.[61] The value of this culture is beyond price, and it is a public interest. Although few are chosen, the many are called: so long as it exists, it is open like higher education to all who can benefit from it. This universal culture does not judge nor dispute with popular culture nor the many sub-cultures. In so far as all are genuine expressions and sustainers of vitality, all are citizens of one world. Moreover, there are no precise frontiers in this world and no privileged immunities: the superior cultivated person may not seldom be mistaken or down-right silly. Even in the best regulated societies, the whirligig often brings in poetic justice to redress the blessed inequalities of nature.

The idea that democracy means that the many are the measure of all things is hasty. Featureless assimilated masses with the power of the vote, helplessly dependent on a leader and jealously imitative, this is a picture of a destructive beast. The beast is not a chimera, it is found in the natural history books , and no doubt it is not extinct; but like certain parasites, it does not appear until the health of the dominant organism is impaired. If we know how to keep and im-prove the health of our society, we need not fear this manifestation.

Hume more than once observed that general opinion was the only conclusive standard by which questions of morals or of aesthetics could ever be decided. No such statement without qualification can be expected to be true, and this is as true as any. It does not mean that a majority vote can settle the relative value of two works of art more conclusively than the opinion of connoisseurs; it does mean that a democracy can be trusted to be public spirited enough to maintain the conditions of plural culture if its citizens are edu-cated in a way that makes them personally interested.

6. RESTORED COMMUNITY

The sparks of living kindled by general education will flicker and die out if the climate is too damp. Society cannot exert control through its schools unless the education provided is education for what follows. Unless there are jobs available to those who have been trained for them, careers open to those who have chosen them, frustration is liable sooner or later to produce political catastrophe. For these economic floods and droughts are not nowadays acts of God to be endured with high fortitude or dumb resignation. Govern-ment is, or is held, responsible.

If work is normally available and secure, what matters next is place, work-place and home and public-place: the visible community for use and enjoyment. The city was always the focus of loyalties and the symbol of aspiration and achievement.

'The city is a fact in nature, like a cave, a run of mackerel or an ant-heap. But it is also a conscious work of art, and it holds within its communal framework many simpler and more personal forms of art. Mind *takes form* in the city; and in turn, urban forms condition mind. . . . With language itself, it remains man's greatest work of art.'*

It is largely because the village locally balanced on sturdy self-sufficiency has been destroyed, because industrial blight spread over the face of the countryside, much of it now derelict, because house has been joined to house and town laid to town until there is no room, that there has been a justified lament for lost culture, folk and fine, a loss visible in prevalent meanness. The shapeless conurbation is projected into the future as symbol of the ruin brought and wrought by industrial millions.

The resolute attempt in our time to halt the devastation, to preserve or redeem the inheritance, to restore form and significance to community in its physical aspect, to institute control, is itself in the concrete case, say in TVA, a symbol, a symbol of the power and promise of creative social control in every field in which it is intelligently applied. But in this field faith and hope will not be sustained by quick results. This is a long-term programme. The inheritance over large areas is shocking. New mistakes are being made. Departmental demands are private vandalism writ large, and departmental rivalries delay or prevent the right decisions. Human stupidity and insensibility, here as everywhere, limit achievement. But first steps have been taken, exemplary achievement can be seen, progress will be made.

The Geddes-Mumford inspiration has triumphed in the main,[62] the humanist, sympathetic, empirical approach, adopting and adapting what is there, intervening decisively, but little, and after study and reflection on the spot: all in contrast with the grid-iron plan of the municipal engineer. There is planning orthodoxy and there are rival schools and cults, breeding a doctrinaire outlook, as always, but the extent and intensity of the discussion in print and at the frequent well-arranged and well-attended conferences, and the lively interest taken by many well-informed local councillors, help to ensure that this field of prime public interest shall not fall under the domination of narrow professionalism. Again, the teamwork which is necessary and the painstaking statistical studies which keep up to date for when it is required information about the actual habits of people living in a place and the trends that are revealed, all help to keep this type of planning from the abstract, conformable to the needs and wishes of the people affected.

The local development plan itself is a model instrument of social

* Lewis Mumford: Introduction to *The Culture of Cities*.

control, in so far as it is based on exhaustive studies and is an exercise in intelligent foresight and imaginative projection. It is more than a prudent provision against unsightly and unsuitable building, for it is an attempt to evoke and realize the physical possibilities of the community: it expresses aspiration.[63]

The question of the optimum size for a community has been much discussed. The small face to face community has often been idealized.[64] Rousseau thought that this was a condition of virtue and of democracy. Burke, with eyes on a different model, was not far from saying the same. Recently, Arthur E. Morgan, first chairman of TVA, having a lifelong first-hand experience of both small and large communities, has gone so far as to assert that man is a small-community animal, that what destroys the small community destroys man, that the cultural inheritance transmitted in small communities is as necessary to survival as man's biological inheritance.[65] What he has in mind is that the social control of power, the prevention of the subordination of human relations to techniques and of the destruction of human affections by large-scale manipulation, depends on decentralization. This was also the argument of Aldous Huxley in his Preface to the Penguin edition of *Brave New World*: the small community is our sole recourse if we wish to escape from Brave New World and its worse alternatives.

Mr Morgan believes, and demonstrates, that the small community (and with it the human personality) can survive and flourish, that it can survive, and will, because it can be improved, because it can enjoy metropolitan standards without the inconvenience and inhuman conditions of the great city, and will therefore attract the best types who want the best conditions for their children's upbringing. Thus, on Confucian principles, by attracting the best dynamic types of cultivated people, the small communities will flourish and propagate themselves, and more than hold their own against the inhuman and demoralizing cities. They will initiate a social regeneration that will save mankind.

The small community as a cell in the personal resistance movement against modern scale and number overriding individual differences has its attractive heroes, but the cause may not be worth quite all that is devoted to it. After all, only yesterday the small community was a byword for every kind of petty oppression and suffocating mediocrity. The escape from this into the large, loose, amorphous, anonymous urban mass was, after all, a celebrated escape, a documented epoch. To idealize now the old prison is perhaps an ironical specimen of advanced thinking, respectable enough, however, if it is frank repentance and abandonment of ancient aspirations. As pioneering, it needs to be looked at rather critically. For one thing, all forms of association are conditioned by the larger society, and the old small community tended to create despair in so far as it tended to be the great society writ large, so to speak, bringing home in binding particular requirements all that was most conventional and popularly received. As victim of both locally enforced conventions of the time and possibly personal forms of local oppression, the individual was not likely to find in his small community a home which encouraged his personal development, apart altogether from restricted opportunity for choice of employment and for search for like-mindedness.

Of course the modern ideal is to combine the vitality and humanity of genuine community with the freedom and amenity of modern ideas and standards; but this battle is not to be won on the narrow front of local community, although experiment here may make a gallant and striking special contribution to the campaign. If what is important is to save people from feeling helpless and insignificant,[66] to encourage them to become self-dependent, to enjoy lives of their own, and to find a place and play a part in the life around them, this can be done by any society and not by resistance to society nor by escape from it, that is to say, by educational policy, social opportunity, and public opinion. Unless and until these positions are won, the *élite* small community, like the 'progressive' school, offers a lead which can hardly be followed.

If one creates space and light where there was huddle and squalor, introduces form and function into the townscape, settles some urbanity in the mess and some humanity in the mass, surely the big city need not be sacrificed to the dogma of small community? Town and country planning as a form of social control is limited to the physical environment. No more than anything else does it offer a solution of the whole social problem. There may not be good management nor good human relations in the modern factory, perfectly sited with every amenity. The new town has produced unneighbourliness and neurosis unknown in the old slum. Modern schools are not a substitute for nor a guarantee of modern education. The physical conditions are nevertheless important enough to write promise in the place of doom, to supply incentives and provide opportunities, to encourage and facilitate good patterns of living. The remodelled small community offers to do this in one way, a very attractive way, but not in the one way needful: it is not a gospel. Rather, it is a restored choice, with a promising future, and, like all good options, with a balance of advantage and disadvantage over other possibilities. The immense significance of the restored small community, of the possibility of its restoration, is the token of successful resistance to modern scale, which does loom large enough to menace with manipulation the face to face relations and day by day decisions of local communities. Transcending the value of the small community itself is the experimentation it exemplifies, the multiplication not the reduction of possibilities, the use of modern techniques for variety of life and for individual purposes and patterns of living, not the subordination to them of all personalism, the example of 'intentional' social activity.[67]

The values of the old folk-culture can be restored and developed in the primary and secondary modern schools; the values of the old village and small town can be restored and developed in the modern small cultivated community; the values of the old aristocratic or bourgeois *élite* can be restored and developed by the modern dynamic types. This form of conservatism, inseparable from experiment and diversity, is alone valid and viable, and can shame if not stop the conservative lament that all is handed over to the clamour of unrestrained appetites, that the reduction of all values to efficiency in increasing the production and widening the distribution of consumer goods[68] has begun to bring to an end the distinctive dignity of being human.

As to place, though not primary it is precious. The individualism founded and nurtured by general education in the schools, the common source of happy co-operation and of diverse patterns of living, can be met by options, experimental and established, in scale and types of community, an elaboration of modern idiom and idiosyncrasy in place and local character and way of life, which helps to make anywhere dear to the inhabitants and interesting to the visitor.

7. THE PUBLIC INTEREST

There is no bottom to hold these foundations, interior and exterior, of a life worthy to be called human unless government can control economic fluctuations and otherwise maintain for its people a certain place in the world. Unless the future is reasonably calculable, nothing matters: today's efforts are poured into the void. There is nothing new in this, it is the substance of history, but our time has posed decisive issues for democratic national government, namely, whether or not it can manage a free economy, and whether or not it can in consort with totalitarian government make the infinitely hazardous passage into perpetual peace.

Even in the plural society of many forms of independent association, government is not just one form amongst others,[69] a special function, for it is the paramount authority whose initiatives and maintained directives control and affect all lives and interests. This does not make government totalitarian, of course. There are at least the following specific distinctions: (1) there is continuous surveillance and criticism from a responsible Opposition which will be judged in turn by its own performance in office; (2) the government's policy in essentials has been approved by a majority in the country: (3) legislation in the making and the conduct of administration are informed and legitimately influenced by the interests affected; (4) government is restricted to general policies and provisions which establish public conditions, and does not supersede nor seek to determine other corporate or personal decisions and initiatives; (5) there are established safeguards and procedures which limit the powers and regulate the actions of government.

The distinction between any political party and the Communist Party, a total distinction, makes the difference clear. The Party demands and exacts from its members a total loyalty in all their thinking, activities, interests, and relationships. In power, the Party does not fill merely ministerial offices but also nominates its members to take over the key positions in every kind of organized activity throughout the country.[70] Moreover, the Party secretary may control the central committee of the Party and its political bureau, and thereby control the policy and conduct of every minister without being a member of the government. The Party moves in, not to play the party game but (in theory) to bring politics to an end.

Government, then, by what it does, refrains from doing, or fails to do, affects more powerfully than any other single influence the happiness of everyone. This is equally true of totalitarian and of democratic government. Yet democratic government at best is party government, biased in favour of the sectional interests it is drawn from, and can never be anything like a government of sages and saints. Here are life and death problems of national and human survival, and here are the political parties deploying their big battalions in sham fights, scoring partisan points, manoeuvring for advantage, no side thinking first, if at all, of the public interest. Not only are time and energies wasted in this way of dealing and double dealing with public business, but also the talents of the parties are dissipated. Could they and should they not be combined in a Council of State which would govern the country to the best of the available ability, integrity, and experience? Or might not Seven Wise Men be found to steer us out of our troubles?[71]

This is an old and persistently seductive idea. Eminent persons who should know better continue to flirt with its attractions. For experience has shown,[72] and would show again, that the Council of State will not solve our problems, that the prior problem is to prevent the Council of State's falling into the hands of the most astute or the most fanatical or the most unscrupulous politicians. Politics can be ignominiously driven out with the best of intentions for a new and clean order, but nothing can prevent their coming back with sevenfold evil, and the last state becomes worse than the first. The business of the Assembly, the constituencies, public opinion, have to be organized somehow; there have to be working incentives and deterrents, accustomed channels of communication, an accepted chain of responsibility, a basis of support for power, a reliable executive. Put all this complicated and delicate machinery in question and every hope and fear is touched, all interests are jeopardized, the most aggressive and the most cunning elements take the first and swiftest steps to seize advantage. This is all too old a story at this date to bear elaboration. Not to put it too strongly: if one thinks in terms of real alternatives instead of in terms of impossible ideals, there are no disadvantages in parliamentary party government.

The established conditions of party government in Britain are the conditions of maximum popular control at the national level: the Cabinet and the People predominate in the constitution. There are serious drawbacks, notably, subordination of the politician to the party machine and consequently reduction in the prestige and attraction of the House of Commons and impoverishment of the soil for ministerial timber.[73] There are drawbacks in other systems, in every system. And there are abuses. Although it would be fatal to get rid of the party system in favour of some alternative which would be supposed to serve the public interest, there is (always) room for improvement in working the party system on whatever model it is practised, and in some cases more than in others.

Where there are only two parties, or two effective parties, and the force of circumstances tends to drive both along the same road in a national situation which narrows the way, party policies may become factious and factitious in their differences. Even in this case, the party system remains useful and necessary in allowing controlled scope to the personal struggle for power and providing the machinery for responsible surveillance and alternative government. But actually there are likely to be real differences of principle and policy in the parties corresponding to differences of opinion and interest in the country. What becomes really important is to define with some sharpness the agreement and difference, and to

M

accept collaboration in the areas of agreement, which are likely to be those of prime national importance.

For instance, a foreign policy which is not candid and stable because not unreservedly backed by the overwhelming majority of the nation and by successive policy-makers, creates doubt, danger, and difficulty and is injurious to the national interest. At the present time, when world order or international anarchy are at issue, this is recognized to be of decisive importance, although party politicians may frequently speak against their better judgement.

We are committed to a managed economy, as much as to parliamentary government, and without the knowledge and experience which give confidence of success. To add to the trouble, the economic situation of Britain is extremely precarious, since it is necessary to import nearly half the food supply and nearly all the raw materials before a man can be put to work. This vulnerable position, with livelihood and efforts constantly imperilled by events outside national control, and the business of national control itself uncertain, asks for an unusually persistent attempt to collaborate on the part of all interests.

The pattern of a sustained collaboration of all interests engaged in learning to run a managed economy is extremely elaborate. Primarily involved are the Government and Opposition with the employers and trade unions and financial institutions; secondarily involved are the experts, economists and officials; thirdly, foreign governments and foreign interests, since nowadays economic co-operation is necessarily international even whilst it is not international enough. To produce a policy to promote industrial expansion with controlled inflation to which all these interests are party, which they take responsibility for carrying out, to which they re-adjust their position in the light of results, and which they help to revise for a better informed initiative, is perhaps impossible. To multiply responsibility and divide allegiance in this way, to cut across departmental and organizational boundaries and to cut into their integrities, to harness conflicting interests in the same team, merely to bring together such and so many diversities for any common purpose, this is perhaps too much to ask. All the same, it would be no more than a conscious development, a deliberate extension, of what has become modern statesmanship and modern administration, and goes on every day officially and unofficially. This new climate of statesmanship and administration, encouraging administrative invention and flexibility and multiple co-operation, is not without storms and frosts and droughts, heart-breaking vagaries and unsettlement, but it brings to logical flower and fruit the complexities of a highly organized society, and it will improve.

A common experimental policy for the control of a managed economy, in which everyone had enough confidence to make it workable, and which would be designed for learning and revision as well as for present management, would impose many compromises, restraints, and tensions, but it would not be impossible, for administrative experience and techniques are equal to it.

This necessary economic collaboration of all interests, including the political parties, would not necessarily bring to an end the conflict between the parties nor the conflicts between organized employers and organized workers. Politics would go on and industrial disputes would go on, and it would be in the public interest that they should, since the alternative is not harmony but repression. Nevertheless, these conflicts are and will be mitigated by the enormous increase in the volume of public interest, genuine common interest, now the submerged four-fifths of the iceberg.[74] These historical gains to be conserved include civil liberties and the constitutional conventions and procedures of democratic party government, with regulated and open access to power and regulated and popularly controlled exercise of it, social legislation enacted and social policies laid down, public institutions working, voluntary associations assisted. If economic policy could now be nationalized, tentatively, flexibly, and with international interests built in (and also foreign policy in so far as it is not now fragmented into separate issues, like defence and the international aspect of every policy and every question), the public interest would be completed and wear a crown it does not yet have.

Politics will, and would, go on. Enough agreement to learn how to work a managed economy by providing enough continuity and common understanding would not require either party to sacrifice its fiscal interests and principles. The Labour Party in office will continue the drive towards equality, will seek to raise the revenue for public purposes, to be spent on education, health, assistance to the poorer or weaker groups, improvement in the status and terms of employment of the workers. The Conservative Party in office will be committed to reducing taxation and public expenditure. Here in plenty is the legitimate stuff of party politics, likely to remain on the agenda for some time to come. Differences of interest are involved as well as differences of opinion, and they will not be resolved without a political struggle. The electorate chooses the party, and that fraction of the party programme that is practical politics. In office, the party makes the decisions and takes the responsibility, has its own way. It would be silly to pretend that there could be a national economic policy which would remain the same whatever the Administration. But there could and should be Labour and Tory versions of a national economic policy, loyally worked whoever is in office. A party in office has its own way, but not regardless, or democracy is at an end.

(When an enlightened exponent of modern American capitalism argues that the economy is so buoyant and productive that the production and distribution of frivolities is inevitable and unimportant, being merely the symptom of abundance, at the same time as Federal money is not available for demonstrable needs in education, the scope of party politics in modern successful democracies is indicated, not closed.)

Industrial disputes, too, will, and would, go on. The drive of the political Left for more private wealth for public uses is paralleled by the drive of the Trade Unions for higher wages and shorter hours, more pay for less work. Many people think this is reprehensible. It may be so. To suppose that it is decadent, however, a modern lack of restraint, the greediness of a pampered proletariat, is a mistake. The resolute attempt of one set of people to better their position at the expense of another set, met by an equally resolute resistance, is history *tout court*. In the political case, the trial of strength is taken at the polls. It is as unjustified, and unnecessary, to say that the solution is just as to say that it is unjust. Each side thinks of justice in different terms, and the question is decided by convention, or by those whose interest is numerically the stronger. In the industrial case, bargaining explores the strength of the parties; expansion or economies may give room for manoeuvre; arbitration may be invoked to settle the question. The political parties may resort to fraud, the industrial parties to force, that is, to strike or lock-out. This is a bad thing and a sad thing. Disputes can always be settled by the weaker party's giving way. The question is, which is the weaker party? A trial of strength answers that question. There is, unfortunately, no principle of abstract morality or justice to settle such questions. Neither the political Left nor the industrial workers are morally required to accept existing conditions as final.

Although morality consists primarily in fulfilling engagements and in meeting legitimate expectations, the engagements and expectations may be changed, and changed in a way that alters the relative advantage of the parties; and this may be done by a build-up of power to enforce a claim. The moral order is not violated so long as the changes are brought about in accepted ways. In industrial disputes, these include the right to strike. Objectively, strikes have been barren and ruinous. Actually, following Sir Walter Citrine, the trade union leadership has abandoned use of the strike as a weapon in a cold war with employers, still more decisively as an instrument of political action, and has embraced a policy of co-operation with employers and the government in the management of industry.[75] The strike remains a necessary *ultima ratio* at the disposal of the unions, but is more often used unofficially by a local body of workers against their management or against their union.

A healthy moral order does not consist in preventing at all costs any appeal to the *ultima ratio*, but, rather, in finding room for it whilst doing everything possible to avoid recourse to it. A healthy moral order is one in which men are satisfied that what is expected of them is right and proper, and therefore to be faithfully fulfilled. This gives room for dispute and requires ways of settling disputes without disrupting the order. In this way, a strike may be in the public interest, in so far as it may be the only way in which a satisfactory settlement of a grievance or a claim can be made the active and prior interest not only of the workers involved but also of the employers, the government, and the public.

Of course group pressure for a higher standard of living and envious levelling policies could handicap, impoverish, and even wreck the economy. There is no reason to suppose that the trade union leadership does not understand this as well as anybody. There is enough evidence to show that they have grasped the essential truth: that their struggle for an increasing share of expanding trade returns is conditioned not only by the prosperity of industry but also by the viability of the whole system, the managed mixed economy and the political democracy, in which they are resolutely loyal partners. There are uncertainties, disagreements, and different assumptions about the working of the system, but if practical agreement can be reached on short-term policies to be tried out and revised, there is an instrument of control. Most of the moral obligation in the question is found in the good faith in coming to agreements and in working and revising them. Apart from the age-old obligation of a day's work for a day's pay, which is fundamental, there seems to be very little moral obligation to constrain decisions. Differential pay and conditions are usual for different grades of employment carrying different levels of responsibility and requiring different levels of qualification. But there is no absolute entitlement to them, nor claim against them. Those who fill the higher grades have been, or increasingly will be, educated and trained at public cost, and they enjoy the power, prestige, and satisfaction of exercising their native gifts and acquired skills. As a category they are not worthier as persons than the wage-earners. There is no moral objection to the pressure of trade unions to gain a higher proportion of the product for their members. There is no moral objection to the political drive to tax inheritance or otherwise to raise more public money for improving social services, assisting needy categories, or closing the gap in the terms of employment between salaried staff and wage earners. In practice, social expediency, hard facts, and public interest, all that is genuinely a common interest, limit what can actually be done or properly attempted under these heads.

How far is the public interest a genuinely general interest, in widest commonalty spread; our institutions and way of life, the managed economy, the social legislation enacted, the welfare society in the making, are they all really bound together, and do they together bind all citizens in a real common interest and common purpose?

There are obviously beneficiaries of the present order: the very many who never had it so good, who enjoy something like equality of opportunity, full employment, social security, more leisure and pleasure, more goods and services; the defective, physically or mentally, the diseased, physically or mentally, the deprived, the delinquent, the aged, the feckless, the underprivileged young, the destitute, the unemployed, were never so well cared and provided for. That the business and professional middle classes have anything to be thankful for, still less to look forward to, is not so obvious. They cannot follow the style of life their fathers enjoyed, and their children will find themselves even more confined in hope and scope, in work and pleasure and culture. Many consider themselves under attack from the Labour Party. The Conservative Party cannot dream of restoring their privileges, and is not in a position even to save them from further losses. All walks of life are being harried and kept on the move until they end in being penned in the common public routes. The most enterprising and ablest of the younger men of these classes, it is sometimes said, are leaving the country, to bring up their families in climates more favourable to their energies.

The public interest, however, never has been nor will be defined in a way that can include all possible private interests, especially past privileges and personal dreams. The privileged classes in Britain have been required to share their privileges at a time when the Empire has gone and population at home has greatly increased. In no circumstances can they ever again have it so good. If some of the most energetic are being attracted abroad by younger lands of more abundant natural resources and ampler social opportunity, or even by wealthier industrial societies with a higher standard of living, that is their choice, and may, or may not, be Britain's loss. The public interest could be affected. If what is going on and is in prospect does not on the whole hold the interest and even fire the enthusiasm of the great majority of the young and able, with the result that in proportion to their enterprise and talent they are restless and look abroad and try to engage their energies elsewhere, the outlook would be black indeed, so black that it would lead to a policy of *sauve qui peut*, that is, to an abandonment of the public interest. Attachment to the public interest on the part of all classes and reconciliation of private interests with it, sometimes even the sacrifice of them to it,[76] have been the only conditions on which any society has thrived. They are not easy conditions in a free society, but, as in the case of domestic affections or any happy impulse that has to bear the heat and burden of the day, the discipline required may be light because the rewards are sweet and sufficient.

8. CHARACTER OF A HAPPY LIFE

Things are and remain in the saddle so long as mankind is trying to rely on impossible forms of control: self-regulating systems, laws of historical development, spontaneous adaptability. Nobody doubts that they can be brought under a high degree of social control by a dictatorship. This is a rather desperate simplification of all interests, a drastic impoverishment of human possibilities, a profound reduction in status of human dignity. In the political democracies, it is not simply the case that if only we would forget our differences, and form a common mind and purpose, the technical means are available to bring things under control—a hopeless prerequisite. The case is, rather, that in a loose way things are under control, that in social legislation and social policy, and in much else that embodies a public interest, a common mind and purpose is formed, that it is highly composite and not a forgetting of differences, that it initiates intended social changes of which the different interests involved have different expectations and from which they gain different benefits. The way to make this loose control strict is not by more direct methods, but by becoming more fully conscious of what we are doing and doing it more conscientiously and intelligently; that is to say, completing each stage thoroughly, actually doing what is planned, and revising motives, means, and ends in the light of what is learned. This is social self-determination, social free-will, the highest form of social existence, of which the British people in their present historical phase are eminently capable.

In actual practice, the partnership in a managed economy and the collaboration in social policies are at least as close as in NATO or in the forms of European co-operation, in which there is an acknowledged high degree of common interest and urgent need to develop it. To say this, of course, is to acknowledge grave imperfection. In perhaps each case, the sustained initiative is deficient and defective, defective in that unless and until a common programme has been hammered out, however limited by differences, there is no initiative, deficient in that unless and until the programme is actually worked and its results carefully studied, the initiative is not sustained. But this type of control, social self-determination, is there already with us in the rough, in the making.

Social self-determination, limited naturally to the open possibilities of a certain geographical and historical situation, is a form of social discovery and creation. It is a collective enterprise, however far short of integration the parties fall in their composite intention in any plan or policy, but parties and persons make different selections from what is achieved and different uses of what they select. A political democracy allows and a liberal education promotes diverse patterns of living and more than one interpretation of life. Self-dependence leading to a life of one's own is the psychological and moral basis of dependable citizenship. Although this self-dependence is founded in infancy and developed with the acquisition of competence and skills, it is not purely technical but also moral, for it involves renunciations and choices, attitudes and decisions, beliefs and ideals. Where do these come from? No doubt they take practical shape very largely under the constraints and influences of the expectations we customarily have one of another in the various relations and social functions of life, of the opportunities that come our way and the alternatives that are offered, and of the rules and procedures by which are settled claims as to who shall have what and who shall rule whom, bringing under social control the appetites for power and for goods. But this practical social determination is supplemented, and somtimes supplanted, by a more theoretical teaching or reflection. In the ancient world, the Stoics went as far as possible in teaching self-dependence, allowing value only to what was in a man's own power, his will. They went too far, far too far. But when we have gone as far as possible in the other direction and have created a human providence which can be relied on normally to satisfy our multiplied human wants, some discipline of the kind will still be necessary, will be more than ever necessary, or they will not be satisfied.

Therefore, religions, philosophies, interpretations of the world, discussion of values, are highly important to society as to individuals. But they are highly improper subjects for public initiative on a national basis. Monopoly is outrageous mockery of the truth and degradation of the human mind. Any sort of amalgamation is intellectually grotesque. The compromises that are necessary, the mutual toleration required are not socially disadvantageous. Freedom of thought is more sacred than any gospel. 'The eager, critical constructive labour of the mind in liberty is the historical force, the irreplaceable religion.' Social self-determination makes room for and protects this historical force. In shaping and re-shaping together their practical ends free citizens do not attempt to dominate each other, nor aspire to a universal church. If one is learning from experience, there is no plainer lesson of history.

NOTES: CHAPTER IV

1. *it has been assumed:*
   for the author's qualification of this eighteenth century assumption, see below p. 146.
2. *The most useful political science:*
   a good critical survey of contemporary political research is D. E. Butler's *The Study of Political Behaviour* (London, 1958). For a recent re-statement of political theory on traditional lines, see H. R. G. Greaves's *The Foundations of Political Theory* (London, 1958); also Schneider's *Three Dimensions of Public Morality*, cited above.
3. *analysis of . . . spontaneous motion:*
   cp. the celebrated techniques of F. M. Alexander for physical re-education, described in a series of books: *Man's Supreme Inheritance* (1918), *Constructive Conscious Control of the Individual* (1932), *The Use of the Self* (1931). Also Bentham's *An Essay on Political Tactics.*
4. *advanced forms of primitive . . . behaviour:*
   e.g., democratic procedures institutionalize factious strife and intrigue, collective bargaining (with the sanctions of strikes and lock-outs) the hiring and firing of primitive *laissez-faire.*
5. *not merely a system of principles:*
   how little a system of principles Barbara Wootton makes evident in *The Social Foundations of Wage Policy* (London, 1955). All the same, it is possible for collective bargaining to be concerned with principles of wage determination rather than with every question of a rise as it arises—the cost of living, the price of the product, the productivity of labour, or the profits of the industry has furnished a basis for agreement on automatic adjustment of wages.
6. *Not even by . . . the Dictatorship of the Proletariat:*
   this has not been the method in the advanced industrial countries where the class struggle has been real.
7. *the system . . . worked:*
   a conspicuously fair and informed examination of the working system in the context of contemporary problems and possibilities was made by R. G. Hawtrey in *Economic Destiny* (London, 1944).
8. *the classical concepts:*
   cp. J. B. Bury's *The Idea of Progress* (London, 1920).

9. *these notions . . . demanded the classical ideals:*
the notion of development in Hegel or Comte or Marx works to a consummation close at hand.

10. *from Locke to Lippmann:*
Walter Lippmann, *The Good Society* (London, 1937). Cp. Sir Roland
Wilson's *The Province of the State*, cited above, and Lord Percy's *The
Heresy of Democracy*.

11. *Mr Lippmann wants to revive it:*
in *The Public Philosophy*, cited above.

12 *'a sudden and vast expansion . . .':*
quoted by Edward Hughes in 'The Changes in Parliamentary Procedure,
1808-82', *Essays Presented to Sir Lewis Namier.*

13. *'the great problem of our civilization:*
speech on the Radical Programme at Warrington, September 8, 1885
(*Speeches*, ed. Lucy, 1885, pp. 188f). It may be recalled that Radical intellectuals, like Shaw and Webb, put their faith in Chamberlain, rather
than in the newly formed Labour Representation Committee, at that
time.

14. *G. M. Young:*
in *Victorian England*, pp. 134f.

15. *Keynes, Beveridge, Salter, Mannheim:*
The General Theory of Unemployment, Interest, and Money (1936) and
Full Employment in a Free Society (1944) are classics of their kind. Sir
Arthur Salter in the years of the depression was preoccupied with the
idea of a planned economy to supplement and correct the working of the
market system: e.g., *Recovery* (sec. ed., 1933) pp. 14-15 or *The Listener*,
December 12, 1934. Mannheim's *Man and Society in an Age of Reconstruction* (1940) was a study of social controls and of the transmutation
of controls, with a view to understanding the type of freedom open to a
mass industrial society. R. G. Hawtrey's explorations in *Economic
Destiny* are referred to above. As a sign of the times, the best document is
The Next Five Years (1935) an essay in political agreement, with some
150 eminent signatories rallied by their acceptance of the need for
political design and economic planning.

16. *Professor Hayek:*
notably in *The Road to Serfdom* (1944).

17. *legislation . . . has been empirical planning:*
see Sir Courtney Ilbert's *Legislative Methods and Forms* (Oxford, 1901)
passim. Also Sir Carleton Allen's *Law in the Making*, pp. 410-13 (5th ed.,
1951).

18. *planning to . . . no purpose:*
'The business of planning amounted . . . to a review of experiments in
induced and controlled social change, and involved the most intricate
problems of social organization and method'—conclusion to a discussion
on a paper read by Prof T. S. Simey 'The Contribution of the Sociologist
to Town Planning', reported in the *Journal of the Town Planning Institute*, vol. xxxix, no. 6, May 1953. This paper and its discussion makes a
useful starting point for some of the problems, principles, and techniques
of social planning in one important field, and in a democratic context.

19. *so closely . . . organized:*
one main method of this organization is studied by K. C. Wheare in
Government by Committee (1955): 'with governments committed to

planning and control of economic life . . . it is essential to obtain the co-operation of those affected by government policy . . . the understanding and co-operation of those expected to carry it out must be sought from the beginning', p. 53.

20. *can be only the government:*
Herbert Morrison gives the reasons why the parliamentary party (Labour or Conservative) does not and ought not to control the government, determine its policy, and instruct the Cabinet (*Government and Parliament*, Oxford, 1954, pp. 135-46; 301-2). The early radical idea that the leader of the Parliamentary Labour Party was a mere spokesman of decisions ultimately derived from the Party Conference and the conformity in practice to the constitutional requirements of cabinet government, even during the test of bitter frustration after the crisis of 1931 (and the frustration of early parliamentary insignificance, 1919-22), is described by R. T. McKenzie in *British Political Parties* (London, 1955) chaps. vi and vii, esp. pp. 317-23; 407-11, 439, 444.

21. *State planning:*
targetting is not in itself planning, even if realistic: it is a call for comprehensive and detailed planning.

22. *sabotage:*
even so valued an established control as the doctrine of *ultra vires* may seem to authority to be 'judicial sabotage' if it threatens to put in question administrative policy which can claim the cover of a general statute; but such administrative impatience is short-sighted. (Allen, *Law in the Making*, pp. 543, 573).

23. *by dealing concretely with claims and representations:*
cp. the routine of modern administration as described, for example, by W. J. M. Mackenzie and J. W. Grove in *Central Administration in Britain* (London, 1957), 'Consultation with Organizations', pp. 460-2, with the practice some four generations ago: 'In every session of parliament measures were proposed deeply affecting the interests of the trading community, and of the details of these they were generally unaware until they were passed into laws, when, if mischievous, it was too late to oppose them' (speech of G. W. Wood at a Town's Meeting on January 30, 1822, called to give increased support to the Manchester Chamber of Commerce, quoted in a footnote by Donald Read in *Peterloo*, p. 178, London, 1958). As Mr Read points out, the purpose of the Chamber was to protect the commercial interests of Manchester with the Government more continuously and effectively than by special public meetings and deputations, and its foundation was a half-way stage in the representation of the Manchester business interests in national politics. On the other hand, the Manchester magistrates were consulted by ministers in framing the 'Six Acts', a draft of the Seditious Meetings Prevention Bill was sent down for comment, p. 188.

24. *and to the public:*
Morrison, *Government and Parliament*, pp. 240-1; 303-6.

25. *continuous responsiveness:*
'There are formal consultations and informal day-to-day dealings which are even more important than what is done through committees' (Wheare, *Government by Committee*, p. 32). 'Committees to advise may be consulted at any stage in the process of government—in the formulation of policy, in its application or administration, or in the review of

policy and its application. In practice it is at the stage of application or administration that committees to advise are most widely used, while the committee to inquire is more usually found either at the stage of formulation or at the stage of the review of policy', p. 45. Also, Mackenzie and Grove, *Central Administration in Britain*, pp. 457-64.

26. *not . . . an experiment:*

Mr D. E. Butler argues that there is too little deliberate experimentation in politics and administration, although he qualifies this by saying: 'Scientific rigour is unfortunately impracticable and the factors responsible for the success or failure of a course of action can seldom be isolated with complete certainty' (op. cit., pp. 92-3). My argument in the text is not merely that scientific rigour cannot be expected and that more experimentation should nevertheless be undertaken; it is that politics and administration have become continuously experimental, not in the scientific sense of being conducted simply and solely for knowledge, but in the sense of inducing controlled social changes and of being open to revisions of intention, policy, and programme in the light of the experience induced; and that this continuous experimentation in social achievement can be controlled and developed to better purpose (that is, to the better purpose of the greatest number) by methodical attention to its phasing, and understanding use of techniques.

27. *an element of . . . knowledge:*

what may be called the PEP element, search for the relevant facts and submission to the constraint of facts, is, fortunately, a much bigger and more decisive factor in politics than is widely recognized. Cp. Morrison, op. cit., p. 302.

28. *instincts of the herd:*

the reference is to Wilfred Trotter's influential book, several times reprinted, *Instincts of the Herd in Peace and War* (London, 1916).

29. *industrial enterprise:*

there have of course been notable studies in recent years of the institutionalizing of practical success in business management: Elliot Jaques's *Changing Culture of a Factory* (London, 1951); L. F. Urwick's *The Pattern of Management* (London, 1956); Elton Mayo's *The Social Problems of an Industrial Civilization* (London, 1949); R. P. Lynton's *Incentives and Management in British Industry* (London, 1949).

30. *'sense of the meeting':*

see A. D. Lindsay's essay *Essentials of Democracy.*

31. *no more unrealistic:*

for a justification of an empirical political philosophy that learns from social experience what the pursuit of rational ends by rational means may mean, see Schneider, *Three Dimensions of Public Morality*, pp. 123-5.

32. *endless process:*

of course *a* plan may end, having achieved its end.

33. *nothing is made a success:*

the Moscow Underground as a symbol of spectacular popular success in the midst of daily deficiencies is a memorable example of astute political management.

34. *legislation-administration-evaluation:*

this formula can of course be applied to the political process in non-democratic regimes, but it can also be used, as here, to distinguish the democratic process by defining the political function of independently organized interests and by interpreting the political process as political, that is to say, democratic, by separating the phases of legislation and evaluation from administration (not nominally nor merely technically, but essentially) as political.

35. *adequate separation, integration, and working of the . . . phases:*
of course the three phases interpenetrate; preparation of new legislation involves evaluation of experience determined by previous legislation, administration involves planning the policy enacted and evaluation of its results, not merely carrying out an instruction. Nevertheless, in each successive phase the process is concentrated in different hands, in parliament, in the public administration, in voluntary associations (including firms, trade unions, political parties, research institutes); all have parts to play all the time but different roles dominate each of the three Acts. Only in so far as each agent keeps to its role and genuinely plays its role are the major political evils contained—bureaucracy, overcentralization, doctrinaire policy, on the one hand, anarchy or inefficiency, or mere muddling through, on the other.

Urwick insists on the separation of planning from performance in business management (op. cit., p. 86) for the sake of calculation beforehand, to make sure that everything is taken care of from the overall point of view and little or nothing left to take care of itself on the spot and when the time comes. But this is no less necessary for the sake of learning from the events afterwards. This determinism is the necessary condition of control, and of being able to learn what we want and what we can get. Cp. p. 153 above.

For the complications and frustrations which follow from the failure clearly to separate the phases of the political cycle, see Acheson's *A Citizen Looks at Congress*: the importance of the issue is not underestimated by Mr Acheson; it is the future of representative institutions.

36. *The phase of evaluation:*
over the wide field of social security services there is recognized need for systematic critical evaluation of their development. A leader in *The Times* of May 27, 1959, 'The Long View' recalled the proposal in the Beveridge Report for a statutory standing committee for this purpose, and reviewed the deplorable tale of decisions and schemes of political expediency that have been substituted for investigation and report. This was followed by a letter (May 28th) from Sir Keith Joseph advocating operational research techniques organized as a service to the Government and the social service departments, to improve current practice and to evaluate alternative programmes. Mr Vladimir Rys (June 2nd) wanted an independent institute capable of carrying out fully comprehensive studies of the working of the social security system as a necessary complement to the scheme, sponsored and subsidized by the Government, with the participation of trade unions, and employers or other public bodies. On June 8th, a vigorous leader 'Overcoming Inertia' glanced at various 'projects for securing the study and information necessary for the formation of consistent policies for sectors or for the whole of the welfare state', and deplored official inertia in face of unquestionable need. Here is groping for a method of systematic evaluation and information, to be related to government administration, to public opinion, and to party programmes.

37. *a State which provided only security:*
see Sir Roland Wilson's *The Province of the State*, cited above.

38. *The most conspicuous feature:*
Professor Carr has shown in his history of the Bolshevik revolution that there was no theory of economic planning at that time, and that this was forced on the party after abortive attempts at workers' control of industrial policy in factories. The parallel with Victorian social legislation is solely in their both being forced by the exigencies of a situation. Otherwise, they were very different situations: industrialization in Czarist Russia was already inspired and controlled by the State; the problem, without individualism and a free market, was to enforce abstinence for capital investment and maintain incentive; whereas the Victorian problem was to maintain the worker as a productive agent. Cp. chap. i, above, pp. 43-4. For a detailed study of the development from the early days of the Revolution by experience and discussion of methods of financing a planned economy, see R. W. Davies' *The Development of the Soviet Budgetary System* (Cambridge, 1958)

39. *The State may not wither away:*
Mr Khruschev in the course of a seven-hour speech to the twenty-first Communist Party Congress repudiated the marxist idea of the withering away of the State and pictured instead a highly organized society in which 'everybody will have to fulfil within a definite time and in a definite order his work function and his social duty'.

40. *the shocking indignity of it all:*
that is, of political servitude, not of the necessary determinism of administration and management, without which there are not the conditions which make possible control and choice.

41. *renounces liberty:*
the accent is on 'renounces'; where political liberty has never been enjoyed, a different language is to be employed.

42. *The philosophical conservative:*
to the examples cited in chapters i and ii above may be added the arguments of Michael Oakeshott in 'Rational Conduct' (*Cambridge Journal*, vol. 4) and *Political Education* (Cambridge, 1951). But the temperament and philosophical attitude are well exemplified in people who are not primarily political thinkers, like Samuel Johnson or Boris Pasternak (not forgetting Mr Eliot). Johnson's view of the Whigs, in its deep-rooted aversion, is well analysed by James L. Clifford in his *Young Samuel Johnson* (1955), p. 100. Although a novel, *Dr Zhivago* expresses unmistakably the feelings and convictions of its author, that life as it is, as it renews itself, is infinitely beyond any theory of it and any attempt to shape it: pp. 226, 258, 269, 305, 447. Pascal's idea that the pursuit of justice is chimerical, endless and fruitless restlessness, and should be renounced for the sake of inward and outward peace and self-transcendence, with private works of charity and due support for the established order and all customary ways, is a personal position which it is legitimate to try to win others to adopt; as the theoretical basis of an absolute regime, it is another matter. Here, again, conservatism is bound up with a religious view. But there is (perhaps) a distinction between the view that custom manifests a wisdom that transcends human reason and the view that custom, however stupid, keeps men within bounds, and thus gives them the inestimable blessing of social and inner peace.

43. *not to be identified with the democratic cycle:*
nor is the concept of the political cycle to be identified with the complex

idea of democracy; it is, however, an essential constituent of that complex, the regulative part of it, which preserves the idea of democracy as a system of conditions and procedures, and saves it from degradation to the notion of a popular programme or a simple administrative task. The idea of democracy is not a Platonic definition of justice; it is the apprehension of an historically elaborate technique for developing *pari passu* the notion of justice and the realization of it.

44. *shaped in the statute:*
of course not merely nor mainly in draftsmanship, but by all the means which bring to bear on legislation in the making representations from the interests affected. What a political party conference may be said to want is far from being a government policy or a proposable bill, it has to be reduced to practical politics for electioneering purposes, and then, if it gains the suffrage, account has to be taken in the bill of much data and many considerations and representations to which it is rough hewn before the final shaping in the course of its passage through Parliament. Lord Salisbury's paradox, that only uncontentious legislation should be brought before Parliament (Young's *Victorian England*, p. 134), is a vicious political doctrine. (For the intricacies of the American system, in which this practice was, and even is, a serious danger, see Acheson, *A Citizen Looks at Congress*, esp. chap. i.) But although in modern societies it is necessary to act—or else one is left to re-act, to follow after events with too little too late—the legislative initiative is just as stultified if its Acts fail to win sufficient co-operation as when it is reduced to unimportance by meeting every objection. It is the narrow passage between these rocks that political seamanship has repeatedly to negotiate. The statute is not a mere resultant of forces, and without adequate statesmanship democracy cannot survive.

45. *In an adult society:*
the preoccupation of the parties during a great part of the term of any Adminstration with election issues framed for vote-catching is a heavy price which has to be paid for the decisive advantages of the democratic system.

46. *This is the dangerous idea:*
is there, then, no political obligation? Of course there is. Human interdependence in society necessarily requires definite and accepted ways of living and working together which make a first claim on loyalty; and this mutuality is today extended to the interdependence of societies in one world—although there is yet only a rudimentary and fragmentary world order. One's own interest is normally central, but it always involves the interests of others and is always limited by other interests, and my rights, claims, and dues have always to be taken equally with the rights, claims, and dues of others, raising the question of justice when it is not accepted as settled. This inescapable political situation is the condition of political obligation. This is the situation in which I have to act and to justify my views, decisions, and conduct to the satisfaction of my fellows as well as my own. What really has to be justified is any unwillingness to accept the obligation to uphold and work established institutions in spirit and in truth. But the ultimate appeal, even on these fundamental questions of public interest, is to agreement, to what real people really want, not to awesome laws nor to commandments of any authority whatever: 'browbeating' and 'kotowing' are not words in the vocabulary of moral obligation.

47. *preparing for experimentation:*
education is no longer thought of as fixed, even for a generation. It has been said: 'to do their work effectively in society schools will need to have powers of growth and change unlike anything known in education hitherto.'

48. *continuous discussion:*
the note of public enthusiasm was struck early, and the phase of evaluation began to run concurrently with the phase of administration. For example, H. C. Dent in the *Preface to Secondary Education for All* (London, 1949) wrote: 'An unprecedented experiment, of the utmost importance, has thus been launched. What course will it take? How valuable will it prove? Many years must elapse before full answers to these questions will be known. But they will be known the sooner, and with more certainty, if continuous critical study of the experiment is made as it proceeds'.

49. *The awakening to the power of education is world-wide:*
the social expediency of education is one thing, the claim to it as a simple human right another. Consider the implications of the following passage from Humayun Kabir's book *Education in New India* (London, 1956), p. 181: 'in all countries, students are maintained by the effort of others and draw their sustenance from the wealth of the community. In a country like India, where our *per capita* annual income is not even Rs 300, a school pupil costs the community not less than Rs 500-600 a year, while a student in a college or university costs much nearer a thousand. Some pupils contribute hardly anything to the production of the total wealth during their tutelage, this means that the *per capita* income of three persons is required to maintain a school child. Similarly, the cost of maintenance of a college student amounts to the *per capita* income of four or five persons.

50. *the food and raw materials . . . which only these experts can provide:*
for what this really means, see *The Next Hundred Years* by Harrison Brown, James Bonner, and John Weir (London, 1957).

51. *general education:*
the problem for our democratic societies has not been better examined than in the Report of the Harvard Committee *General Education in a Free Society* (Camb., Mass., 1946). For a reflective digest of a decade of experience and discussion, see G. D. Parikh, *General Education and Indian Universities* (Bombay, 1959).

52. *These have been the 'progressive' schools of the public system:*
the authors of the Education Bill of 1944 and of the White Paper on the Bill purposed to give the primary schools their freedom for enlightened educational ideals, their freedom from the constraints of grammar school requirements; intensive nation-wide competition for places in the grammar schools has drawn them from independent courses into the narrow channel of Eleven-plus. Moreover, the friction and fear occasioned by the competition seem to have destroyed, at least for a generation, the more generous possibilities of the 'modern' type of secondary education. If the 'modern' schools are to be more or less dilute grammar schools, a series of lower streams tackling the same or similar curricula, this is educational sacrifice and educational tragedy, a flying in the face of experience and of intention, a deep and perverse social stupidity: there is no language too harsh and resentful to describe this trend. Of course the sacrifice of the many to the few is an old story in education; we are paying now

for our traditional concentration on an educational *élite*. For illustrations in a study of the London grammar schools in this century, see Flann Campbell's *Eleven-plus and All That* (London, 1956). The most sustained and best documented attack on the intellectualist academic bias of our education is Herbert Read's *Education through Art* (revised ed., London, 1958). Even worse, is the technical bias which is drawing the intellectual after it. Herbert Read writes: 'I have spent the best part of a lifetime protesting that an education that ignores the mental processes which lead to the creation of the most permanent achievements of mankind can be no true education. Our whole conception of education has become functional—conceived by serving the provisional interests of a social economy and not as a conquest of reality. Education is today a system exactly corresponding to the technical organization of our society and instead of realizing and regretting the enormous limitation that such a system imposes on the development of the human personality we take a pride in the inhuman efficiency of such a machine'.

A unique review of the role and scope of higher education in our society, with a view to avoiding the establishment of a 'meritocracy', is contained in a paper published in *Socialist Commentary*, September, 1959, the report of a group convened under the chairmanship of Robin Marris.

53. *What the child needs:*
for example, the following tasks of general education are of main importance:

   (i) socially necessary personal habits (e.g. cleanliness) are to be induced by a firm and tactful control that does not allow the child to become afraid of and repress his own aggressive hostility under correction and does enable him to deal realistically with the ambivalence of his feelings and to learn to evaluate realistically the feelings of adults in authority, and thus in due course to evaluate the world realistically;

   (ii) the child is to be encouraged to explore activities, and enabled to acquire rudimentary skills and to become capable of achievement, so that he is stimulated and developed and can be morally weaned (become self-dependent) and socialized (become dependable and co-operative);

   (iii) the child is in due course to be given *reflective* possession of himself by being shown how to analyse and remedy failure, how to make a method of success, how to solve problems, how to make decisions and choices, in a word, how to learn from and apply experience, as well as why and in what ways he should be self-dependent, dependable, and public spirited;

   (iv) the adolescent cannot be fully and fairly given his choice of life unless, all along, the fields of his possible interests have been made accessible to him.

54. *the moral order of a free society:*
cp. chap. i above, p. 23.

55. *a public basis for the development of professional services:*
'the professions are being socialized and the social and public services are being professionalized' (T. H. Marshall's *Citizenship and Social Class*, Cambridge, 1950, p. 147). For one examination of the meaning of this, see *Professional People* by Roy Lewis and Angus Maude (London, 1952) esp.

N

pp. 77-81 and chaps. xi and xii. For the effect of educational selection on social class, see Marshall, op. cit., pp. 62-68.

56. *Worth is still by poverty depressed:*
for measurement of this, see *Social Class and Educational Opportunity* by Floud, Malsey, and Martin (London, 1956).

57. *The dynamic type:*
'In his Army Pay Book, Hamilton, as a young Revolutionary officer, made various notes and jotted down a variety of quotations. One of them is surprisingly self-revealing. It is from an oration of Demosthenes, and, as entered by Hamilton, reads: "As a general marches at the head of his troops, so ought wise politicians, if I dare use the expression, to march at the head of affairs; insomuch that they ought not to wait the *event*, to know what measures to take; but the measures which they have taken ought to produce the *event*".' (Richard B. Morris, ed., *The Basic Ideas of Alexander Hamilton*, New York, 1957, p. xix). Hamilton is a superb example of the dynamic type. But the argument of this book is not merely that a wise politician should take measures to produce the event; whatever politicians may do, the meaning of democracy is that the whole of society is organized to sustain an initiative in producing the events from which its constituent interests may best learn what they most need to know in order to attain ends which are truly desired and compossible one with another, within each monad and in all the configurations of striving interests. The contrast between the professional or business man, an individualist who makes his own way by his own efforts, and the workers who lever themselves up as a group by the power of collective action complicates this picture, but fits neatly enough into its design.

58. *spoils have ever been sought:*
'the idea that the politically active part of the nation had a claim to maintenance on the State was generally accepted, even if it remained subconscious' (Sir Lewis Namier, *The Structure of Politics at the Accession of George III*, p. 16 and pp. 224-5).

59. *Contemporary culture:*
see Richard Hoggart's *The Uses of Literacy* (London, 1957), and Raymond Williams's *Culture and Society* (London, 1958). A neglected treatment of the question is R. C. Churchill's *Disagreements* (London, 1950). Cp. Santayana's 'The Aristocratic Ideal', chap. iv. of 'Reason in Society' (*The Life of Reason*, 1 vol. ed., London, 1954, pp. 130f). In so far as current phenomena reflect and are the product of widespread failure, frustration, immaturity (one possible reading of the situation), it is a teachers' problem. An early attempt to tackle it in the school is to be found in *Culture and Environment* by F. R. Leavis and Denys Thompson (London, 1933). See also Reports on Conferences and Forums published by the Joint Council for Education through Art, 1957-59, 13 Prince of Wales Terrace, London, W.8. *Television and the Child* (Oxford, 1958) was the quietus of extreme hopes and fears.

60. *Cultural diversity . . . does not entail anarchy:*
cp. Kabir, op. cit., p. 208: 'Communication and understanding are thus the essence of education, and a democracy offers the best medium where it can flourish. An uneducated person lives in his immediate physical and mental environment. The purpose of education is to liberate him from the bondage of environment without at the same time destroying his connexions with it. Education makes man aware of the different types

of society and civilization. It enables him to view the present in the light of the past.' This educational ideal may be framed in terms of the highest wisdom and learning or pitched at the lowly level of local comparisons and choices.

61. *it will depend on subsidies:*
the problem of sustaining the arts and scholarship by grants from public funds and private foundations is being tackled by trial and error and by fits and starts; however, the Ford Foundation began its programme 'Humanities and the Arts' with a systematic exploration of the needs to be met, and this is a precedent to be followed in future development.

62. *The Geddes-Mumford inspiration:*
for a review of the field by an experienced and gifted disciple of Geddes, see *Town and Country Planning* by Patrick Abercrombie, third ed., revised by D. Rigby Childs (Oxford, 1959).

63. *it expresses aspiration:*
against the physical attempt to restore and remodel communities has to be set the long-term and large-scale administrative and social changes which have had the effect of making the local population rootless and irresponsible. Documentation of these typical changes and their effects is in A. H. Birch's *Small Town Politics* (Oxford, 1958). Physical re-planning is of course not an answer to this aspect of local decay.

64. *has often been idealized:*
The Heavenly City has always its counterpart in Babylon—the Garden City and the mechanized town. See Helen Rosenau: *The Ideal City* (London, 1959).

65. *Arthur E. Morgan:*
The Future of Community and the Community of the Future (Yellow Springs, Ohio, 1957).

66. *feeling helpless and insignificant:*
it is important to recognize that people seek refuge in collectivism, and do not merely feel victimized. Cp. Martin Buber, *Between Man and Man*, pp. 200-1.

67. *the example of 'intentional' social activity:*
'The creation of new communities, and the more deep-seated of the efforts for creation of new patterns and ways of life in and among existing communities, have been among the more important and universal ways in which societies the world over have maintained their vitality and have advanced in type' (Morgan, op. cit., p. 140); chap. xv for an examination of some present-day 'intentional communities'.

68. *consumer goods:*
even here, efficiency has included widespread and sustained improvement in design. 'At least, after more than a century of frustration, it seems that we have hopes of solving a problem which has baffled industry ever since the development of power-driven machinery removed design from the control of the individual craftsman' (Sir Charles Tennyson in a special article in *The Times*, February 9, 1959).

69. *not just one form amongst others:*
the channel is narrow here between the metaphysical State, on the one hand, and types of voluntary association, on the other; but the case does not present difficulties to reflection, and the pursuit of exact classification and definition is not rewarding. Cp. Greaves, op. cit., chap. i.

70. *in every kind of organized activity:*
thus when in 1956 Mr Khruschev's decentralization policy required a
stimulus to the participation of workers in management, it was proposed
to revive 'production meetings' and to enlarge the powers of the trade
union committees, and decrees to this purpose were issued in 1958 by the
Presidium of the Supreme Soviet and the Council of Ministers; but this
did nothing to take the trade union committee (which was explicitly
given direction of the 'production meetings') out of the control of the
Party.

71. *Seven Wise Men:*
' . . . seven or more wise men, able to create confidence in everybody,
should be appointed jointly by the chief parties to our predicament'—
Archbishop of Canterbury in a sermon reported in *The Times*, November
25, 1957.

72. *experience has shown:*
see chaps. i and ii above.

73. *subordination of the politician:*
the backbencher MP, like the medical GP, has suffered a fall in status, with
increasing specialization and multiplying petty consumer demands; the
legislator or the physician has been taken out of him, leaving a necessary
link, a go-between. Nobody is to blame, and something can, and perhaps
will, be done about it, within the bounds of modern requirements.

74. *the public interest:*
the notion that there is a 'public interest' has a bad press today, perhaps
for two different, even opposite, reasons: on the one hand, is the marxist
sociological analysis which explodes the hypocrisy or naïvety of a 'common interest', and forces the issue between two major interests in conflict;
on the other, is fear of the oppressive claims of society in the name of
the 'general will' or the 'common good' (cp. Greaves, op. cit., chap. ix,
esp. pp. 143-5). Mr Greaves also rejects the 'public interest' as a useless
tool of political analysis because it may be identified with so many different things (p. 154). All the same, he uses the concept of 'the social good'
and finds its criteria in 'the system of co-operation, and the methods and
forms this takes', and the purposes embodied in it. True, the institutional
machinery represents the public interest in a democratic state, but the
content of the social legislation enacted in the political cycle, also becomes
a public interest. Love and care for the instrument is promoted by enthusiasm for the work it has to do and has done: the two cannot be
separated and survive. Cp. Morrison, op. cit., *passim.*

75. *Sir Walter Citrine:*
see Allan Flanders' *Trade Unions* (London, 1952), pp. 137-9. See also Alan
Bullock's account of Bevin's part in the reconstruction of employer-worker
relations after the General Strike in *The Life and Times of Ernest Bevin*
Vol. I (London, 1960).

76. *sometimes even . . . sacrifice:*
'The "ethical harmony" is one achieved by the sacrifice of interests, which
is necessary precisely because no natural harmony of interests exists. In
the national community, appeals to self-sacrifice are constantly and successfully made, even when the sacrifice asked for is the sacrifice of life.
But even in the national community, it would be erroneous to suppose that
the so-called "harmony" is established solely through voluntary self-
sacrifice. The sacrifice required is frequently a forced one, and the "har-

mony" is based on the realistic consideration that it is in the "interest" of the individual to sacrifice voluntarily what would otherwise be taken from him by force. Harmony in the national order is achieved by this blend of morality and power' (E. H. Carr, *Twenty Years Crisis*, pp. 210-15, London, 1939; p. 212).

CHAPTER V

Perpetual Peace

ARGUMENT

ANY CONFIDENCE restored by reflection upon an analysis of social process at home cannot be stretched by any ingenuity to cover what is going on in the field of international relations. Other things being equal, it is the micro-climate of the field which affects most closely the health of the crop, but when the weather threatens one of the major natural disasters, other things are not equal.

In modern times in Europe, the 'balance of power' has been the maxim of prudent foreign policy for the preservation, or restoration, of peace. This works as a voluntary system of collective security, if it does work, and it has worked at best very imperfectly, and during the last seventy years has been totally inadequate to cope with the arms race which has made the world increasingly and at present insanely insecure. The idea voiced today impressively by American liberals that the nuclear deterrent, the 'balance of terror', can keep the world safe for power diplomacy, which high-minded Western statesmanship will use to build up an international system for the free nations, is tragically deceived. Even if the arms race is not a mill-race swelling in volume and accelerating in velocity and drawing in ever more of the nation's brains, energies, and resources, it is a distraction or a preoccupation likely to end in unprecedented destruction unless it is ended soon by a deliberate decision of the Powers. Until there is an effective decision to halt what is going on and has been going on and to institute an altogether different system of defence, a world-wide system of collective security, danger increases and the decision becomes more difficult. Verbal declarations in the highest quarters that this is ultimately necessary cover drift on in the old policies and active cultivation of disastrous alternatives. At the same time, serious objections to a collective system and the old motives against it diminish. Time is against hope, and the agonizing reappraisal has not yet taken place.

I. INDEFENSIBLE DEFENCE

Suppose the basic conditions for creative social control have been established in Britain, that there is a working party system, a preponderant volume of public interest, and in the making a sound educational system and a managed economy, and suppose that the principles, rules, and techniques of a planning democracy are thoroughly understood and accepted, the confidence that might spring up and the hopes one might nurse are blasted by the prospect abroad. If historically on the domestic front things were never in so good a form for organic development, incipient enthusiasm turns to anguish unless some way can be found to disperse the gathering gloom. Nobody can take much interest in a tender plant that is doomed to a climate it cannot survive. A generation that has lived through two world wars is liable to be paralysed by the drift to a third and overwhelming disaster.

Nobody, certainly, has any confidence in present defence policies. Since defence has become technically impossible, deterrence is relied on for the prevention of war. Nobody knows who is deterred from what: the powers are possibly prepared for instant obliterating retaliation the moment an unspecified act of aggression is committed. There was never so infinitely dangerous a situation. Either the threat is bluff, and will sooner or later be called, or else it is likely sooner or later to involve an unprecedented act of devastating and irretrievable inhumanity. In that case, a disaster of unimaginable magnitude is imminent, implicit in certain uncertain political acts, hitherto normal, for which no regular substitute has been found. The appalling consequences of retaliation are relied on to prevent any act that might provoke it, and they may also be relied on to nerve the assumption that retaliation will not lightly follow any injury and is not likely to follow many injuries. This is the military situation in which a cold war between the Soviet bloc and NATO powers is being prosecuted, in which the Western powers fear the Communists have the initiative, and in which racial tinder and nationalist current distribute danger in many places throughout the world.*

To exaggerate the risks of the present situation is quite impossible. Indeed, the danger is so total and so obvious that people find it diffi-

* This paragraph needs some modification since the retreat from Mr Dulles's threat of massive retaliation. In particular, it seems to be the firm intention of the military command in Europe to use the shield forces of NATO to halt any act of aggression and interpose a pause which would impose on the aggressor responsibility for a deliberate decision to invoke all-out nuclear war or revoke aggression. The deterrent of nuclear capability is made credible by the deterrent of conventional capability in a system of graduated defence designed to limit the first phase of any local attack to restraint and prevention, combining the disarming deterrence of offering the other cheek with the assurance of unlimited retaliation if the offer is accepted.

cult to take seriously, may be inclined to think that it provides its own remedy in being so certain and so appalling, or become fatalistic. This takes us a long way nearer the edge. Officially it is admitted that present defence policies are makeshifts,[1] waiting on disarmament and world security arrangements, that the stalemate balance of power is not a method of keeping the peace, a permanent form of social control, but a precarious understanding which cannot endure and provides a last opportunity for reaching a durable arrangement. Meanwhile, strenuous unofficial efforts are being made to break out of the dilemma, to blaze a path out of the jungle, chiefly by campaigning for unilateral disarmament, whether or not reckoning with the consequent communist menace. To the inevitable resolutions on the question passed by every form of association, and the ballots and tests of canvassed opinion, are to be added the more significant studies and thinking of independent groups of more or less specially qualified persons. The total volume of unofficial thought and agitation may well exceed that of passive indifference if not of acquiescence in official policy, but an unofficial line is very unlikely to rally the country and lead to a reorientation of public policy.

Yet if anything is clear, it is that this is not a case in which performance can be improved by learning to look at what is being done in order to see how it can be done better; this is a case in which failure can be avoided and disaster averted only by the prevention of what is being done and the doing of something else. In this sense, the international case is far different from the domestic case, and social control on that front has to be achieved by different means. This is not wholly true because some of the things which are being done in the international field, of course, are on the right lines, but the main traditional assumptions, attitudes, approaches, and actions are such that they cannot produce anything but war. Unless and until this can be altered, there can be no hope.

As a first step in the analysis, in order to see clearly the traditional forms of international political behaviour and their inevitable consequences, it is useful to look back over modern European history, and in particular at the theory and practice of the balance of power. In this connexion, the treatment of the idea of perpetual peace by eighteenth-century philosophers is instructive. It ought also to be compulsory reading for those who follow the intellectual fashion in deriding these philosophers for the naïveté of their faith, the imbecility, if not perversity, of their universalist assumptions and aspirations. If these critics would read Rousseau they would learn that their real enemy in this sector of the field was an abbé, Charles-Irénée de Saint-Pierre.

2. THE BALANCE OF POWER

In his brilliant restatement of Saint-Pierre's scheme for collective security, *Projet de Paix Perpétuelle*, Rousseau's argument of the case puts it as strongly as it can be put, and it is intellectually unanswerable: this is the intelligent, and only, method of establishing perpetual peace, with all the advantages that would bring in providing the indispensable condition for good government, real safety, and a sound economy. In a critical examination of the project (*Jugement sur la Paix Perpétuelle*), he goes on to say why he thinks a scheme of collective security is nevertheless not likely to be adopted by the nations. Everyone can see, he says, that society is formed by common interests and that conflicts come from opposed interests. But interests fluctuate continuously, and common interests do not long remain solid and binding unless they are enforced by a superior power. Moreover, a favourable moment for putting the scheme into operation has to be waited for, and is extremely unlikely to occur by chance, for it has to be a moment when there is no nation with unsatisfied ambitions able and anxious to profit by the international anarchy, when all nations are equally interested, each for its own advantage, in the pooling of strength for common defence. In these circumstances, there is only one way in which the scheme can be brought into operation: instead of writing a book, it will be necessary to raise an army. Perhaps the remedy is worse than the disease.

Kant, who owed and showed that he owed so much to Rousseau,[2] took a more hopeful view of perpetual peace. Not that his view was coloured by any more romantic idea of human nature. He wrote bitingly about 'European savages'. He knew perfectly well that the current maxims of actual statecraft not only conduced to war but also maintained a continuous state of cold war, and that no statesman was ashamed of these maxims and these policies, since political honour consisted only in extending the power of the State, no matter by what means that succeeded. He knew perfectly well also that perpetual peace meant turning the back once for ever on all these ways and ends, and pursuing opposite courses. How did he think that was possible?

There was, he recognized, no possibility of perpetual peace unless and until it was deliberately instituted by a federation of free States which laid down, accepted, and observed the necessary conditions.

Without this guarantee, there could only be war or the threat of war, for without a guarantee of this kind the sovereign nations existed in a state of nature and not in any form of international society: without a guarantee, their very mutual proximity was mutual injury. The main hope of a solution sprang from this very fact. 'The problem of founding a constitution, however difficult it sounds, can be solved even by a nation of devils (if only they have sense).' The special international treaty which would guarantee perpetual peace could be brought about in the way in which society in the first place had come about, and for the same reason, but with greater deliberation, intelligence, speed, and completeness. And if man does not do it intelligently and economically in the short run, Nature will do it painfully and wastefully in the long run. Hope did not rely on the moral perfectibility of man, for the problem was 'how the mechanism of nature, not the moral perfectibility of man, may be used so to direct the hostile inclinations of a people that they mutually force each other to submit to laws and thus to bring about the state of peace in which laws have sanctions'. Kant thus believed in the order expressed in Whitehead's dictum 'the instability of evil is the moral order of the world'. This order was further shown in the need and tendency of commercial and other such forms of self-interest to work for and develop international arrangements dependent on good faith.

Kant would not have been Kant if he had thought this was all and sufficient. As he put it, 'a good constitution in a State does not depend on intrinsic morality: on the contrary, the moral improvement of a people depends on a good constitution in their State'. But once the necessary condition had been established, the moral improvement was all-important; mere external behaviour approximating to what the conception of justice prescribed was not enough. Practical politicians and lawyers, Kant notes, 'boast of knowing men (which is probably true since they have to do with many) without knowing man and what can be made of him (which demands a higher standard of anthropological observation)'. The moral conscience of mankind was evident even in the hypocrisy which was the tribute the statesman paid to the philosopher. When the statesman saw that perpetual peace is a moral obligation and a practical possibility he would make this, without any equivocation, the first and last word in the determination of his policy. Moral progress is sure but slow, and we reasonably can hope for an increasing tempo.

Hume's view of the problem was more orthodox,[3] for he accepted the maxim of preserving the balance of power as the sensible and sufficient principle of foreign policy. Whether explicitly formulated

or not, this was the maxim on which 'all the wiser and more experienced princes and politicians', ancient and modern, had proceeded. Policy, then, in so far as it is on these orthodox lines is on
the right lines, and improvement requires only that practice shall
conform more closely to the model. Hume, examining the contemporary policy of Great Britain, found that she had not failed to
oppose herself to bids for preponderant power in Europe but that
she had employed excessive means for this end, prolonged her wars
far beyond what was necessary to check foreign ambition: 'above
half of our wars with France, and all our public debts, are owing
more to our own imprudent vehemence than to the ambition of our
neighbours.' This excess had also the effect of encouraging Britain's
allies to be demanding and inflexible in a way that prevented agreement and peace. Not only were the wars prolonged beyond what
was necessary, Britain's resources were also recklessly drained to
make the war more devastating: she ruined herself to ruin the foe.
These excesses were likely to have the ultimate consequence of
making us withdraw from Europe and abandon the attempt to
maintain a balance of power. Hume's own passion for moderation
made it easy for him to point the moral here, and to make the
balance of power a principle of political prudence applied to keeping or as soon and by as little as possible restoring the tranquillity
of Europe. This made the balance of power a security system in
which force was used only to halt an act of aggression or check a
policy of aggrandisement, and not for the ruin or humiliation of a
neighbour and rival, nor for expansion.

   After 1815 a new diplomatic language, inspired by the politics of
Tsar Alexander's Holy Alliance, spoke of the 'European order'; and,
more notably, a new diplomatic method was instituted with the in-
novation that brought the Great Powers together in periodic conferences to consult on the maintenance of their common interests,
to confront one another's point of view, to search for a basis of
compromise, to recognize, or at least to announce, a collective duty.
'This concert of the great powers implied the idea of a control which
they could exercise of one accord for the purpose of maintaining
peace.' Nobody was deceived. 'In the course of each of these con-
gresses, it is in words only that there is any question of a "European
interest"; in reality, the particular interests of the States are paramount.' By 1823 not even the appearances survived.*

   The rest of the nineteenth century saw the further course of that
aggressive nationalism which since the Renaissance and the Refor-

* Histoire des relations internationales. Tome 5 ième. Le XIXe Siècle I de 1815
à 1871. Pierre Renouvin, 1954. Chap. iii.

mation, and with doctrinal zeal in the seventeenth century, has supplied the drive of European politics. Cavour unified Italy and Bismarck Germany on 'reasons of state', that is to say, by force and fraud. Kant's analysis had not yet been justified by events. Hume's balance of power as a theory of control required a moderation it was powerless to induce. Rousseau's reading of the situation was amply confirmed. New hope, however, shone on the workers' front of international solidarity which the socialists imagined would cut across and block the imperialism of the powers. When this collapsed at the first shock, the train of nationalist politics exploded a war to end war.

3. THE LOST PEACE

The Allied Powers who won the first world war lost the peace and were embroiled in a second world war twenty years later. How this happened has been traced many times,[4] by those who were mixed up in the events and saw them close at hand and by professional students who have analysed the voluminous documentary evidence. It would be speculative if not useless to discuss what might have been, to try to determine the point at which events had passed out of control and the points at which a little, possible, difference could have made all the difference. What is not speculative is the spectacle of political ineptitude displayed by the victorious powers, and it is this unhappy unforgotten sight combined with the increase in our hands of unimaginable power that unnerves the present generation.

The Allied Powers as victors were responsible for the peace. It need not have mattered finally that they failed at Versailles to create a viable Europe, for necessities might have asserted themselves without disaster, if they had with vigour and confidence either instituted a general security system or maintained Franco-British hegemony in Europe through the French alliances. Both to lay unstable foundations and to fail to follow any clear or consistent or co-ordinated policies opened the way for Germany to solve real problems by new methods, political, economic, and military. Conservative thinking, unprepared to institute a new world of any description and inevitably losing confidence in the cherished world of the past beyond recall, made shift from crisis to crisis and drifted with events to catastrophe. That Germany in turn failed equally by follies of a different character ought not to be any consolation. It is human political ineptitude combined with annihilating technical powers that is so terrifying.

That favourable moment to put into operation a scheme of collective security which Rousseau thought so extremely unlikely to occur by chance certainly did come with the cessation of hostilities in 1918. The institution of the League of Nations shows that the opportunity was not thrown away; but it was lost all the same. The League came into existence, there was a vast amount of paper work and of discussion, but collective security remained a phrase. Mr E. H. Carr has argued that the failure of the League was not due to the wickedness nor to the stupidity of anybody, that it was not a failure to live up to the right idea, because, rather, the idea itself was false or inapplicable, in so far as collective security was a remote ideal unrelated to the realities of power and of politics, or else a means of maintaining the *status quo* useful to the victorious powers and for that reason unlikely to appeal to the unsatisfied powers.[5] In other words, as Rousseau foresaw, collective security could be made a common interest if there was a power which was in the mind and strong enough to impose it, but not otherwise. There was an exceptional opportunity for the Allied Powers to do just this after the war with a minimum of force and hostility, but the resolution and common purpose were lacking, and without this the idea of itself, as Professor Carr said, was false or inapplicable, because it did not and could not take the place of political realities.

All the same, the failure of the Allied Powers to impose on Europe a system of collective security *was* a stupidity and a dereliction of duty. At that time it could have corresponded to political realities, and it could have offered a way out of the dilemmas of national defence and the international anarchy. The Great Powers in virtue of their power are responsible for international order. They may be evenly matched and may maintain peace by holding the balance of power. One or more may make a bid for preponderant power, and precipitate war. As an outcome, one or more may establish an hegemony. This regime may be oppressive, and eventually provoke an opposition that will destroy it. Or it may be and remain powerful, statesmanlike, and moderate enough to prove beneficial and gain widespread support. These are the changes and chances incidental to a flexible system which answers to the realities of power and the moralities of responsibility. The implication of Professor Carr's argument is that an inflexible system of collective security, which could only have been established by the imposition of the dominant powers, would have perpetuated the interests of the dominant powers by automatically depriving all other powers of any chance of opposition and every opportunity of change. The dominant powers would continue to enjoy the fruits of power without its responsibility and risks, and the subordinate powers would lose

their hopes and their means of redress. Those, therefore, who identified the League and collective security with international morality
were blind idealists or mere hypocrites.

The only real answer to this argument is that the dangers of living
in the midst of the rivalries of armed powers are so real and the
strains so injurious and the chance of living long under an hegemony
continuously powerful and consistently moderate is so slight that
the advantage is all with the alternative of a system of collective
security if it could be established, even at the expense of perpetuating certain existing privileges. To close certain questions and remove certain possibilties may not be a limitation or a reduction,
it may be the condition of opening more important questions
and founding more advantageous possibilities. If the only legitimate
use of force is to suppress the use of force, that may be the condition
for new possibilities of liberty and equality. All told, then, the loss
of the peace by the victors in the first world war by their failure to
establish and enforce a system of collective security was the tragedy
of European man. A unique opportunity of immense magnitude was
irretrievably lost.

The victors of the second world war by their immediate division
into hostile camps gave themselves no opportunity of instituting a
system of collective security. The world has become, inescapably,
the theatre of operations, and the drama that will be played out is
the immense rivalry of East and West. With the extinction of the
means of national defence, the balance of power has become a
balance of terror. Nobody supposes that this is a system of international security, even of the rough and ready kind history has provided up till now. It is assumed by some that the novelty of the situation, the obsolescence of all traditional methods, and the intolerable
risk and strain of the actual predicament, will at last bring the idea
of a collective security system into practical politics. This is an assumption to be examined.

4. PRACTICAL POLITICS

The general advantage of a collective system which bought maximum security at minimum cost has not been as attractive to
politicians as to intellectuals. The main reasons are obvious, and
have been decisive. (1) The international anarchy is a spoils system
for those powerful enough to profit by it, and ambitions are not
easily satisfied, and power can be obtained at a price. In any case,
the 'great powers' have disposed of sufficient power both to count
on being able to hold their own and to make it worth while to en-

tertain schemes designed to improve their position. (2) Any regime which governs by fear is itself fearful at home, and the most certain and convenient way of relieving home-made insecurity is to foster fear of what may come from abroad. This both closes the ranks in the country and puts into the hands of the regime armed power which faces outward but may be ordered to turn about. (3) Defence with all its ramifications on the modern scale accounts for a sizeable sector of the economy in terms of money, men, plant, and material. The vested interest here is a national interest. A change of policy which involved a drastic cut in this expenditure might be attractive in theory and in the long run, but in practice and immediately it would give the government a headache and be likely to occasion severe dislocation and widespread discontent. (4) Not least, national sovereignty, with the free hand and the prestige which go with it, are hard to part with, for people and politicians. Emasculation is a hard choice. A farewell to 'greatness' is said with extreme reluctance and only under necessity.

These objections, and their like, to the obvious advantages of a collective system are insubstantial as arguments, but the solid obstacles which they represent remain invulnerable to even the gentlest pooh-pooh.

All the same, if the obstacles have not been completely shattered by the change in the actual situation, they have been reduced, dislodged, undermined, or otherwise impaired as a barrier. Towering over all is the destructive power of modern weapons and their mounting cost. Complacency is impossible, and statesmen are driven to seek a remedy, even a remedy they would avoid, if it is the sole workable recourse. The risk of war has become too great for an adventurous foreign policy. Only the most 'vital' national interest is worth the uttermost resistance to an attack. In the last resort, however, only annihilating prevention can defend the vital interest. The paradoxes of the predicament are more practically powerful than the old unanswerable arguments for collective security because they represent an intolerable actual dilemma, they light up a position in which all the traditional lines of policy lead only into a trap; they do not merely indicate an alternative that is more high-minded, or more advantageous to more people. And since the possibility of national independence in the field of defence and of foreign policy has gone with the obsolete weapons, national sovereignty has in fact gone the way of absolute monarchy. Its prestige may yet be inflated to legendary popular glory to compensate for the power that is irretrievably lost, but there will be no illusions in the world of practical politics.

Part of what is meant, then, by saying that the international situation today is totally new is that the age-old incentives to build up preponderant national power or to seek and rely on a balance of power are considerably reduced, and, correspondingly, that the weak incentives to prefer a rational system of collective security are considerably reinforced. Collective security which offered one alternative among several in a disjunction, an exhaustive set of mutually exclusive alternatives, now offers the only alternative to a dilemma. This is the theoretical measure of the difference which has come about, virtually the elimination of choice.

Cogent as this argument is, practice is unlikely to follow meekly and neatly. Collective security, even if it is the only way of escape from a real dilemma, is not likely to be achieved by a common decision that it shall take place on an appointed day. The technical difficulties are not too great perhaps, but the psychological and political difficulties are still so great that the prospect looks extremely dubious.

Communist and other authoritarian powers still have reason to play up and play on popular fear of foreign aggression or hostility. The democracies are more or less deeply divided internally, and one from another, on the lines of their defence policy. The immense powers disposed of by powers profoundly antagonistic and mutually suspicious are not going to be renounced in a hurry for the benefits of a common system they would have to control and work together. The power they have not renounced is being used every day to further their interests and attain their conflicting ends, trusting to the common fear of all-out war to keep this side the brink. This easy, if illusory, way out of the dilemma is likely to be preferred as long as it lasts. That is, the real problem will be forgotten or postponed until it is too late. There is nothing in history to console one with the thought that this is not really the way in which things do happen. On the other hand, one can also learn from history what the conditions and the methods are which do promise some measure of control.

5. FOREIGN POLICY IN THE WEST

Unless and until a system of collective security is instituted, the full weight of the risks of war and the responsibility for peace is borne by statesmen holding national power. They make war or maintain peace as an outcome of the foreign policy they pursue which in turn is based on the power they wield. This amount and this method of control are not reassuring. As a matter of plain history, political ineptitude combined with the constraints, often amounting to compulsion, of situations not under control has made war inevitable. The statement that statesmen in power are responsible has to be qualified by mindfulness of the pressures and resistances which in the political democracies limit the statesman's power. In some circumstances this may prove a restraint and a safeguard, and in general democracies do not encourage an aggressive and onerous foreign policy, but so long as so much does depend on the character and conduct of foreign policy it is prudent to recognize that these are liable to lack in the democracies the coherence, consistency, drive, and clear responsibility which make them a method of control. The war which was to have made the world safe for democracy created the opportunity which was lost. The opportunity can be regained by the democracies only by a foreign policy directed to that end. Here, we are stumbling in some general direction by a tangle of paths, and the desired road is still to seek.

Since traditionally an effectual foreign policy is based on national power, reasonable hopes and anxieties in the West are fixed on the influences that go to the making of American foreign policy. When Mr Dean Acheson, or Mr George Kennan, expounds his views at convenient length and with admirable candour, troubled minds in the West are offered a conceptual nucleus on which to lay hold in order to rescue their own thinking on the question at issue from the swirling flux of current opinions.

Mr Acheson* looks back on the disintegration of a world system based on the European empires of the nineteenth century, maintained by a balance of power and economic expansion, with the diplomatic, commercial, and managerial skills and disciplines which these policies required. In this system, Britain played a major role. The Second World War was the final act. Today, the Soviet Union with a powerful initiative and a world programme has no alternative and must prevail unless the United States can build a countervailing international system.

'The disappearance of a world system and of the power which sustained it, together with the growth of Soviet power and ambitions, means that the nations which wish to preserve independent national identity can do so only if the material strength and the political and economic leadership of the United States are enlisted in the effort. However much all of us may dislike this thought, the requisite power does not reside anywhere else.'†

* *Power and Diplomacy*, 1958.
† *Ibid*, p. 7.

O

If the United States is to inspire and lead a coalition of free peoples who are determined and able to maintain their independence, and who can offer security and aid to other peoples not attracted by the Soviet system, certain policies are requisite, in Mr Acheson's view. These are hard policies. In the first place, American industrial productive power must be developed for the primary purpose of making the United States and its allies militarily strong and economically expanding, and not for the primary purpose of meeting and increasing the appetites of American consumers. In the second place, there is no easy way out by relying on the nuclear deterrent. Simple reliance on this, 'brinkmanship', is an abandonment of leadership, because everybody can see that the policy of massive retaliation is a recipe for disaster. The essence of deterrence is that the threat shall be credible and not suspected of bluff. Therefore, nuclear weapons and the forces that operate with them should be held in reserve as the preventive by deterrence of total war, and separate forces should be maintained to take the field and meet aggression with direct and local opposition, employing the minimum of force required to stop an invasion of interests wherever it may take place. In the third place, America as inspirer and leader of a coalition of free States, beyond the creation of power, must aid their development, forbear criticism and resentment, and refrain from policies which divide and weaken the coalition, e.g. China.

Such a policy would run counter to many of the things which are actually being done or said with the authority of Congress or of the Executive. But it would not be a new policy, in that it would only serve more adequately and intelligently the purpose of NATO and the present Administration. The principal contribution of Mr Acheson is a more realistic analysis of the world situation, with a refusal to dream that there is a way to avoid sacrifices and risks on a long, dangerous, and toilsome road by quick or easy agreements to end the cold war. The initiative of the Soviet Union will prevail throughout the world unless it is met by a counter initiative which offers hope, leadership, and strength to peoples who value their independence; and no such offer is possible without a clear-sighted, resolute, and costly plan.

Mr Kennan's Reith Lectures* might be read as a supplement to Mr Acheson's Clayton Lectures. He makes the same presupposition that the Soviet system and policy constitute a total challenge to the West; he is equally convinced that the demands necessary to meet it are harsh and that prevalent hopes of avoiding them (summit meetings, global solutions, coalition diplomacy, the United Nations, dis-

* *Russia, the Atom, and the West*, 1958.

armament) are illusory; he is not less confident that persistence in meeting these demands can restore and maintain the Western position; he is equally insistent on the need for forbearance and mutual understanding in overcoming divisions in the coalition. But his contribution is distinctive. Essentially, he is saying that the competition of the West with the Soviet Union is not a bid to outdo each other in doing the same things, whether in increasing military might or in space achievements, or in rushing to the aid of underdeveloped regions. The real competition is rather a different kind of match: to see in the two systems which peoples will the sooner and better solve their own problems and perfect their way of life and make available to others who wish to avail themselves of it their experience and their help and their example. Seeing the challenge this way, one is able to meet it with more deliberation and serenity, though not with less effort; one is released from certain prevalent anxieties and can relax to that extent; one need not oppose the Russians at every point nor vie with them in every activity; one need not seek to obstruct their progress nor find reason to rejoice in every difficulty and discomfiture. At the same time, Mr Kennan has no illusions about the intention of the rulers of the Soviet Union to do everything in their power to undermine and destroy the position of the Western powers. In the last resort, this can be prevented only by armed strength. However, that does not involve an arms race, which is senseless, ruinous, and fatal.

'The beginning of understanding rests, in this appalling problem, with the recognition that the weapon of mass destruction is a sterile and hopeless weapon which may for a time serve as an answer of sorts to itself as an uncertain sort of a shield against utter cataclysm, but which cannot in any way serve the purposes of a constructive and hopeful foreign policy. . . . The suicidal nature of this weapon renders it unsuitable both as a sanction of diplomacy and as the basis of an alliance. . . . There can be no coherent relations between such a weapon and the normal objects of national policy. A defence posture built around a weapon suicidal in its implications can serve in the long run only to paralyse national policy, to undermine alliances, and to drive everyone deeper and deeper into the hopeless exertions of the weapons race.'*

Mr Kennan underlines the intense danger of the highly provisional situation in Europe, for which the victors over Germany are again responsible. The first aim of policy should be to remove piecemeal

* *Russia, the Atom, and the West*, p. 56.

by negotiation and compromise this major source of military danger. In regard to Asia and Africa and the Middle East, we should seek to provide a basis for independent policy by reducing our dependence on these regions, and by defining the frontier of our vital interests.

'Once people in Moscow see that such a point does exist, and that what lies to our side of it is enough to assure our security and to leave us the ability to carry on indefinitely as a major factor in world affairs—once they see, in other words, that we are not really to be outflanked in the Asian and African theatres or any other— then I am sure they will not be long in appreciating the advantages to themselves of a fair settlement of political differences in the key areas of Europe and of North-East Asia.'*

Finally, the West should not scorn to answer patiently and indefatigably Soviet lies, and to proclaim the truth as we see it, since only in this way can the intellectual climate of the West be maintained as an influence in the world.

Thus these two civilized Americans reaffirm in the temper and style of Hume the maxim on which 'all the wiser and more experienced princes and politicians', ancient and modern, have proceeded: to preserve the balance of power by maintaining and exerting the minimum force needed for the purpose. They define the conditions on which this ancient maxim may be preserved even in the nuclear age and in a world situation of bi-polar tension.

These conditions involve formidable difficulties, which are not ignored, for although the purpose of the policy is the avowed purpose of NATO, the conditions run counter to strong current tendencies: renunciation of the hope of any easier alternative, sacrifice of consumer goods, manning of conventional forces and abstention from bidding up competition in nuclear weapons, strengthening of government initiative in the United States and collaboration of private interests in support of public policy, negotiation with the Soviet Union through personal diplomatic channels, patience with allies on points of difference and misunderstanding. This might be unkindly described as an unrealistic attempt to restore the field for an old-fashioned diplomatic policy. That judgement has to be tested by the alternatives which are open to be preferred. What can be said immediately is that an equally unpopular foreign policy was made to work in Britain in the nineteenth century, only because it was fundamentally in accord with the public interest. The other

* *Russia, the Atom, and the West*, p. 85.

remark worth making at once is that these two spokesmen of Western civilization exemplify, without a word of cant, in what they say and in their manner of saying it what it is that is at stake and invites efforts to preserve it.

6. THE ALTERNATIVES TO A FOREIGN POLICY

If the peoples and politicians of NATO are not prepared for the restraints and sacrifices required by a foreign policy based on the maxim which 'all the wiser and more experienced princes and politicians', ancient and modern, have followed, by what alternative initiatives can they hope to control the changes which will affect their position in the world? Setting aside wishful thinking, which can never make a policy, two initiatives alternative to a modern form of traditional power diplomacy have been proposed. One is the renunciation of nuclear weapons by the NATO powers or, if necessary, by Britain alone (since this is a proposed British initiative). The other is an attempt to build up opinion and pressure leading to the establishment of a World Security Authority, under the United Nations or in association with the United Nations.

The arguments for and against renunciation of nuclear weapons have been conveniently presented by Mr Philip Toynbee.* Mr Toynbee's position is substantially that of Earl Russell, Mr J. B. Priestley, Mr Kingsley Martin, and other promoters of the British campaign for nuclear disarmament. He states it graphically with intense feeling in a memorandum which he circulated to some seventy-five prominent people, inviting their comment. His little book reproduces the memorandum with a selection from the comment he received, mainly from the disagreement, and his own reply.

Briefly, Mr Toynbee's argument is that nuclear weapons are of no use to anyone who is not both wicked and insane, since to use them is to invite retaliation and retaliation is futile annihilation. No political ends can be gained by such means. Nevertheless, the arms race goes on, and there is no ceiling. The situation is extremely dangerous because unless and until it is altered it will lead in all probability to an accidental and catastrophic nuclear war. The situation must be changed, for the sake of the human race, and if the Americans cannot be persuaded to give the lead in a renunciation of these insane and wicked weapons, Britain should strive to build up a neutral bloc throughout the world dedicated to the repudiation of all nuclear weapons.

Some of Mr Toynbee's critics are not understanding the situation

* *The Fearful Choice: A Debate on Nuclear Policy*, 1958.

or not taking it seriously enough, and can be ignored. Others, who possibly understand the situation better than Mr Toynbee and feel its doubts, dangers, and difficulties as deeply and sincerely, do take a different view. They argue that unilateral disarmament by Britain might well increase the danger by tempting the Russians and creating panic, that it is not practical politics, anyhow, that the arms race has a rationale and is not just a mad scramble, that the deterrent does deter and has been and is a stabilizing factor, that the extent of the destructive power of nuclear weapons and of survival in a nuclear war are problematical, that renunciation of nuclear weapons is not a policy and raises the question of the type and scale of arms retained and developed (unless total pacifism is intended), that the risk of an accidental nuclear war can be greatly exaggerated. On the other hand, these critics fully agree with Mr Toynbee in wanting negotiation with the Russians in order to get a political settlement and disarmament. Many of them agree with a great part of Mr Toynbee's thesis. Mr Nigel Gosling of the *Observer* who says that he differs only in not believing that war is imminent nor that it would necessarily mean the end of the human race, sums up the situation in these words:

'The present strategy of the West, what has been called the 'Balance of Terror' is no more than a new term for the oldest of concepts—the balance of power. This policy has been consistently applied for two hundred years. During that time it has not succeeded in averting war *except over short periods*, nor has it led to any visible slow bettering of conditions in which war *could* be averted. By its very nature it preserves the old conditions—those which always end in war. There is no reason to suppose that history will suddenly change its course. Unless an entirely new approach is tried, war is a certainty by the form-book.'

In replying, Mr Toynbee insists that none of his critics has told him in what circumstances the use of nuclear weapons would be morally and politically justified. If they are not going to be used in retaliation, it is wrong and foolish to pretend that they will be; and if it is intended to use them in such a situation, they will not have deterred and their use will be wantonly wicked. On the question of the extent of damage inflicted by these weapons, he reiterates Dr Arnold Toynbee's point that no country has the right to threaten to use weapons which may destroy uncommitted peoples. On the arms race, he quotes from an American correspondent who wants the West to engage in an all-out arms race in the hope of reaching overwhelming military superiority in order to be able to dictate terms; and he suggests that this is a widespread view in the United States of what the arms race means. To the majority of his critics, who say that they are taking a calculated risk, that they hope for disarmament by negotiation, and if this cannot be had on 'satisfactory' terms the Russians must be 'contained' by deterrence ('This, they say, will be a sad state of things—a dangerous state of things—but it is the best that we can do'), he replies that they should at least *face* the nuclear warfare they are prepared for, and not continue to think and speak in outmoded terms like Mr Duncan Sandys: 'To me it is inconceivable that the free peoples would surrender their liberties without a fight.' We should no longer talk of dying to the last man, Mr Toynbee says, quoting Mr Alex Comfort, but of killing to the last child; and he adds, 'I would say, of torturing to the last child'. Finally, Mr Toynbee admits that total and immediate disarmament by the West (of which he is in favour) is not practical politics, but he would be happier if the West would turn in the direction of peace-making and the construction of common prosperity and make signs and take steps, and though deeds are better than words, words are better than nothing; and if negotiations fail, his hope is in Britain's unilateral repudiation of nuclear weapons.

Mr Toynbee's proposals, as he well knows, appeal to some of those who share his assumptions and convictions as an act of faith and courage justifying high optimism, and others may accept them as a lesser evil, a counsel of despair for all short-term purposes. That the world is waiting for an act of moral leadership, a demonstration of a return to common sense that will dispel the nuclear nightmare and halt the arms race, and that Britain has the authority to speak the word of deliverance, is not an idea that any historian would be likely to entertain. The mere force of moral example can have little effect in politics. The powers that depend on NATO for security and aid would be alarmed and discouraged by British withdrawal. There would be a resettlement of forces after the small earthquake, a replacement of Britain by Western Germany. The world would go on as before, without Britain. And Britain would survive without the dignity or the claims of a Chelsea pensioner. On the other hand, as an alternative to a futile and fatal arms race, even Mr Kennan would repudiate the nuclear weapon and stake national safety on good conscience, common sense, and an appeal to humanity. So much is there in this fearful question of contingency and assumption and speculation, so little of absolute principle and reliable calculation.

There are, however, certain political assumptions which deserve the utmost respect, and any policy or judgement or action which ignores or flouts them is bound to be false and dangerous. The first is that the nuclear weapon or any weapon which is unlimited and indiscriminate in the havoc it wreaks is futile and fatal as an instrument or sanction of diplomacy. The second is that, *a fortiori*, an arms race in such weapons for the sake of security or of overwhelming superiority is futile and fatal. The third is that dangerous tensions and provisional situations exist all over the world which are the likely occasion sooner or later of hostile actions and counter offensives liable to ignite the fuse which lets off total war, quite possibly on an issue not vital to anybody.

The comfortable assurance that the deterrent does deter, and because it does so it keeps and will continue to keep policy within bounds, and therefore there will be no total war, that although it is not a suitable instrument or sanction of diplomacy it is a new and useful condition which restrains the diplomacy of all the powers, this is a prevalent assumption which supplants the above political assumptions and allays the fears they prompt. Because it has a certain happy truth for the time being, it is liable to provide a false foundation for the thinking and operations of statesmen, with the result that instead of making it their first and urgent business to seek political settlements and stable situations the world over, together with disarmament and the joint and common control of nuclear weapons, they go on pursuing balance of power diplomacy in the balance of terror situation. The balance of power system never induced the moderation required to make it a system of continuous peace-making, nor the concert and moderation required to make it a system of limited war-making rapidly terminated. There *is* just a possibility that the balance of terror has introduced and will maintain this required inducement to restraint which will make the world safe for diplomacy.*

* An absolute stalemate between the strategic atomic striking forces of the USSR and the USA might be reached in five to ten years, a position in which *both* would be able to launch long-range rockets from invulnerable sites *within* their own territories to deliver 'clean' H-bombs of high power. In this situation, both powers would be independent of allies, equally 'invincible', equally anxious to avoid an all-out war, equally able to employ the H-bomb for a limited purpose as an instrument and sanction of diplomacy, e.g. to destroy, after warning, an evacuated city. Such a situation might induce the USSR and the USA to arrange a political settlement and to undertake together to police the world, through the UN. This kind of possibility, with its variants (developed by Dr Leo Szilard in a paper privately circulated) shows how treacherous the assumptions are liable to be in all our arguments on this question of international security. There are no sure means of knowing which we can trust.

Now this is the assumption of Mr Acheson and, with marked recent uneasiness, of Mr Kennan. They represent the American awakening to the responsibilities of world power and the realities of world politics, and a repudiation of the American diplomatic legacy, an embarrassing record of naïveté, resounding phrase-making, moralistic declarations, and legalistic paper triumphs, made possible by American immunities and American ignorance of the real problems, interests, and policies of other nations. It is not insignificant that Mr Acheson gives the title *Power and Diplomacy* to his published lectures, and Mr Kennan's Walgreen lectures published in 1951* were a searching examination of the record, and an explicit plea for a realistic power-based and (for that reason) restrained diplomacy. In his closing lecture, he said:

'. . . I see the most serious fault of our past policy formulation to lie in something that I might call the legalistic-moralistic approach to international problems. This approach runs like a red skein through our foreign policy of the last fifty years. It has in it something of the old emphasis on arbitration treaties, something of the Hague Conferences and schemes of universal disarmament, something of the more ambitious American concepts of the role of international law, something of the League of Nations and the United Nations, something of the Kellogg Pact, something of the idea of a universal "Article 51" pact, something of the belief in World Law and World Government. But it is none of these entirely . . .'†

Here he was identifying actual American diplomacy with the hopeful internationalism and lay political thinking of the century, what he called 'diplomacy by dilettantism'. He went on to make the same general analysis of the unsoundness of this view which Mr E. H. Carr had made in his criticism of League of Nations policies‡ earlier. It is the wish of a satisfied Power to rule out all violent change.

'The function of a system of international relationships is not to inhibit this process of change by imposing a legal strait jacket upon it but rather to facilitate it: to ease its transitions, to temper the asperities to which it often leads, to isolate and moderate the conflicts to which it gives rise, and to see that these conflicts do not assume forms too unsettling for international life in general. But this is a task for diplomacy, in the most old-fashioned sense of the

* *American Diplomacy 1900-1950.*
† *Ibid*, p. 95.
‡ *The Twenty Years Crisis.*

term. For this, law is too abstract, too inflexible, too hard to adjust to the demands of the unpredictable and the unexpected.'*

The worst of the legalistic approach is that it imposes an absolutist international morality, which, if it does not conceal the wish of the dominant powers to forbid change, is liable to end by their taking action which cannot rest short of their total domination.

'It is a curious thing, but it is true, that the legalistic approach to world affairs, rooted as it unquestionably is in a desire to do away with war and violence, makes violence more enduring, more terrible, and more destructive to political stability than did the older motives of national interest. A war fought in the name of high moral principle finds no early end short of some form of total domination.'†

We are still in the situation which Rousseau described: instead of writing a book, it will be necessary to raise an army. Perhaps the remedy is worse than the disease. It has not been so easy as Kant thought it was for devils to found a constitution.

Is it true, then, that the larger hopes of internationalism are, and are likely to remain, phrases, that enlightened hope clings even more closely to the wisdom, restraint, skill, and information of statesmen and trained diplomats, that institutions in this field are a snare and a delusion? Before hearing the advocates of these institutions, it may be worth while to take a glance at what the meaning may be of that national interest which has been the foundation of diplomacy.

7. NATIONAL INTEREST

Joseph Schumpeter has argued that imperialism and modern nationalism and militarism are examples of 'the ancient truth that the dead always rule the living'. What he tries to show in his essay *The Sociology of Imperialism* is that these aggressive policies are associated with structural elements and organizational forms once essential to a society but long since serving no useful purpose, and injurious to the rational and permanent interests of the people. In particular, imperialism is not a development of capitalism, but an outcome of autocracy. Absolutist national states were established in Europe in the sixteenth and seventeenth centuries, though not in England. This unity under the royal power was achieved by the

* *American Diplomacy*, p. 98.
† *Ibid*, p. 101.

creation of a military machine and a military caste, which persisted as a war party and made war in order to persist. This pattern was never superseded by the commercial pattern of pacific relations because commercial development took place in the matrix of autocracy; the commercial interests of peoples were subordinated to the profit of kings; commercial incentives were added to other motives making for war, and commercial objects might be the declared pretexts of war: but imperialism was autocracy in action or militant nationalism, and not a capitalist policy. If the interests of peoples were consulted, if cheap plenty for all was the real concern, then pacifism and free trade, Cobden's principles, would have prevailed. Indeed, the case of England, in which absolutism was resisted and destroyed, shows that this is what happens when commercial and popular interests are allowed to become dominant. The characteristic foreign policy that developed in England under liberal and radical influences 'may be summarized under the following principles: never to intervene, unless vital interests are gravely and immediately threatened; never to be concerned about the "balance of power" on the Continent; not to arm for war; to reduce, by means of understandings, those areas of friction with other spheres of interest that were particularly extensive because of the lack of planning in the global structure of empire; to relieve tension and conflict by appropriate yielding, to the point where the remaining British sphere would be at least half-way tenable'. Such a policy was not easy, and suffered set-backs at home, but it prevailed because it was in accord with the objective interests of the politically important segments of the population. Imperialism and aggressive nationalism can survive only so long as the objective interests of the people are subordinated to certain useless surviving dominant elements oriented toward war, objectless war, so long, that is, as the dead continue to rule the living.

Dr Gunnar Myrdal also finds that the dead continue to rule the living—in economic theory.

'The emergence in under-developed countries of this common urge to economic development as a major political issue, and the definition of economic development as a rise in the levels of living of the common people, the agreement that economic development is a task for governments and that governments must prepare and enforce a general economic plan, containing a system of purposefully applied controls and impulses to get development started and to keep it going—all this amounts to something entirely new in history. It represents, indeed, an attempt at a complete reversal of what once happened in the now developed countries as described by the Schumpeterian model.' (p. 80)

The main thesis of Dr Myrdal's *Economic Theory and Under-developed Regions* (1957) is that a tendency towards inequality is inherent in the unhampered play of market forces, the rich get richer and the poor poorer, and particularly so when the general development is low. Since there is no world government to interfere with these forces and integrate the economy as in the national case, and since development is usually very low in the poorer regions, the operation of the tendency is most marked in the international field. Colonies and independent territories have been affected alike by this tendency, but colonies benefited potentially, though seldom actually, in so far as they acquired many of the basic conditions for general economic development (transport facilities, law and order, education, administration). The present inevitable liquidation of the colonial system leaves the former dependencies still subject to the tendency to become poorer, unless and until national governments in these countries set to work deliberately and intelligently to plan economic development in the interests of the whole people. In all these circumstances, economic nationalism is necessary and constructive in so far as it follows national economic interests, for it moves towards international equality which is a condition of international solidarity as a basis for an integrated world policy. Military strength does not avail in the interests of the rich nations against this movement, because this movement is world-wide and irresistible, because in the rich countries there is no popular interest in nor support for repression, and because military action has become too dangerous to use lightly. This situation has already introduced an unprecedented measure of international equality, which provides the conditions for economic nationalism.

Thus Schumpeter had argued that economic nationalism was the fruit of autocracy, retrogressive and contrary to the objective interests of the people, and Dr Myrdal argues that the welfare state is, and can only be, nationalistic, that economic nationalism is progressive and in conformity with the permanent interests of the people. Of course, there is no necessary contradiction between the theses, since they relate to different phases of development; and Schumpeter allows that autocratic policy in the earlier phase made a seed bed for economic growth that could neither have sprung up nor maintained itself without it—an excrescence in his system which Myrdal makes the head of the corner in his. However, the main point of both arguments, in connexion with national interest, is that military power is an anachronism, that it cannot any longer be used to advance national interests, neither by the rich countries nor by the poor. Why, then, this paradox that when arms have become useless as an instrument of policy for the advancement of real national interests, the nations are engaged in an unprecedented arms race? Is it simply that the dead always rule the living?

8. THE ARMS RACE

The general principle of Schumpeter's thesis on imperialism is even better exemplified in the arms race. Science, even more than capitalism, is universal, a free exchange and a development beneficial to all, and, even more than capitalism, is used for, and feeds, aggressive purposes only because it is developed in sovereign national states with armaments and a military technology which it is applied to improve and perfect, and it is in the interests of scientists to be destructive even less than it is in the interests of capitalists to be aggressive. In a word, Schumpeter's argument of the relation of capitalism to imperialism is true *a fortiori* and with fewer qualifications of the relation between science and the arms race. Of course there is less point in this application of the argument, because it is not so generally assumed that the arms race is a necessary development of science, a natural fruit. All the same, it is widely assumed that men are morally too immature to be safe with scientific knowledge, which they will pervert to destructive purposes. This is a false sociology of the arms race, which Schumpeter's sociology of imperialism could be used to correct. Surviving institutions, persisting professional castes and their traditions, real situations, have far more to do with the logic and compulsions of the arms race than simple moral obliquity or even immaturity. After all, under these constraints, in war time, men of outstanding integrity, humanity, genius, and culture, ornaments of the race, like Einstein and Oppenheimer, have had not a little to do with this application of science. The dilemma of such men has been a major tragedy of the human spirit in our time. It has involved our intellectual *élite*.

Dr Myrdal's thesis also has a precise and grim application to the arms race. It started some seventy years ago by deliberate national policies. Even then, and long before, it was recognized that international anarchy constituted a vicious circle: a nation armed in self-defence, and her neighbour felt bound in self-defence to get ahead in arms, provoking a counter effort, until the inevitable preventive war was provoked. With the development of science, administra-

tion, wealth, and other social factors, each acting and reacting on
the defence problem, the old-fashioned vicious circle has become a
rapid spiral, the 'take-off into sustained growth' has taken place with
a vengeance. In particular, the intensive and massive concentration
of science on weapons is influencing military thinking which is
influencing political decisions which have far-reaching unintended
consequences. Moreover, with the increasing scale and pace of this
development more and more of the nation's thought, energy, and
resources are involved. It is a dynamic movement, on Myrdal's
'principle of interlocking, circular inter-dependence within a process
of cumulative causation', never achieves a stable equilibrium, and
disappears into the night of fantasy. Nothing can stop it, and save
us, short of deliberate interference to bring it to a halt; and that
means an agreement of the major powers.

Myrdal's general analysis can be applied to the arms race, but
what has actually been happening to bear it out is documented by
Mr Philip Noel-Baker in *The Arms Race* (1958). Mr Noel-Baker is
a veteran internationalist, not only as a theorist but also as a politician with official and ministerial experience. He is a life-long
advocate of disarmament, and his book, in addition to being a
compendium of the facts, is A Programme for World Disarmament.

Every statesman repeats duly and almost daily that war has
become an anachronism, that the nations must disarm and learn to
live with one another, that nothing else makes sense today, that the
alternative is too appalling to contemplate. There is no reason to
think that these are moral platitudes with which popular speeches
are always larded, and not sincere personal convictions. Yet these
earnest speeches neither inaugurate nor indicate a new epoch. As
under the regime of the Holy Alliance, the words are at variance
with the deeds. Not quite. If the attempts at disarmament have been
abortive, they have been made. The assumption that disarmament
with collective security is a utopian scheme entertained seriously
only by internationalists like Mr Noel-Baker is at variance with the
history of official disarmament discussions both between the wars
and since. Under the League of Nations and the United Nations,
Commissions have been set up by unanimous votes charged with the
task of preparing draft treaties of comprehensive disarmament.
Genuine initiatives have been made by the great powers to bring
about drastic disarmament. In particular at the outset of the UN,
the United States adopted the Lilienthal Report, 'as revolutionary as
atomic energy itself', and proposed to commit the monopoly of the
control and development of atomic power to an international

authority. The Russians destroyed the plan. Mr Noel-Baker writes:

'It would be hard to guess from . . . Communist speeches that what the United States had actually proposed was that the source of power in a new, world-wide industrial revolution should be handed over to a publicly owned International Authority, in which all nations should have fair and equal rights and shares; to which the United States would give, for nothing, the most valuable industrial secret ever known; to which it would hand over capital assets worth at least $4,000m. It would be just as hard to guess that the United States had proposed to give up the A-bomb, which it alone possessed; to distribute the vitally important strategic industry of atomic energy on an agreed and equitable basis around the world; and to dedicate all the knowledge and experience at its command to ensuring that no more nuclear weapons should ever again be made. The greatest capitalist nation had proposed the international socialist control of the source of world prosperity for centuries to come; the greatest military power had proposed a total nuclear disarmament, in order that the rule of law through the United Nations should prevail.'*

For the first ten years of the UN in all these discussions the Russians for their own reasons, good or bad, and understandable enough, were unco-operative. Then there seems to have been a genuine change of line, and by that time the United States had become altogether mistrustful: the moment had passed, the attempt to achieve universal and comprehensive disarmament was abandoned, partial measures only were proposed, because the Americans had come to think that NATO, the 'atomic shield', and the readiness and ability of Western forces to deal promptly with Communist aggression anywhere, could effectively defend the free nations, and that with the state of deadlock on major political issues a drastic reduction of armaments would increase the danger that a local outbreak might become world war. 'Time is showing that the United States rejection of the Russian offer of May 10, 1955, may have been a terrible mistake.' The United States had a case, and it would be wrong to turn the tangled story into high tragedy with hero and villain. The fact remains that the arms race is on and that there were other possibilities.

The arms race means the development of atomic power and scientific research on a nationalist basis. Research is the dynamic of the race, and it is applied to every branch of warfare, maintaining

* *The Arms Race*, p. 192-3.

continuous improvements and innovations in the struggle to gain and keep the technological lead. What is entirely new is the pace and scale of development in the powers of destruction, applied continuously to all weapons and methods of warfare: to conventional weapons as well as to the nuclear deterrent, to submarines as well as to chemical, bacteriological, and incendiary methods of warfare. In these circumstances, the military technologists and service chiefs tend to determine policy, and with weapons and methods developed on this scale and at this pace, the offensive determines strategic thinking. In an all-out nuclear war, whole fleets, cities, regions are considered expendable, so long as the mission of massive retaliation can be performed. Land armies are being converted to combat units adapted and equipped for nuclear, chemical, and biological war and with immensely increased fire-power and mobility. The longer the delay in reaching agreement on disarmament, the more difficult it becomes to reach agreement, far-reaching developments have taken control,[6] and decisions pass more firmly and irrevocably into the hands of the technologists and strategists who have done all the thinking and demanded and obtained so high a proportion of the nation's money, brains, skill, and production.

The colossal waste and frustration might be borne with the resignation and patience that have been so often in human affairs the only alternative to ignorance and apathy, if there were any assurance that these frightful powers of destruction will never be used because they are known to be so frightful. Unfortunately, there is no reason for any such assurance: if the arms race goes on, they will almost certainly be used. In the first place, in the event of war no nation is going to accept defeat without resorting to its 'best' weapons. In the second place, weapons that on their first use caused widespread horror and moral revolt (poison gas, the bombing of cities, the atom bomb) are subsequently thought necessary and legitimate, in so far as one side uses them: there are no moral restraints — and can be none unless and until there is a universally enforced world order. In the third place, the atomic powers have officially declared their intention of using these weapons whenever it is in their essential interests to do so. Weapons up to two and a half times the calibre of the Hiroshima bomb are being christened 'tactical' and described as suitable for use against military targets in conventional warfare.

There is no exaggeration when Mr Noel-Baker declares that the arms race has become the most evil thing in human history. He sees no sane alternative to a disarmament treaty without further delay, comprehensive and detailed in its provisions, phased over several years, but with terms that end in total disarmament with collective security under a world authority. Similarly, Grenville Clark and Louis B. Sohn have argued* that complete disarmament, rather than reduction or limitation, is necessary, that the time is past for generalized recognition of this need in the speeches of statesmen and others, that the only useful talk now is in terms of alternative detailed plans which could lead to a draft treaty, and that only the acceptance of international institutions and the abandonment of reliance on national armaments, the 'balance of terror', and diplomacy can save the world and lead humanity into the way of peace. The alternatives have become plain enough. The time for political decision is now.

9. CONDITIONS OF PEACE

Mr Acheson was chairman of the departmental committee which he set up and which appointed and worked with a Board of Consultants that included Mr David Lilienthal and Dr Robert Oppenheimer and which issued in 1946 the Acheson-Lilienthal Report. Instead, the McMahon Act became law. Had it been otherwise, Dr Oppenheimer has recently said, 'there would be neither atomic bombs nor atomic secrets'. It would have been, he thinks now, a broader initiative than was then envisaged, promoting and controlling science and technology in its constructive applications on a world scale. He goes on to say that strategic plenty has been obtained and tactical plenty cannot be far away. 'Total nuclear war has begun to take on that desperate, perhaps genocidal, perhaps suicidal, quality which was anticipated from the beginning.' Yet in the same paper he shows himself resigned to acceptance of current American policy as without alternative.

'To discourage the planned, deliberate, all-out atomic war, we need to look both to defense and to deterrence, defense that may not always in the wavering fortunes of a changing technology be trivial or even inadequate, deterrence which maintains a reasonably invulnerable capability for retaliation. In order to prevent the unsought, unplanned, eruption of all-out nuclear war, entrained by the growth of an initially limited conflict, we need to be prepared in equipment, men, training, planning, and doctrine to keep wars limited: limited in objective, in terrain, in tactics, and in means. These are not easy assignments; they are expensive, they are uncertain.'†

* World Peace through World Law, 1958.
† Atoms for Power. The American Assembly, Columbia University, 1957, p. 32.

P

The big question is whether this wise, generous, patient, persistent, moderate, skilful, flexible, sacrificing, long-term diplomacy backed by armed strength advocated by Mr Acheson can be practised by the United States, whether it can offer to free peoples assistance to self-help and a shield against communist aggression and penetration, whether it can prevent nuclear war, whether in default of a common world system in the UN it can build up for free peoples an alternative to the communist world system, whether this is the only realistic hope for the West, and whether the assumptions on which it rests are valid and reliable. It is a policy with strong attractions for many liberal persons. It enables the liberal democracies under United States leadership to create and sustain their own international order based on their own virtues and values, without compromise and without retreat. It involves no necessary hostility to the communist world. It is a long-term policy in which they can be consistent and persistent. It is a challenge to great historical achievement. On the other hand, the assignments are not easy; they are expensive, they are uncertain. Can the arms race be halted with the possession of strategic and tactical plenty? Can limited war be practised? Can statesmen determine the decisions for which they are responsible? Can statesmen and peoples maintain the high virtues on which the successful and safe conduct of such a diplomacy wholly depend? Unless these questions can be confidently answered in the affirmative, there is no bottom to the policy proposed; it is based on unrealistic assumptions, and is perhaps more utopian than disarmament.

Mr Acheson, Mr Kennan, and Dr Oppenheimer are extremely intelligent persons and admirable and admired human beings, but in these life and death matters it is safer to be guided by the generalized experience of mankind than to trust to the insight or wisdom of any contemporary. The analysis of a Schumpeter, a Myrdal, a Noel-Baker, which shows that the arms race will not halt nor be halted with the production of enough, that nationalist and militarist considerations will prevail and increasingly direct research, that the possession of arms and the competition in arms, with all that goes with it, is the biggest cause of war, that in such a situation all the factors interact in a way that initiates an accelerating spiral movement in a given direction which can be checked only by deliberate intervention and planned reorientation: this analysis, as a generalization of what usually happens, with supporting reasons, is worth more to anxious and threatened humanity than the best of contemporary intentions to be wiser and do better than our forefathers.

The analysis which undermines trust in the concepts of American neo-diplomacy backed by a discriminating doctrine of arms is the same analysis which supports confidence in a policy of planned general disarmament and collective security. For such an initiative starts a self-sustaining movement in the direction of world collaboration and integration. The United Nations, which has been a little more than words and gestures, a moral and political ritual, would, once it had become the locus and focus of real politics, develop genuine institutions which would serve both as the basis and guarantee of world order and as the method of political conflict and social change: what is now the shadow would become the real thing. This can happen only with general disarmament, and the creation of a World Security Authority. Until then, the realists are right, but fatally right, right as imperialists are right, in terms of a system that has no future except disaster.

However, disarmament and collective security are not to be had for the wishing, nor for the argument, any more today than when Rousseau wrote. There is no power strong enough to enforce it, and there is no cheerful prospect of getting it by agreement. That, again, is a major assumption, or basic conviction, of American policy. One can hardly say, on the lines of Schumpeter's argument, that disarmament will come because it is the objective interest of the people, and they are and increasingly will be the dominant influence in politics; since the argument is, rather, that it will not come unless and until there is a deliberate intervention and plan to bring it about, and meanwhile delay makes a political decision to do this more difficult and more unlikely.[7] Of course, the people of more nations than one, and soon, may decide that disarmament is their objective interest and enforce it on their leaders. Indeed, it is precisely upon this, reinforced by the mutual pressure of 'the balance of terror', that Clark and Sohn rely in putting forward their plan as practical politics. But this calculation may be discounted as unrealistic, inasmuch as at present the people of the Soviet Union have the utmost confidence in their leaders on questions of foreign policy, and the peoples of NATO are extremely unlikely to demand of their governments unilateral disarmament, and their governments have not found it practicable to get multilateral disarmament on their own terms.

Thus, in every direction, the alternatives seem to lead only to risk, uncertainty, impracticability, disaster; and the more one broods on them the menace of the future grows. This anxiety is partly the nervous apprehension of the looker-on. Governments alone are responsible for day to day decisions and for the formulation and implementation of policy, since they alone have the information — and no one is more sensitive to this than an ex-minister like Mr Acheson or an ex-adviser like Mr Kennan. If it is improper, useless, and ridiculous to offer advice to governments or to formulate for them the policies they should follow, it is not less intolerable to be expected to resign oneself helplessly (and hopelessly) into their hands, when one looks back on the gross errors and tragic ineptitudes of the past. To study these things and think about and discuss them has point and purpose in so far as one has the right to know what policy is being followed, to raise questions about it and have them answered, to make proposals and to have them considered. In a democracy this right is recognized and there are appropriate methods for giving effect to it. If one is to avail oneself of them to any purpose, one must have studied and thought about and discussed the policy being followed, in the light of alternatives that are practicable. Under any regime, there are always plenty of armchair politicians who do otherwise, but their value is no use anywhere, and although a democracy must never fail to guarantee their right to talk, it stands only to lose by the results.

Although the intelligence, the telegrams, the privy information are in the hands only of the officials and the politicians who bear the responsibility and make the policy, and there is no substitute in foreign politics, nor at home, for statesmen and statesmanship,[8] there are certain constants and conditions in the general situation which help one responsibly to probe and question and attempt to assess what is being done. These can be learned only from a study of the present in the light of the past. Two comprehensive conclusions as a test of policy seem to emerge from such a study.

(1) Although political settlement may not be obtainable at any given time and although multilateral disarmament may not be obtainable, these remain the proper objects of policy, and renunciation of them as unobtainable is a counsel of despair. There is grave danger that after failure they remain on the agenda as phrases and items of disillusionment down for postponement. A policy that does not pursue them actively and resourcefully, that turns away from them and builds up an alternative to make the future, is not a tolerable foreign policy today.

Whether political settlement is easier than disarmament and comes first or whether disarmament makes political settlement easier, is arguable, and the priority may vary with the situation; but they belong together, both are constant objectives of policy, and advance towards one is a move towards the other which brings the first still nearer.

Partial disarmament or a halt to the arms race would be something, and a settlement in Europe or establishment of a demilitarized zone, but there are powerful arguments which would show that a comprehensive settlement for Europe and the Middle East (and Formosa?) and a plan for total disarmament would be safer, more attractive, more negotiable,[9] if the implementation of the treaties were carried out by easy stages over several years: the comprehensiveness of the treaty would help to establish confidence through definition of intentions and the undertaking of a definitive solution of serious problems, whilst the easy stages would make the plans flexible and workable. Here again, these are arguable positions which give scope not only for discussion but also for diplomatic tactics in the effort to achieve results in the movement towards settlement and disarmament.

If there is a single objective of strategy, a single test and measure of policy, it is the United Nations. At present it provides convenient services and is otherwise the plaything or the tool of the powers. Whilst there are at least two groups of powers who aspire and strive to build up international systems of their own, no world order can be established, and the longer this goes on, the nearer the danger that other rival systems will enter the field. The UN is unlikely to exercise an effective collective role unless and until it is made responsible for world security, with general disarmament. If and when it does so the foundation will have been laid for rapid and orderly world development. This is the strait gate that alone leads to salvation, although the road to it may prove circuitous, steep, and hazardous.

(2) To have a constant objective of foreign policy, pursued consistently and persistently, if it is openly declared, and if it is intelligible as conformable to objective and permanent interests, is a formal condition of mutual trust. Similarly, if policy is not hostile, not seeking to confound the politics and frustrate the knavish tricks of the enemy, not afraid of other powers and therefore not out to hamper and harm them and make it difficult or impossible for them to solve their problems, if, on the contrary, policy demonstrates the good neighbour, then it is disarming, and without preaching or practising non-resistance can evoke new responses. In the same way, international relations as much as personal relations, if not more, require psychological understanding which makes allowances for the constraints and effects of situations. Germany between the wars, Russia after 1917, Egypt after the war, but also most nations at most times, might have been dealt with more successfully by tact than by tactics. Nations like persons are of course responsible for their behaviour, but their behaviour like that of persons is largely

determined by their situation and by the treatment they get.

Thus, candour and continuity in foreign policy, understanding and respect for the situation and problems and aims of other powers, and actual assistance to them in their difficulties are moral conditions without which negotiations can hardly prosper nor disarmament take place (in spite of Kant's belief that even sensible devils could produce a constitution easily enough). Fortunately, these virtues are becoming easier for the powers to practise, with the liquidation of imperialism and the prohibitive risks of an 'adventurous' foreign policy. The Western powers do not have to wait for the Soviet Union to set an example; and if their own policy is concentrated on negotiating a political settlement and disarmament and instituting a system of collective security, the moral conditions which make these things possible are made possible by concentration on these things. We can perhaps have more easily than we know what we ought to want, and certainly what we ought to want is not now far from what we do really want when we understand well enough what the alternatives really are.*

What is to be understood by perpetual peace? There are two prophecies in Isaiah: 'and they shall beat their swords into plowshares, and their spears into pruning hooks; nation shall not lift up

---

* The practical alternatives offered to policy and political decision are not all the time, nor at any time, the big alternatives of unlimited war or general disarmament which frame the issue within which particular decisions have to be taken and particular policies formed and followed. At great cost during the past ten years the governments and peoples of NATO have striven to put themselves in a position to defend themselves, and they enjoy perhaps a measure of confidence in the security achieved by their system of graduated defence. They are not likely to be willing to throw this measure of security away nor to allow it to be whittled down for any guarantee that does not provide at least comparably reliable assurance. At the same time, they know this system of graduated defence and NATO interdependence to be extremely costly, risky, and unstable. Military thinking, now preoccupied with prevention and security, is prepared to accept the feasibility and desirability of the security offered by a reliable system of international inspection and control over a wide enough area, as a guarantee against surprise attack and as a preliminary, after test, to general disarmament. Political initiative is committed to finding the way to this mutual security by reliable and acceptable guarantees. Thus what has had to be thought of as an unlikely jump into a new orbit can begin now to be seen as movement along a continuous road made by current thinking and actual initiatives which can effect the transition from one order to another by piecemeal and tested exchanges of an obsolescent type of guarantee for one that has already replaced it in theory. This movement will not go on inevitably to a destined end; it needs to be sustained by an alert, informed, and urgent public opinion; but this public can perhaps soon begin to enjoy the inestimable happiness of working with the grain of events and pushing and directing a load under way.

sword against nation, neither shall they learn war any more' (Isaiah ii, 4). That is perfectly possible. The other begins 'and the wolf shall dwell with the lamb' (Isaiah xi, 6-9). Not even eighteenth century philosophers thought that—because they had abandoned Isaiah's faith in the creation of 'new heavens and a new earth'. We cannot aspire to change human nature. We can hope to control human behaviour, to reduce inevitable conflicts to manageable proportions.

NOTES: CHAPTER V

1. *Officially . . . admitted:*
   see, successive White Papers on Defence, e.g. the White Paper for 1957. Cp. *British Foreign Policy* (Central Office of Information, 1956) pp. 2-3. Also, *A World Security Authority*, by ten Conservative MPs (Conservative Political Centre, No. 190, 1958).

2. *Kant . . . owed . . . so much to Rousseau:*
   see Ernst Cassirer's *Rousseau, Kant, Goethe* (Princeton, 1945). The summary of Kant's views is the argument of his *Perpetual Peace* (Zum ewigen Frieden).

3. *Hume:*
   in *Essays* Part II, Essay VII 'Of the Balance of Power'.

4. *How this happened:*
   one unpretentious but authoritative view is in Harold Butler's book from which the title of this section is borrowed, *The Lost Peace* (1941).

5. *E. H. Carr has argued:*
   The Twenty Years Crisis, 1919-39, esp. pp. 40-2, 111-12, 254-63, 52-3, 287-9. And *Conditions of Peace* (1942) pp. 6-8 for a summary statement of why, in Professor Carr's view, Great Britain and France lost the initiative (and the peace) after victory in the first world war.

6. *far-reaching developments:*
   the pace, scale, and complexity of these developments are such that there is a modern gap between the thinking of even the instructed public interested in defence questions and policy-makers. A partial remedy is in the study devoted to the development of strategic thinking in American universities. Because there is little or no counterpart to this in Europe, an Institute for Strategic Studies has recently been set up in London with American Foundation money, 'to promote on a non-party basis the study and discussion of, and the exchange of information upon, the influence of modern nuclear weapons and methods of warfare upon the problems of defence, strategy, disarmament and international relations'.

7. *delay makes . . . more unlikely:*
   it should be noticed that this is the opposite of Kant's view or that of anyone who believes that the dialectic of events will eventually teach those who refuse to learn by experience in intelligent anticipation. Man's intelligent development of his means of defence has ruled out this hope that the nature of things will in good time save him from the worst consequences of his stupidity in spite of himself. The thought that at worst, if not now, sooner or later philosophic hopes would be realized has been falsified by the supervention of a situation of the 'now-or-never', 'all-or-none' type.

8. *no substitute . . . for . . . statesmanship:*

it has been one of the worst illusions of radical and idealistic thinking that politics and statesmanship (dubious if not evil things) ought to be and would be superseded by rational institutions, open diplomacy, and the sovereignty of peoples. There never will be nor can be this substitution, and this is one of the important lessons to have been learned from the attempts to translate eighteenth century (and Wilsonian) ideals into practice. Of course politics and statesmanship are profoundly qualified by institutions and popular power, and the job is to exert this influence more intelligently and systematically, which presupposes full appreciation of the nature of politics and the role of statesmanship.

9. *a comprehensive settlement:*

chiefly because unless there is an equal will to seek a settlement in *all* areas of tension, temporary disengagement in one area may be feared on one side and desired on the other as facilitating ambitions elsewhere. See, e.g. Michael Howard's Penguin Special *Disengagement in Europe* (1958). 'It seems impossible to hope for a settlement in Europe as an isolated act.'

CHAPTER VI

Order and Progress

ARGUMENT

HUMAN PROGRESS by the spread of enlightenment and emancipation was the gospel of eighteenth century missionary humanism which makes no converts today. Yet scientists cultivate daily great acquisitions and push the frontiers of knowledge abroad and make more widely available increasing resources, and machine industry has a like momentum and expansion, and administration does not lag far behind, and backward peoples demand their freedom and strive to gain their share in the use and enjoyment of this modern science, industry, and administration. Enlightenment and emancipation are still making the future, and we can see plainly enough the rough-hewn ends we have to shape in the present historical phase.

What the eighteenth century thinkers underestimated was the class and national appropriations of the universal benefit which they expected to flow from this expansion of science and industry and the freedom which promoted it and which it promoted. If this strife goes on, the worse possibilities of the already fashioned future will be realized. This does not mean that intellectual development and techniques have outstripped moral development, for the moral question can hardly be raised so long as the international anarchy persists. An institutional solution of this problem is absolutely requisite not only to avert the universal calamity of total war but also to release the universal benefit of science and industry.

However, although this benefit is in universal demand, there is no assurance that it will increase virtue and happiness; and there is present evidence that its consequences are disliked as regimentation and feared as social rejection. In this sense we live after Utopia, that we are bogged in the consequences of progress, not riding on high hopes of it. Nevertheless, the life of one's own which is a legitimate personal aspiration and a social imperative is not to be gained by a retreat to individualism, nor by escape into personalism, but only by social advance through organization and education. Parallel to this, our political thinking has left behind speculation and declaration and is engaged in empirical studies and analysis, disclosing what we have and what we are doing. By these means it becomes possible

*to formulate the general method by which to perfect what we have
and what we are doing, and so to enter into possession of a society
advanced far in the making. But the primitive methods still employed by nations living in the state of nature warn the intelligence
of man of a universal tragedy advanced far in the making.*

*The last word has not been said. It remains possible to learn
from experience. In general, the thinking of an earlier phase can be
brought up to date in the light of results. In particular, the notion
of a set of laws or of institutions which could reconcile and regulate
all interests and the notion of laws of historical development can
usefully be replaced by the concept of informed social planning in a
democratic regime integrated into the concept of self-advancing
social processes mutually advancing one another in a universal
order. This complex concept is close enough to current practices
and trends to be a guide to action and a vision of the better possibilities of the rough-hewn future.*

I. DECLINE AND FALL

The professor of history whose lectures I was attending at the time
when Dean Inge was debunking the Victorian idea of progress exclaimed with exasperation, 'Of course there is progress: why, the
Swiss army today would defeat Julius Caesar.' Since then this progress has hurried on down, and although a child, suitably trained,
could now not only construe *Caesare duce* but also defeat his legions
single-handed, there are stiff-necked people still demanding a sign.
Would the professor, whose picturesqueness has, alas, vanished, accept that his argument had suffered a *reductio ad absurdum*? Might
he not have clinched his point: science is even forcing us out of war,
and threatening nations with the happiness of having no history
and professors with the inconvenience of having no employment?
For since the invention of gunpowder the application of science to
the art of war has seemed to philosophers to be progressive. It gave
wealthy and civilized nations an easy security against poor and
barbarous tribes, an advantage they did not enjoy in Roman times,
and of course brought barbarians into the imperial fold. 'The invention of fire-arms, an invention which at first sight appears to be so
pernicious, is certainly favourable both to the permanency and to
the extension of civilization,' wrote Adam Smith. Science applied to
war, Condorcet recalls, abolished the knight, the militarist, and he
hoped that it would abolish militarism, because it had given the
nations security and a footing of equality through permanent con-
federations, and they would learn that their interests had nothing to

gain and everything to lose by commercial wars, even more certainly than they had learned the ruinous futility of religious wars.
It is this development of the argument for the progressive consequences of science which has in our time reached the zenith of
unanswerable logic and the nadir of practical nullity.

The arguments of eighteenth century philosophers, however,
were not confined to nor concentrated upon the abolition of war
as the promise and sign of progress. The improvement of agriculture
and of manufactures, the extension of foreign commerce, the ac-
quirement of higher proficiency in the arts and sciences, these
universal consequences of the division of labour and discovery of
the method of inquiry were 'real improvements of the world we
live in'; mankind was benefited, human nature was ennobled by
them, and it was the purpose of, say, Adam Smith or Condorcet to
describe the conditions on which these benefits and dignities were to
be had and how they were to be used to general advantage.

The basic document for the idea of progress is still Condorcet's
Sketch for a Historical Picture of the Progress of the Human Mind,[1]
his testament written in hiding from the Terror. After all the
debunking of the idea of progress, it can be intelligently read today
with the utmost respect.

'We observe that the labours of recent ages have done much for the
progress of the human mind, but little for the perfection of the
human race; that they have done much for the honour of man,
something for his liberty, but so far almost nothing for his happiness. At a few points our eyes are dazzled with a brilliant light; but
thick darkness still covers an immense stretch of the horizon.'*

This is the perfect summing-up at the end of the eighteenth
century from the point of view of a man versed in all the knowledge of his time who valued scientific philosophy above everything
and valued it for its importance to the great mass of the human race,
whose interests constitute 'the true subject matter of philosophy'.
Condorcet looked back on the stormy passage of the small number
of enlightened and free nations to the degree of civilization they
enjoyed, and traced the reasons why the progress of the mind had
not always resulted in the progress of society towards happiness and
virtue. In his time, the progress of philosophy and of the dissemina-
tion of enlightenment had reached the stage when its influence upon
public opinion 'ceases to be a slow, imperceptible affair, and
produces a revolution in the whole order of several nations, a
* Condorcet, p. 169.

certain earnest of the revolution that must one day include in its scope the whole of the human race'. The doctrine of the indefinite perfectibility of the human race ('of which Turgot, Price and Priestley were the first and most brilliant apostles') was necessary to consolidate these tendencies and give reason the vision and faith to combat obscurantist and conservative philosophies that resisted and opposed the movement of enlightenment and emancipation.

In his final chapter 'The Tenth Stage', Condorcet considered 'The future progress of the human mind', this indefinite perfectibility of which his predecessors had written. His hopes he subsumed under three heads: 'the abolition of inequality between nations, the progress of equality within each nation, and the true perfection of mankind.' By the first he meant the attainment in due course by all nations of the enlightenment and freedom enjoyed by the most civilized. By the second he meant that the social art would succeed in time in achieving a real equality, 'in which even the effects of the natural differences between men will be mitigated and the only kind of inequality to persist will be that which is in the interests of all and which favours the progress of civilization, of education, and of industry, without entailing either poverty, humiliation, or dependence'. By the third he meant betterment of the human race (1) by discoveries in the arts and sciences as means to individual welfare and general prosperity, (2) by progress in the principles of conduct and in practical morality, and (3) by improvement in the faculties of man, either by the perfection of instruments or genetically. He puts as a question whether nature or the conditions of civilization had set limits to progress in this sense under these heads, and found in past progress evidence for believing that there are no limits. He went on to discuss prospects under these heads, and the policies by means of which the progress might be brought about, anticipating remarkably so much that has since been achieved. The whole work is but the hasty outline of a project put forward by a man hounded to death, but it bears the vital impress of the brilliant, spirited, generous Condorcet.

In his Introduction and in the final chapter, Condorcet drew on the analogy of the physical sciences to warrant his essay in sketching 'with some pretence to truth, the future destiny of man on the basis of his history'. Comte flattered this project with enthusiastic imitation, and himself with the idea that, unlike Condorcet, he had formulated the laws of historical development with scientific exactitude and certainty, and thus settled a new science on permanent foundations. Condorcet looked for, and Comte found, the general laws directing social phenomena in necessary uniformities in the development of the intellectual and moral faculties of man. Marx argued that the necessity was not in any order of ideological succession but in the need to provide the material means of life; the successive methods by which this was organized provided the clue to the necessary order on which the future could be predicted with scientific exactitude and certainty. In both cases, science was the means of progress, but in the one case this proceeded by enlightenment and education, in the other by technological and political revolution. Equally, Herbert Spencer, claiming scientific exactitude and certainty, predicted social progress as necessary natural evolution which conservatives could do little to stay and radicals little to hasten: an inevitable long-term process which all parties might as well make up their minds to accept gracefully.

Since those days, ideas of moral and social development have been refined by further research and reflection, and their statement has been far more genuinely scientific and generally acceptable.[2] None the less, the notion is in ruins, and stirs little or no contemporary interest. The reasons are interesting and important. They are also many. Perhaps they can be comprehended under the two heads of academic and practical.

I will merely mention typical academic objections to the notion of progress. All arguments by which a formulation is attempted of exact laws of social development on the basis of history and by analogy with physical sciences are discredited.[3] The phenomena are too various and central identifiable features are too closely linked with too many variables for drastic simplification and highly general abstraction to prove useful and reliable in this case, and there is no possibility of experimental testing of such comprehensive theories. Similarly, arguments based on the analogy of the evolution of species are of little logical value, and have led to erroneous predictions. There are many linguistic difficulties. Chief of them is to make sense of the absolute use of the term. The notion of progress, like the notion of 'ought', is perfectly intelligible so long as it is used relatively: 'Disarmament negotiations have/have not made progress'; 'You ought to do this if you want that'. But 'progress' like 'ought', used absolutely makes an interminable, perhaps gratuitous, problem: 'If one believes in original sin one cannot believe in human progress'; 'You ought not to bear false witness'. Here one has to break down 'progress', 'ought' into more explicit terms, or else contend that they are ultimate notions which cannot be defined. This can be maintained much more plausibly in the case of 'ought' than in the case of 'progress'. One can hardly speak of progress without having in mind some ideal goal of history or at least some definite idea of improvement. The incompatibility of original sin with human progress, for example, entails some such judgement as that human behaviour will never, as a general rule, attain such restraint and disinterestedness as will enable men to live together in harmony. The ideal goal or limited idea always implied in the notion means either that the concept of progress varies with the presuppositions held (Christian progress is achieved in the preaching of the gospel to all mankind, marxists expect it by the dictatorship of the proletariat everywhere, the romantic socialist looks forward, or back, to *News from Nowhere*, and so on), or else that the progress in question is a particular and partial improvement or advance, say, material progress or scientific progress. Thus there are no difficulties in using the word 'progress' relatively and nothing but difficulty, and perhaps no sense, in using it absolutely.

On the practical side, the utility of the notion has also declined. The purpose it served as the slogan of rationalists and radicals against the forces of tyranny and superstition is now mainly if not only the purpose of convinced marxists, and it survives mainly if not only in the marxist version. Apart from doctrinaire or romantic socialists, others mostly feel that indubitable material and scientific progress is a mixed blessing, and that the age of universal co-operation for the resolution of common problems and the amelioration of the human lot not merely seems as far aff as ever but, rather, is now seen to be for ever beyond reasonable human aspiration, since it is clear that man is not rational and moral by nature, given a chance, that his release from the power of kings and priests who kept him in bondage and ignorance or from capitalists and land-lords or from any and every particular frustration does not have the proclaimed and expected consequences. Secular sectarians there are, but most people, it can be fairly stated, have no vital faith in man which they feel they must uphold against visible but doomed enemies who hold him down or keep him back. If it is felt, however obscurely, that man given every possible chance will continue to give the same performance as an average human being, the notion of progress breaks down into expectations of improvement in those standard performances for which records are indeed broken every day; and these, although they are watched with great interest and acclaimed by the many, would hardly, even in the aggregate, be written down by any as human progress *tout court*.

A notion that has lost both its rationality and its utility does not survive. Practice is the tribute which twentieth century superiority pays to eighteenth century common sense.

Nevertheless, when leading academics have stamped on the idea and it has been trampled by the intellectual herd, and when ordinary thoughtful people do not trouble themselves about the idea, unless sometimes a little ruefully, the last word has not necessarily been said. It may not be simply splendid that there is no general and reasonable secular faith, not confined to doctrinaire or romantic sects. Indeed, unless such a faith is recovered and kept in repair, the mythical marxist version must prevail. At this time of day, we do not look for a new renaissance nor reformation, nor new industrial nor political revolutions. Contemporary intellectual, moral, and social changes have been and are vast and fast enough. What we most need is to know how with reasonable confidence to act effectively and work hopefully for possible and worthwhile achievements in the social field, so that there is a favourable climate and a permanent context for our personal endeavours, otherwise in some way frustrated and in some sense illicit. Is any such faith entirely groundless in sober estimates? Is there sense and prospect in the advancement only of science, and not also of that learning which results in cumulative changes in behaviour?

2. ENLIGHTENMENT AND EMANCIPATION REVISITED

To go back to Condorcet's text, for there is much in it superior to Comte's attempt to better it, and one must try to assess the strength and the weakness of the position if one is to revalue one's own hopes and fears and redirect one's practical efforts. First, however, there is the point to be considered that, *a priori*, enlightenment and emancipation *are* the conditions of human advancement, on the assumption, that is, that human dignity consists in personal spontaneity and integrity, in human nature managed by reason. Only in so far as men are informed and able responsibly to make or mar their lives are they distinctively human: knowledge is peculiarly sacred as the condition of humanity. This recognition coupled with the perception that knowledge is cumulative and irreversible ('Ignorance', remarked Tom Paine, 'is of a peculiar nature: you can keep man ignorant, but you can't make him ignorant') founded if it did not justify the faith of the Enlightenment. Of course, it was a much earlier recognition, which is enshrined in the myth of the Garden of Eden. Once man had eaten of the fruit of the forbidden tree, he was a changed creature, forfeiting his primal privilege of ignorance and innocence, thrown on his own responsibility, aided and guided in his stormy, difficult, tragic existence only by the light he had acquired, the sole source and resource of his changed status, unless visited and redeemed by his Creator. The myth which in one form or another celebrates the birth of civilization seals the unique and sacred function of knowledge. The Enlightenment sought and thought to transform the myth into a concept which would furnish reason in its full impersonality as the demiurge of civilization, recognized if not worshipped. The equivocal question of happiness was not necessarily involved. Civilized nations, Condorcet allowed, 'may well seem to primitive races to be richer, more powerful, more educated and more active than they, but also more depraved, and, above all, unhappier; and so savages, instead of being impressed by the superiority of civilized nations, must often have been terrified by the extent and multiplicity of their needs, by the torments they suffer through avarice, and by the eternal agitation of their always active and never satisfied desires'. Philosophers were divided on the question of whether the savage view of civilization was justified or not. Yet, regardless of his happiness, having ceased to be ignorant, as Tom Paine said, man could not be made ignorant again: knowledge, ever-increasing knowledge, was his tragic dignity and fate. To make this knowledge the source of increasing benefits was the duty of the enlightened and the hope of mankind, but knowledge itself was the superb and supreme benefit. Progress in knowledge was assured, and this was the most valid assurance possible of general progress, but in any case knowledge, as the condition both of their dignity and of their ability, was the highest term in which human beings could think of their advancement.

Knowledge was inseparable from freedom,[4] since it presupposed freedom of inquiry and of criticism, and because it increased practicability of purpose, revealed and multiplied alternatives, and imposed moral responsibility for choice and decision. Therefore it was the condition of human maturity, whether or not that was what it did in fact produce.

If this *a priori* argument that mankind is matured by progress in knowledge with its implicated freedom is countered from experience with the demonstration that men disuse and misuse this knowledge and freedom and are made worse by the establishment of these conditions of their perfection, and if, moreover, it is argued that in order to establish this knowledge it is necessary to multiply specialists and subdivide specialisms until perhaps informed men know far more about far less than informed men previously did, then part of the answer is that this knowledge and this freedom are not merely the knowledge and freedom of individual men and women but mainly a collective achievement, not necessarily an increase in the rationality and morality of men and women but an increase in the resources of mankind,[5] permanent, stored in institutions, and available for the making of more excellent patterns of personal and collective living, but not necessarily resulting in that, since it is also an enlargement of the possibilities of evil.

Put formally, what the eighteenth century called enlightenment and emancipation are necessary but not sufficient conditions of human progress. Perhaps philosophers of that period, in the midst of signal achievements and signs and portents of vast transformations, rashly concluded that they were both necessary and sufficient. But the truth is that the goal of progress is unattainable if it is to establish the sufficient conditions on which virtue, happiness, and cultural achievement necessarily supervene. There is no reason to hope that human life can be perfectly determinable.

3. CONDORCET'S ARGUMENT EXAMINED

Knowledge as meant by Condorcet was empirical verifiable knowledge built up on the principles of Locke's analysis. In itself, he noted, Locke's analysis was an immense emancipation, for it enabled men to understand the nature, objects, and limits of human knowledge, and the kind and degree of certainty that attached to any opinion, and thus set them free from the tyranny of authority and of tradition. This method could be applied to all the objects of human understanding, and would therefore show us how we got our moral ideas and what motives we have for conforming to them. The independence it gave men would be confirmed in education, whose chief function it would be to assure that independence, so that men were able and ready to profit by each other's ability and knowledge without there being a class of ignorant persons necessarily dependent on and exploited by men of superior ability and understanding. Such independence made the functions of law and government more simple and rational, regulating and reinforcing the natural interdependence of men instead of keeping some in subjection to others and providing remedies for the ill consequenes. Arts are the application of sciences, and laws and institutions, like the practice of morality itself, might reasonably be expected to come to perfection with the development of their corresponding sciences. When the social art had reconciled (identified) the interests of each with the interests of all, virtue would no longer be arduous nor temptation strong. This art was informed by a relevant science which made it clear what the social power ought and ought not to do.

'How, with all the astounding multifariousness of labour and production, supply and demand, with all the frightening complexity of conflicting interests that link the survival and well-being of one individual to the general organization of societies, that make his well-being dependent on every accident of nature and every political event, his pain and pleasure on what is happening in the remotest corner of the globe, how, with all this seeming chaos, is it that, by a universal moral law, the efforts made by each individual on his own behalf minister to the welfare of all, and that the interests of society demand that everyone should understand where his own interests lie, and should be able to follow them without hindrance?'

But *laissez-faire* must be supplemented by many public initiatives of an appropriate kind.

Above all, it is the interdependence and mutual reinforcement of all these factors of progress which is the dynamic of the movement. When Condorcet exclaims that 'nature has linked together in an unbreakable chain truth, happiness and virtue', it need not be supposed that he is naïve, or that this is the sentimental exuberance of the eighteenth century, for the genuine reciprocities to which he constantly refers are in effect as if nature had linked such desirable goods. Just as the several sciences further each other's progress continuously and cumulatively, and the whole system of human labour does the like, so 'All the causes that contribute to the perfection of the human race, all the means that ensure it must by their very nature exercise a perpetual influence and always increase their sphere of action'. It is this he is concerned to prove, and contends that he has proved, and 'in the great work' will elaborate. And it is from this that he concludes that the perfectibility of man is indefinite.

Sciences, education, industry, democratic institutions influencing and advancing each other continuously and cumulatively under the management of the social art which has learned how to release and regulate the energies of nature: that is the picture. But the picture, although a sketch, it too perceptive and sensitive, and too crowded and comprehensive, to be reproduced. The text is there, to be read and re-read, to explore the mind of the Enlightenment in one of its most attractive representatives.

When one reads such men as Diderot and Condorcet, with their dazzling mental gifts, generous humanity, and social enthusiasm, for whom knowledge, liberty, virtue, social sympathies and social intercourse, nature, the arts, respect for all men, are the only real goods that we possess, and who saw the future for all mankind in the prevalence of these cherished values, and when one turns from their dawn to our vulgar day of numbers and plenty, of collectives and commercials, of yesterday's Belsen and today's young hooligans and tomorrow's impending catastrophe, one sees writ large in the event all that which in their own day these enthusiasts believed would soon become old, unhappy, far-off things in the yellow pages of history. One then understands the malicious derision for these men in some quarters today. The golden age of humanism perhaps truly was in the Enlightenment, the dawn when it was bliss to be alive and very heaven to be young, before men could take the full measure of their problems or enter a sober assessment of the probabilities. But every period of history has its privilege and its burden, and to flee in spirit from one's own time is like embracing a faith which one cannot believe. Besides, to have lost faith in idealized notions of nature and human nature, which is the major difference between our day and the Enlightenment, need not be the same as to have lost faith in nature and human nature; what is merely darkness should not be assumed to be a dead-end. On the contrary, it is a necessary passage on the road of enlightenment. Our generation knows far more about the real humanity that is making its own future, and although there may always be in the real, unlike the ideal, much to fear or detest, there is always much that is unknown, discoveries which surprise and delight, features that are hidden: the real is the harsh or healing corrective and the inexhaustible resource, darker but deeper than any ideal or theory.

A realistic faith in nature and human nature survives a reading of, say, Condorcet in the light of subsequent experience and modern knowledge. His recognition of and insistence on the interplay and reciprocal reinforcement of the factors of progress, inducing a continuous, cumulative movement, is the dominant theme of his essay, and the foundation of his faith. This is entirely consonant with the analyses of a Schumpeter or Myrdal.[6] Science and capitalist expansion of industry may be in principle universal processes of increasing unlimited benefit to all men, as Condorcet or Adam Smith thought they were, but in the context of nationalist politics may be destructive. Or, as Myrdal insists, it may require nationalist policies to initiate expansion and establish the conditions on which the tendency to equality sets in. The social factors may further each other continuously and cumulatively in the spiral movement of progress, or in a spiral dive to disaster, or in a similar but slower process of deterioration. A decisive intervention or initiative or event may make the difference between progress and disaster or deterioration. Scientific advance, industrial expansion, education, democratic politics, are interacting social processes, but they are not neces-

sarily 'progressive' in the sense of being universally beneficial
natural processes in the way in which they were assumed to be so by
eighteenth century philosophers. They may or may not be universally beneficial, according to the social context in which they interact. The study of these conditions and consequences is the study to
which Condorcet's text read in the light of experience and modern
theoretical discussion would direct us.

One immediate positive result of being able to look at the situation in this way is release from the dilemma of having to choose
only between two very dubious beliefs as the alternative to chaos,
namely, belief in the power of human beings to replace with conscious purposes and rational social inventions the massive and
obscure movements of history, or belief in general laws of development which show that history is progressive. If the large-scale social
processes which make history and which cannot be halted nor
radically changed (like scientific and industrial development) could
nevertheless be appreciably controlled by a decisive intervention
initiating a calculated change in a particular factor (by a solution of
the defence problem, for example), which by its direct and indirect
and cumulative results would turn a vicious circle or a downward
spiral into a progressive trend, then the outlook would be altogether more favourable to disinterested aspirations.

4. 'PROGRESS' REPHRASED

What, then, is recoverable, if anything, in the idea of progress? Not
a philosophy of history. The quest for a philosophy of history might
be, and usually is, rejected as 'historicism',[7] historical determinism,
a rejection of confused notions of scientific 'law'. With this goes
rejection of the concept of the uniform ascent of man by well-
defined necessary stages from primitive to civilized states. The
comparative method in cultural anthropology has shown no uniformity, but divergence and differentiation leading to distinct and
and distinctive civilizations, together with cases of convergence and
assimilation, by cultural diffusion or borrowing, a process impossible
in organic evolution and characteristic and decisive in cultural
evolution. If at the present time as a total outcome of world history
there is visibly on foot a world-wide convergence of social development, an assimilation of all cultures by the diffusion of the
scientific-technological complex of techniques, that is a general
trend which has to be accepted, in the sense that this is happening,
will probably continue to happen, and cannot in practice be halted.
That it had to work out in this way, that this is 'the meaning of

history,'[8] may be true, but it does not help with the present nor the future.

Neither is a detailed forecast of the future what is wanted in place of the idea of progress. Such forecasts carefully argued on defined and reasonable assumptions are undoubtedly worth attempting.[9] Only by this type of thinking can the technical problems ahead and human capacity and resources for dealing with them be brought to attention and discussion, and no social thinking can be adequately informed and responsible unless it bears in mind the results of such inquiries. Such forecasts, whether in the technological field or in social studies or in administrative departments, and whether for periods of five years or one hundred, might be regarded as specialized divisions and developments of such a view as Condorcet's general sketch, but entirely scientific as far as they go, and totally dissevered from any general doctrine of progress. They certainly serve the purpose of social control, and are no doubt generally regarded nowadays as far more relevant and reliable than any general doctrine.

Similarly, the targets for social action, the Five or Seven Year Plans, the social programmes, to which the forecasts may be preliminary, as deliberately intended phases of progress are not a substitute for nor a residue of a total doctrine of progress. Such social plans[10] aiming at some improvement may be thought of as taking place on the basis of certain understood and reliable uniformities and within the context of certain universal social processes. It is faith in these processes abstracted from philosophies of history, social forecasts, and social programmes that is now in question.

The advancement of agriculture and of manufactures and commerce, of the sciences and arts and of education, in a word, of civilization, seemed in the eighteenth century to be a universal benefit, 'real improvements of the world we live in,' diffusing its blessings at large, not limited to the particular nation promoting the advancement. Adam Smith* in a passage in which he notes all the familiar unneighbourly fear, mistrust, jealousy, and envy characteristic of the relations between nations, makes this remark on the universal benefit of improvements, and goes on: 'In such improvements each nation ought, not only to endeavour itself to excel, but from the love of mankind, to promote, instead of obstructing, the excellence of its neighbours.' He said any other sentiments were beneath the dignity of such nations as France and England; and he seemed to think that love of mankind, in this sense, would prevail with the spread of enlightenment. For this civilization was uni-

* *The Theory of Moral Sentiments*, pt. vi. chap. ii.

versal: the activities which constituted it furthered each other, and in furthering the interests of those who directly benefited, these activities indirectly benefited all, since they increased the human stock of knowledge, of capital, of skill, of wealth in all its forms, and of works of art. In this way, civilization was cumulative and progress inevitable.

The philosophers did not take seriously enough the class and national appropriations and monopolies of the social processes which they studied in their universality, processes which ceased to be universal in so far as they were appropriated. Whether, as Schumpeter argued, the nationalist economic policies in the form of imperialism were mistaken and a frustration of natural process or not, they happened, and created the world situation with its forces and stresses in which we find ourselves. These distortions of natural process, if that is what they are, formed in the matrices of old mercantilist national power states, is what we have to live and reckon with. The question of progress in the eighteenth century sense is whether modern civilization, this complex of social processes (the advancement of science, the production and diffusion of wealth, the spread of education, the diffusion and regulation of political power) can after all gain its 'natural' universality. It was assumed that these social processes belonged together in a harmony in which they all furthered each other continuously and cumulatively, and that the frustration of one could and would throw out all the others; so that if this harmony was not in fact found in contemporary society, there was supposed to be some crucial social change which would institute it and set the total process going: Hobbes's sovereign whose law made morality reasonable and made it prevail universally; *laissez-faire* which by removing the hindrances to individual enterprise allowed the operation of the 'invisible hand' which led men in seeking their own good to promote the general good more effectually than they could intend to promote it; the sovereignty of the people which selected and maintained only able, energetic, and honest rulers; the dictatorship of the proletariat which ensured a regime of plenty by taking over the economic machine without any interest but to produce for all. In each case, and whether the language used describes the harmony as natural or artificial, there is assumed to be some revolutionary or decisive change which will ensure that the social processes of industry, learning, morality, government become natural and easy and advance each other cumulatively in a way that it is beyond the wills of individuals either to promote or to frustrate. The question of progress today is the question of the validity of this type of argument. Was there ever anything in it, and if so what has been learned that can bring it up to date and restore a measure of faith in social processes beyond the helplessness of individual men and women?

5. THE CONCEPT OF UNIVERSAL
PROGRESSIVE SOCIAL PROCESS

The sense in which science is universal and progressive needs no elaboration. It is the universal form of knowledge in that it is built up by reference to and reliance on universal experience, and it constantly and consistently invokes the witness and abides the challenge of universal experience: it is essentially social and organized. It is progressive knowledge in that its verification and its applications lead continuously to further explorations and its extension. Science is universal progressive knowledge, and knowledge is universal and progressive in that it is the quest of all intelligent being and the condition of the development of mind. Indeed, science is the type and model of universal progressive social process. It was for that reason that it seemed to philosophers in the eighteenth century to bear human progress within itself.

Science, because of its universality, seemed to make of education a universal process, the communication of universal knowledge and of an understanding of its nature, methods, and tests. It was progressive in that it put in question all that had been formerly received by tradition and authority, and in that it made the mind ready for change and able to deal with the problems that change brought.

Industry is universal not merely in being necessary in some form everywhere and always for the subsistence of man, but now mainly in sharing by direct dependence the universality and progressiveness of science. The methods of a machine-power economy with mass standard products are obviously spreading throughout the world and displacing previous methods and products; and the mass products are being continuously improved in economy of production and therefore in price and availability, and in the number of types of goods offered and of materials used.

Finally, the sense in which the democratic process of government is, or has been thought of as, universal and progressive needs a few words. It is universal in the most obvious way in being inclusive, referring to the whole people, even when requiring submission to majority rule, since this is qualified by respect and safeguards and opportunities for minorities. It has a moral universality in the sense that personal freedom, mutuality, equal submission to laws that are ultimately a product of agreement, is the basis and sanction of moral responsibility, and not mere submission to traditional authorities backed by personal or sectional coercion. Democratic government is a process and progressive in that it has an ideal tendency towards full integration and perfect agreement, which in practice is embodied in the continuous growth of recognized public interest.

The interplay of these universal progressive social processes is in some aspects obvious, although in detail such interplay is complex and a suitable subject of extensive investigation. Thus, scientific research in its practical applications furthers industry and technical achievements which in turn stimulate and facilitate scientific research. Both require and help to sustain a universal educational programme, making more and more effective use of the nation's intelligence and talent, which in turn furthers scientific and industrial advance. These social processes are clearly reciprocal and cumulative.

The influence of the democratic process on these other three in a social complex is not merely to further and be furthered by them in a similar way. Totalitarian methods of social organization may, by giving priority to these processes and mobilizing all social resources for them, under compulsion, advance them more rapidly, and may in turn itself become more efficient in this purpose. The influence of the democratic process is in tending to maintain a balance of interests, by means of the independent organization and representation of all interests in the community. The workers, for example, by means of their independent organizations can take care that their interests are not sacrificed to mere efficiency, service of the impersonal, universal progressive processes, that their conditions of work and life are humanized, made more favourable to the satisfactions they desire. At the same time, other interests and requirements have their influence, and the democratic process is an attempted reconciliation of all such interests and requirements.

Not least, the democratic process influences education. As the means by which society reproduces itself, with its own peculiar features and traditional culture, education is not a universal and progressive social process. In so far as it merely serves science and industry by selecting and training its personnel, it is not an independent universal social process. But in so far as education is based on child-study, on norms of development, and is adapted to the needs and possibilities of the individual child, so that he is enabled to make the most of himself as a human being and of the opportunities he is afforded, it approximates to a universal process based on the human being as an individual who is not merely to be adapted to certain requirements but who is mainly to be enabled to become himself, unique and original, and who is to have room in society to be himself. Education in this sense comprehends what used to be called natural rights or the rights of man more rationally and radically than any political concept or programme could. At the same time, education as a universal process of this kind is dependent on democratic process, since it is possible only in a society in which education of the masses for themselves and for leisure is possible; in turn, it contributes to the democratic process education for co-operation and tolerance. In such a society, therefore, science and industry are used currently for improving the environment for use and enjoyment, for humane values, for life.[11]

These four social processes in conjunction, then, show a marked tendency to improve the conditions of living for most people, and in this sense together, in conjunction, they constitute the condition of human progress in a society.

However, human progress is a universal concept, the progress of the human race. There is, indeed, nothing exclusive, closed, provincial about these four social processes taken in conjunction in an actual social complex: they are modern, universal, progressive, open, humane, cumulative, expanding in the increase and spread of their benefits. Nevertheless, these processes are inevitably regulated by national policies, which are liable to frustrate the universality of their benefit. A situation which induces the nations to make power the prime object of policy enlists science, industry, education, and, as the situation becomes urgent, all independent organizations for the national purpose. All the social processes cease to be universal and progressive in so far as they are engaged in promoting a nation's power to make war for the sake of its safety, for they help to make the situation in which all nations, to obtain this power, consume resources which increase vastly with the development of their science, industry, and education, and thereby vastly increase insecurity, and thereby intensify the devotion of resources vastly to national power. At any rate, an arms race is not only a handicap on the progress of the nations, but in the end an absolute bar to it: they are as alternative as heaven and hell.

It is this competition for national power, because of mutual fear and general insecurity as well as ambition, an age-old dilemma as well as the old Adam,[12] that has prevented and still prevents real fulfilment of the promise of human progress. This frustration was not and could not have been removed by any of the old prescriptions, not by education and the spread of enlightenment, not by political revolution and the sovereignty of the people, not by free

trade, not by the dictatorship of the proletariat. All these attempts at
universality, these bids for achieving the release of human energies
and the harmony of human interests, whatever they did achieve,
were of no ultimate avail because they did nothing about the
universal situation which perpetuated the need for national power
and stimulated the bid for preponderant national power.

If this situation is resolutely tackled and dealt with in our time,
if the problem of world order is solved, in the sense that national
armed power and imperialism become a closed chapter of history,
and armaments are pooled under a world authority for international
security, so that force is used only to suppress the use of force, then
not only will the four social processes in the countries in which
they are already established in conjunction tend to gain their full
universal and progressive character, but also the whole complex
will tend to establish itself with the spread and development of
industry and science throughout the world. The convergence of development and the assimilation of cultures, making use of and developing international institutions, will be a process towards a
consummation in a universal progressive human culture.

This realization of the vision of Condorcet waits on a solution of
the problem of defence, with which the aggressive and destructive
character of nationalism is bound up. What is required is not an
impossible change of human nature, but a reasonable solution of a
universal and urgent problem for which means and motives are not
lacking. A solution will not exorcize the old Adam and start the
withering away of politics, but it can break the old dilemma and
make international co-operation reasonable. The problem was discussed in the previous chapter. Whether mankind will be capable
of resolving this supreme crisis is the question of the age. But the
responsibility is fairly ours. We know what the situation is, what
the alternatives are, and the power and opportunity to make a
decision that will be effective are tormentingly ours. The torment is
not one of indecision, but the oppressive uncertainty of those who
understand the importance of the decision that enough will soon
enough be brought to share their conviction of what is absolutely
required.

6. INTERPRETATION OF PROGRESS

Assuming, however, that such universal and progressive processes
can be so stabilized in a society that each furthers the universality
and progression of the other, and that the conditions of international
mutuality are institutionally established, what is there in the

character of universality and of progression that is necessarily of value? Art or religion or philosophy is not universal nor progressive in the sense in which science or industry is. Does the idea of progress not entail repudiation of permanent values?

The answer is that it does not, for the following reasons. The argument is not that science and industry, education and democracy are of value in virtue of their universality and progression, or, in other words, that all universal and progressive things are of value. Nor is it even that it is of the character of science and industry, education and democracy, to be universal and progressive, and therefore they are not what they ought to be unless they are so, and their value is in proportion to their being so. These arguments may or may not be justifiable. The argument in the present case, however, is simply that these social processes form a complex which should now become universal and progressive, by being released from the distortion of national power policies, if they are not increasingly to prove vicious and disastrous, that they can continue to serve human life only as a universal and progressive complex. Further, the argument holds that the integration of these processes in this sense is being facilitated by certain trends and the conditions of it can be achieved by certain policies, for which there are strong motives and sufficient means.

Thus the question of whether arts and religions or philosophies embody permanent values in their singular concreteness and/or have their own forms of universality and progression need not be raised here. Indeed, it may be assumed that the historical past is not superseded by an improved state of things in the present, as obsolete science and industry are continuously superseded. For it is not merely works of art, because of their concrete singularity, that resist time and enjoy permanent value. They are not to be separated from the social complex in which they are found. Even the obsolete theories are of some permanent interest and importance. Historical study itself (in so far as this is not included in science) has its own universality and progression, which match the convergence of social development and the assimilation of cultures. But this universality and progress of history are not defined and measured by success in demonstrating the necessity and the sequence of this convergence of social development and this assimilation of cultures: they are realized in the accuracy and completeness of the discovery of the past, and in the reconstruction of the past in all its inexhaustible and incommensurable concreteness as a common human possession, for utility and for imagination, for human consciousness. History in itself is a concrete human resource (like science or industry) available to anyone who can or will avail himself of it for any purpose, and can never be resumed in a philosophy of history, which is a mere abstract idea which must ever be neither universal nor progressive. It is in the perpetual relevance and renewal of history that the permanence and relativity of all things are reconciled; and it is because of this inexhaustible permanence and relativity of all things that there is no absolute, and therefore no perfectibility. The notion of progress must always abide this limit. But this limit is not a limit of life nor of thought. On the contrary, an absolute as the goal of progress would be the limit of life and of thought. If there is no such limit, there is a limit to the notion of progress. This limit means that 'real' progress must be compatible with a situation in which nothing is finally superseded and nothing finally attained, in which past, present, and future co-exist in a continuously new context.

Here it is useful to consider a statement of the kind of view which in our time has taken the place of faith in progress with many reflective and sensitive minds.

'Nothing in the relation of man and the world suggests an established harmony. Insecurity, care is our lot. Nothing gives us any reason to think that this struggle can end soon, nothing encourages us to doubt that it is what makes our situation. The perfection of the world of mankind, then, is not the perfection of an order, as all those philosophies and political ideals would have it which think that man can one day unite the world. It is the perfection of a liberty which fights and is hard pressed.'*

This insight, with its disillusionment and renunciation of hope, its rejection of utopia and acceptance of the tragic structure of action, its embrace of risk and uncertainty as the climate of thought and action, is highly characteristic of our age. Is it a genuine insight, or merely romantic revolt? A reformulation of the idea of progress should provide an adequate critique of this position which has been reached by a rejection of the older humanist faith in progress.

That the divine cannot be organized and possessed, domesticated and administered, may be an important and necessary discovery for the religious mind; and that the perfection of mankind is not the perfection of an order may be an important discovery for the humanist: but this discovery may result in a renewal of the church for the Christian and in a renewal of faith in the possibility of progress for anyone. For it is the perfection of an order which assists,

* Emmanuel Mounier: *Le Personnalisme*, p. 33.

which does all that is humanly possible to assist, the variety of human perfections. There is no reason to think that man can one day unite the world, in the sense of making all men members of Christ or party comrades, or simply human brothers. But there is no sense in thinking that the world cannot and will not be united in the support and operation of certain common institutions by means of which all peoples participate in the maintenance of world security and in the development and regulated use of human resources. There is room for difference in the amount of faith one may have in the power of these conditions to favour and foster (not to produce) human achievements of final value; but one can hardly fail to recognize the far-reaching transformation of the situation the achievement of these conditions would mean.

To the angry young men, then, of yesterday and today, in haste for progress or finding and looking for none, the answer is that those who the day before yesterday thought that the sweeping away of kings and priests and who yesterday thought that the clearing out of tory dunderheads would remove the obstruction to an upsurge of human progress, failed to take the measure of the problem. For the feeling that hopes have been mocked, that the trumpet has sounded and the walls have not fallen, that Church and State are as they were, that the old-new ideas have been accepted and assimilated and no longer have the power to shock nor shake, yet everything remains standing as before, with the age-old ideas inconsistently mixed with the old-new, so that Darwin and Freud, Shaw and Wells, have spoken in vain, and there is cultural and social and moral confusion, hypocrisy, uncertainty, disintegration: for this feeling, there is no mollification because no justification. Actually, there has been far-reaching social change, progressive in character, progressive in the sense of increasing human resources, and this has indeed been forwarded by necessary revolutions and shocking ideas, but neither new ideas nor even new legislation can do more than register the provision of new opportunities for actual achievement in day to day operations on every front of human activity. Therefore, to be looking still for revelations and revolutions when it is really possible to hide, even to lose, one's egoism in anonymous unhistorical constructive work in so many open fields, is what to be young and angry means in the present situation—if it were not that progress in human resources has meant unparalleled increase in human insecurity, the unresolved paradox that puts all in question as in jeopardy.

The answer to angry young men is not a verbal retort. They remain invulnerably in the right unless they manage to learn for themselves the inescapable conditions of human existence, and to discern what is feasible and what is not, and the different requirements of successive phases of a situation, and, not least, contentment with the anonymity of effective work, in which all structural changes, ideological or social, are justified or not.

But the theological critic can be met with a simple verbal answer. The kingdom of heaven, the Christian community of loving persons, can, of course, be had only on Christian terms, the surrender to God in faith, with consequent release from self and servitude to mundane interests, through the sufficiency of the divine love. This must, of course, be fully allowed. But it is not allowable to argue that because the kingdom of heaven cannot be achieved by secular means, no far-reaching transformation of human behaviour can be achieved by such means.

Here it is relevant perhaps to enter a criticism of some contemporary sociologists, who may not be Christians but who are influenced by religious tradition and by modern personalism centred in the I-Thou relationship, who would re-focus social relations on the concept of 'love'. This may have the effect of obscurantism, concealing the need for analysis, information, discrimination. It is true that in classical political philosophy friendship is higher than justice and a model for social relations, just as in religious tradition love is above the law. This stress may be needed to counter legalism in an actual situation, as in the Palestine of Jesus, or to mitigate impersonal giant organization, as in our own day, the twin evils of collectivism and individualism; but in real life neither personal love nor friendship is due to everyone from everyone, and what may be specifically due to a given person from a given person in a given situation is rather more specific and more universal, payment of a grocery bill or justice, kindness, respect, charity. This is not merely a quibble or a linguistic refinement, for the difference indicates different moral ideals and different psychological assumptions. For example, Freud's analysis of group relations, on the model of the army and the church, equal dependence of all on a leader who embodies their common ego-idea, differs profoundly from Buber's, the unique I-Thou relationship as a model for all community.[13] 'Brotherhood' or 'love' is not a simple concept, neither psychologically nor morally. If one thinks of the structure of social relationships in terms of these concepts, nothing can be expected except romanticism or polemics.

7. MEASURES AND LIMITS OF PROGRESS

To sum up, now, in a statement of what justifiable faith in human progress might mean today. Everybody admits the progress of science and industry, in the sense that human knowledge is steadily, sometimes rapidly, becoming more detailed, reliable, extensive, and available the world over, and that industry in the advanced countries is becoming more productive and more technically resourceful, and that the educated people of underdeveloped countries are fully aware of the advantage and the necessity to their countries of scientific knowledge and modern industry and administration, and are determined to acquire them. Everybody admits the progress of education in this sense of the world-wide spread of scientific knowledge and of training in the skills and ways and virtues of industrial civilization. Everybody admits the progress of freedom, in the sense of the emancipation of colonial peoples, the self-assertion of backward races, the economic betterment of the poorer classes in industrial societies, and improvement in equality of opportunity. These are the facts of our time, and there might be a consensus of opinion that this progress which is going on rapidly is necessary to establish decent conditions of human existence. What is not agreed is that there are signs which are a pledge that these decent conditions will produce decent human existence. These conditions may be necessary, they can never be sufficient, and perhaps therefore they are not so necessary.

This reading of the situation has many general formulations: for example, *plus ça change, plus c'est la même chose*; intellectually we have become adult and morally are still children; the social sciences lag behind the physical sciences; men are flawed with original sin and can never create a utopia; the control man has secured over Nature has far outrun his control of himself. Such *obiter dicta* are perhaps not intended to advance us much further. Far more important are the attempts to voice the distresses or to analyse the phenomena which have been the results so far in the advanced industrial societies of the material progress which, it is agreed, is rapidly taking place. Many who are supposedly its beneficiaries do not like it, or dislike it as much as they like it. Social mobility, equality of opportunity, these are agreed social goals, as dear to political tories as to socialists, not only because they are demanded and have been promised, but also because the pressures of a technical age require prudent systematic investment in the nation's intelligence. But the emotional results can be ravaging. If the stress of society is on selection and climbing, and people are routed on to escalators or directed down the lower corridors, failure is conspicuous, noted, and irretrievable, a social award, and there is no independent way up, little chance for the individualist, the latecomer, the misfit, and, always, at the bottom the solid mass of re-jects. The lucky ones, parting from their less fortunate associates, able and willing at every stage to conform to standard requirements, have been channelled along established routes and raised to upper levels, where they are still required to conform but may not always be accepted. This organized educational equality of opportunity in a mass industrial society, selecting, promoting, and rewarding specific types of ability, may serve industrial efficiency and cater to the aspirations of the docile majority of the able population, but at the cost, perhaps, of alienating outstanding individuals, occasioning the development of anti-social sub-cultures, destroying or damaging the nexus of affections and comradeship, and having to rely on a cadre of dubiously satisfied conformists. This is the contemporary picture of a collectivist individualist society, void of community and destructive of personality, the society against which Martin Buber or Erich Fromm has protested. It is an analysis of a social condition of which, in the eyes of some, Burke was the prophet, who cursed the reckless of his generation for wanting number to supersede property as the basis of politics. Anyhow, in so far as there is articulate discontent with conditions and trends in ad-vanced industrial societies, we are not now dealing with theories and speculations; and recriminations are ignorant and pointless.

Effective political thinking is concerned with the better and worse possibilities of the accepted trends summed up in the first paragraph of this section. The worse possibilities might be summed up as Cold War and Organization Man; the better possibilities as Collective Security and a Life of One's Own. If rival armed systems preside over the inevitable advance of backward peoples, progress is indeed to be greatly feared. It is in the context of collective security only that this rivalry could come nearer to what Mr Kennan, in his Reith lectures, would have it be, a civilized pursuit of different social ideals.

'Man is a wolf to man.' 'Man is to man a sacred thing.' Neither of these truths can be disputed on historical evidence. Were a world-wide collective security system to be instituted, man might cease to be a wolf to man on the past scale. There are wolves in sheep's clothing; and even sacred things may be worshipped with more de-votion than intelligence. A world order might give the green light to organization. The patriarchal corporation, the welfare state, the philanthropic society, the human providence, might produce an airless climate of total security at the price of total conformity. Sensitive recoil is drastic and futile. That one is one among many is a basic necessary acceptance. Persons are highly exposed: in their bodies, in their affections, in their aspirations. They cannot retreat from these fronts without withdrawing from their humanity. In so far as, like the Stoics, they try to rely solely on self-protection, they are forced to abandon the means and the meaning of life. Risks are unavoidable if we would live, and it is by social means that they are reduced. If these social means tend to excessive function, if they overdo it, the remedy is social counter-measures, not personal recoil and withdrawal: countervailing organization, wider personal participation in the responsibilities of an organization, fuller organizational participation in the making and working out of social policies directed to individual use and enjoyment of what is made available, and to the encouragement of personal and social experimentation.

One is one among many, and the many are very many. Organization is as necessary as science, as inevitable as science, a cultural achievement and the basis of cultural power. This new 'secondary environment' supplies the social disciplines which supersede the old rough rewards and punishments of the frontier or of *laissez-faire* ('get on or get out', 'pay your way', 'hire and fire', 'work or starve'). Who administers these new disciplines of modern highly organized society? Parents and teachers, social workers and officials, managers and trade union leaders: that is to say, most people in some capacity. What kind of disciplines are they? The element of authority responsible for enforceable decisions is inevitably there; the element of example and the communication of standards ought to be there; but the most important and fundamental element in the new situation is the actual provision of facilities and opportunities and assistance and encouragement in their use, for it is by such means that people learn to acquire standards for themselves and are stabilized and made responsible by realistic aims, and only in so far as this happens can legitimate authority function legitimately or example and the communication of standards become efficacious. The more highly organized a society is, if the mechanism is sound, the more alert, sensitive, mutual, it is, charged with life and potentiality. It is then least like a herd. The disciplines which hold it together and regulate its functions are not one-sided, imposed from above, for they are reciprocal demands mutually enforced: I am dependable myself, I keep the rules; and I require you to do so, too.[14]

This would be all very well, it may be said, if things were working out like that, but the first fruits of plenty and welfare and easier conditions all round and the most highly educated generation ever are hooliganism and delinquency or puerile anger or dull compliance. On this, endless discussion is possible. No topic is better placed to touch off prejudices; the random firing has been deafening, and has not died down. Nothing has happened and nothing has been said with weight enough seriously to discourage what is being attempted. Newsworthy results of welfare and education policies are probably nothing of the kind, for the real results are difficult to assess and will take long to become manifest. Mistakes have been made, the first phases are crude and groping, there is a great deal to learn. Humanity is on trial, now and for long to come. Humanity is to have its chance: that is the meaning of post-war developments. *Noblesse oblige* has passed away, but *l'esprit éclairé s'oblige* can never pass away.

Although humanity is on trial in the sense of what over the generations the many and the few will be and will do, the means which will become available to them and the conditions of living may be expected, calculably, to improve: cultural resources will be increased, and it is by that index that progress is to be measured, and it is for that reason that humanity is on trial. The trial is by opportunity. What is to come, if the strategy of human advancement secures the turning-point of basic international order, is not only a broader front in the wider sharing of scientific knowledge and education, industrial goods and leisure, but also further advance into complete and reliable knowledge and in the invention and mastery of arts and techniques. What will be open to men is a vaster and more penetrating, more god-like, reach of consciousness, and the achievement of more integrated, tempered, capable, and dependable personalities, as well as more marvellous productions. Whether the increase in cultural resources which will make this development possible will have this result is in question. This is a question no man should presume to answer, for it is the personal freedom of man that makes it a question. Human behaviour is socially determinable up to a point: beyond that point are the personal achievements and failures which make and mar the historical record and the common day.

Even modest expectations should suffice. So long as the conditions can be controlled, and improved, on which this world continues to be a place in which human beings come into existence and to maturity, and are able in their multitude to warm their hands and play their parts, and in some cases to feel and to contemplate something of the magnitude of nature and of man, there is enough to satisfy reasonable hopes of men who have outgrown the heavens and hells and the utopias and nightmares of their childhood. But, again, no man can foretell what structures may not be built on the firm ground which secures these modest expectations.

It is sometimes held, against the notion of progress, that the future can hold nothing which has not been realized as well or better in the historical past, that human greatness has been consummately attained, human experience comprehensively explored, human feeling incomparably expressed. It was epicurean doctrine that once a man had learned to live well he had tasted all the good it was open to him to enjoy; life held no more, and death was no privation. Professor Butterfield, as a Christian, writes: 'And neither do I know of any mundane fulness of life which we could pretend to possess and which was not open to people in the age of Isaiah or Plato, Dante or Shakespeare'.* If this kind of statement is intended to remind us that we are not greater nor better than our forefathers or that simple human happiness is immemorial or that common sense can hold its own with every new form of sophistication, then a grateful bow is due for the reminder. But if it is intended to deny or to depreciate the increase of cultural resources by cumulative learning from experience, as an expansion and refinement of possibilities, as human advancement, as an addition to the sum of human good, then the author should be attacked as a pernicious deceiver and a corrupter of youth. To suppose that the great systems of society are merely the framework of human activity, the indifferent circumstances in which men play their part worthily or ill, that the style is all, is, of course, to make God the judge and history a probation. There is more in heaven and earth than is dreamed of in that philosophy. When it was said here that humanity is on trial, that is not at all what was meant, the perverted moralism of that view is here rejected with abhorrence, as a poor and pointless theme for human living. In the first place, the social constructions by means of which the precious fruits of learning from human experience are cultivated and transmitted are themselves among the greatest products of the human spirit, the chief witness to upward striving, the milestones on the way to intellectual and social control in the effort to achieve human self-determination and expansion. In the second place, the style, the achievement is not all, the content is of central importance. No doubt Shakespeare is unapproachable, perhaps Newton has no peer; but a modern sensibility is able to respond to Shakespeare's imaginative and expressive achievement in its own way and at the same time have its own freshness and subtlety conditioned by a later state of consciousness; and a modern physicist does not have personally to excel Newton to have a more penetrating understanding of the physical world. Humanity was here said to be on trial not in a limited sense of the probation of persons measured by a test of faith

* *Christianity and History*, p. 66.

R*

or faithfulness but in the extended sense of what uses will be made of the cultural resources accumulated by learning from experience and institutionalizing the results. These will be personal achievements and failures, but measured by multiplied or pioneered opportunity, and counting the results. Humanity is on trial before itself, and for what contributes to human use and enjoyment and to the expansion of human powers; not in God's balance, for an exhaustive reckoning under infinite scrutiny with each individual soul for its own account and for final justice. The social reckoning is not an inquisition but a result, statistical, but as important to mankind, and thus to every living soul, as the wrath (or the love) of God ever was.

8. EMPIRICAL POLITICAL PHILOSOPHY

Political thinking is occasioned by local and immediately pressing social problems, often aggravated by personal experience in the life of the thinker, but it has claims to general truth, it aspires to universality. The political problem in its highest generality might be said to be the reconciliation of men to themselves and to one another in society. There are theories which are centred on this reconciliation as an objective achievement, a goal of history, and there are theories which find the reconciliation for the individual immediately in the realization of an inward condition; and this difference between historical conditions and inward personal conditions, if it is not a difference between political philosophy and a moral or religious philosophy, is a capital division.

The Stoic philosophy or the Buddhist religion is a good example of this absolute reconciliation here and now of the person to all events and to all other persons. Whatever happens, acceptance, detachment, makes it indifferent; whoever comes, compassion, brotherhood, makes a fellow being, an inseparable identity: suffering and strife are displaced, the political problem is solved by abolishing the source of the trouble. Religious faith may be the secret of this attitude: whatever is, is good, because all things are divinely ordained; or the only reality is undifferentiated being, and therefore the sensorial political world is an illusion from which one should withhold acceptance. Or, possibly, secular nihilism may be at the bottom of this attitude: frustration and disillusionment are inevitable, there is nothing worth suffering nor strife. There are quietistic strains in Christianity which approximate to a personal solution of the political problem, but orthodox Christianity is insistently historical. Nevertheless, the idea that all moments are equidistant from eternity reduces the temporal conditions of human existence to a standstill and the value of action to example. Professor Butterfield, an historian, writes with his left hand a one-dimensional interpretation of history by discounting the value of the future, except as room for a repetition of the past.

The philosophies in which this reconciliation of men is conceived as objectively to be realized in history are primarily political. The reconciliation may be thought of as coming about by human action or by means of historical processes that transcend, although they involve, human action. In the latter case, political philosophy is absorbed in a philosophy of history of the hegelian type. In the former case, the political philosophy specifies the conditions on which the realization can take place, as does the *Republic* or *Leviathan* or *Brave New World* or, more generally, *laissez-faire* capitalism or doctrinaire socialism.

Here, again, Christianity is apart, for in the notion of the kingdom of God it prophesies an objective reconciliation which is a nonhistorical goal that transcends human action; at the same time, human wills are the issue, and the end may be realized within the heart and objectively anticipated in social approximations, whose conditions can be specified. This concept is rich at the expense of paradox, for the need to reconcile not only the necessary wisdom, power, and will of God with the necessary freedom and responsibility of man but also the necessary evidence of the Love of God with what would be worthy of God to invite response from the rationality of man, has imposed a heavy and cumulative tax on theological research.

How, then, does one arrive at a political philosophy? Unless one starts already with some metaphysical assumption about the world or with faith in a divine providence at work in history or with some *a priori* notion of the essence of justice or of the state or with some intuition of political or moral obligation, the answer must be that one learns from social experience; and then the question is, by what standard does one select and reject in interpreting and using social exerience, and how is it justified.

The abstract brief answer is that one both forms standards and justifies them by making comparisons, formulating practicable alternatives (without which no choice is in question), making decisions, giving reasons, and reasons for reasons, hearing objections and the case for alternatives, acting on informed decisions and consolidating, modifying, developing them in the light of new experience determined by them. In the political field, of course, one is not deciding and acting alone, but in co-operation or in conflict with others; and one is not simply testing some idea by publicly accepted techniques and universal criteria, but striving for the satisfaction of some interest or for some advantage. Now, even so brief and abstract a statement plunges one into history, into concrete situations with their choices determined by practicable alternatives, with their assumptions, ideas, and ideals, furnished by contemporary knowledge and current issues and possibilities. We are not now in the eighteenth century, and we have learned that the alternative to personal despotism or oligarchy is not the sovereignty of the people exercised through their elected representatives enacting their general will in the laws of the republic, that this ideal can be approached in practice only by way of the clumsy and frustrating devices and conventions of democratic procedure and party government. By this elaborate and established complex of means an accommodation of interests can be sought and maintained without the collapse of decision and responsibility. So precious an achievement constitutes a standard, and a public interest. This democratic order although established is precarious, and is most seriously threatened by imperfections in practice: what is done politically is always subject to judgement by democratic standards, not least procedural standards; and what is done is always open to improvement by a more conscientious and technically competent attempt to follow the model.

The technique of informed social planning as a sustained learning process stands here as the universal formal standard for the whole democratic order, exemplified equally in legislation and administration, industrial relations and economic policy. The determination of social experience by legislation, plans, policies, services, themselves determined jointly, mainly through their organizations, by the interests affected and with the information available, with the subsequent use of this experience in the re-determination of the legislation, plan, policy, service, for a further chapter of experience, is the form and technique of social self-determination which makes practicable the widest measure of social participation, and is likeliest to facilitate the greatest common measure of personal planning, that is to say, to enlarge for most people practicability of purpose, the substance of freedom.

Democratic procedures, conventions, and traditions, without which social planning is informed, so far as it is informed, only from above, belong only to the advanced industrial societies of the West in which they have been historically established, and, tentatively, to the new constitutions which have followed that general model.

The scientific movement, now world-wide in scope, is in the field of pure knowledge a cumulative learning from experience by the disciplined and organized practice of established techniques. Scientific research as a self-directing movement, a universal cultural inheritance, has developed in the course of three centuries from sporadic discoveries and piecemeal individual beginnings. Similarly, the industrial revolution which has issued in a world-wide conscious programme was in its day a summation of diverse inventions, ventures, and local conditions. These two, now integrated, movements, the common cultural language of mankind, are making the future; and although their course and consequences provoke individual protests and occasion anxieties, it is not fanciful to say that they constitute a common human consciousness and a general will. Of course it is fanciful to speak of these movements in the abstract, since they are inseparable from the social organizations in which they are embodied, and the general will to have and to hold science and industry, like the general will for peace, so inevitable in the abstract, turns out in the actual case to be a set of inevitable conflicts set up under the constraints of social situations. In particular, there are the opposed organizational forms of capitalism and socialism, gravely aggravated by international anarchy and rivalries. There is no reasonable doubt that an overdue institutional solution of the security problem would relax the situational constraints which condition these conflicts, and would facilitate an empirical resolution (not without conflict), of the capitalist-socialist opposition.

To say this is not to suppose that the issue is simply a question of efficiency in industrial organization. That would be, again, to make an abstraction from the actual situations. It is easy to see the advantage of totalitarian methods in forcing through a programme of rapid industrial development in backward countries (although the methods are not without serious disadvantages). It is easy to see that vested interests and obsolescent forms of social organization which stand in the way of science and industry cannot be venerated for ever. But once conditions of near-affluence and near-equality of opportunity and assured national security prevail in a society, the need to sacrifice to the future the past and the present cannot be urgent; and when this relaxation is possible, social planning begins to be informed by all relevant considerations and interests, actively represented, and not merely from above on technical calculations.

Thus the better as well as the worse possibilities of the public situation which oppresses so many today are plain enough. The meaning and value of a democratic order and the method of perfecting its practice are reasonably clear, and the conditions it requires are clear, and are attainable, and are perhaps being attained. The promise of such an order is both modest and maximum: modest because such social self-creation works with men as they are, and humanity is on trial; maximum because in so far as it is methodically practised it makes the utmost of the past, present, and future.

Political philosophy is limited to trying to show what ought to be done that can be done, and has negligible power to induce people who don't read it to want to do what ought to be done; but its readers, it may be assumed, are halfway of that mind anyhow. After all, they have nothing to lose but their worries.

NOTES: CHAPTER VI

1. *The Progress of the Human Mind:*
   tr. by June Barraclough, with an Introduction by Stuart Hampshire, 'Library of Ideas', 1955.
2. *Since those days:*
   there is a considerable literature on the idea of progress since J. B. Bury's *The Idea of Progress* (1920). From the Christian side it has been fashionable to say that the idea of progress is a secular version of either Jewish messianism or the Christian dramatic and Providential view of history, and that the idea is justifiable only in its proper Christian version (Christopher Dawson's *Progress and Religion*, 1929; John Baillie's *The Belief in Progress*, 1950; Herbert Butterfield's *Christianity and History*, 1949; and W. Stark's *Social Theory and Christian Thought*, 1959, ch. 1. sect. 2.). On the humanist side, there has been a sober reassessment, eliminating the spurious, contesting Christian misrepresentations and pessimistic judgements, and reaffirming a modest and reasoned belief in human powers of self-direction (Morris Ginsberg's *The Ideas of Progress*, A Revaluation, 1953; R. V. Sampson's *Progress in the Age of Reason*, 1956; Charles Frankel's *The Case for Modern Man*, 1957; Karl Popper's *The Open Society and its Enemies*, 1945, and *The Poverty of Historicism*, 1958.). Practical disillusionment with the idea of progress could be heavily documented. An extreme statement from the psycho-analytical side is David Eder's 'The Myth of Progress' (1932) reprinted in *David Eder*, ed. by J. B. Hobman, 1945: 'We are born mad, acquire morality and become stupid and unhappy. Then we die. This, the natural history of man under domestication, is so rigid a sequence under a variety of forms and changes in the patterns of civilization, that mankind has invariably found it helpful to find a refuge in myths to relieve its perplexity and to mitigate its unhappiness.' The other main source of pessimism has been economic and political analysis. See, e.g, Peter F. Drucker's *The End of Economic Man* (1939) or Raymond Aron's treatment of Burnham's *Managerial Society* in *L'Homme contre les Tyrans* (1944) pp. 325-42: 'Mais la fin des mythes ne doit pas être la fin de l'esperance.'
3. *laws of social development:*
   Popper makes an extensive examination of these arguments in *The Poverty of Historicism*, showing that there are neither laws of succession nor laws of evolution, and that unconditioned prophecies based on trends are not the same as conditioned scientific predictions based on ascertained

uniformities; these are laws of unlimited validity but of limited application and therefore impose limits upon the social reconstruction that relies
upon them; there is a scientific basis for 'piecemeal social engineering'
but not for 'holistic or utopian engineering' which proposes to remodel
a whole society in accordance with a plan, nor for predictions about the
'movement of society as a whole'. Popper here tries to show the limited
way in which the methods of the physical sciences can properly be applied
to social phenomena. Peter Winch in *The Idea of a Social Science* (1958)
argues that social phenomena are completely misunderstood if treated as
the same in kind as physical phenomena but more complex, to be
analysed and explained on the cause-effect model. He thinks he is con-
tradicting Popper, but the two arguments are, rather, at cross purposes.
Both may be regarded as abstractions from the concrete situation described in Chapter IV above, sects. ii-iv. Winch is taking the point of view
of a descriptive sociology, Popper that of the social art, the reformer.
Both views are necessary if one is asking how to learn from political
experience.

Part of Winch's argument is that rule-following is the condition and
meaning of intelligible behaviour, and to understand behaviour is to
formulate and understand the rules in the social context in which they
are assumed, interpreted, and followed. (Therefore knowledge of society
is obtained by studying the various systems of rule-following in their
social contexts, not by applying to social phenomena the special rules
for investigating physical phenomena.) Part of Popper's argument is that
society can be studied by applying the special rules for investigating
physical phenomena if this is done intelligently and modestly, discovering and applying genuine uniformities of limited use.

Now, Winch's rule-following as the condition of intelligible behaviour
is also the condition of learning from experience. He himself says: 'It is
only because human actions exemplify rules that we can speak of past
experience as relevant to our current behaviour' (p. 62). Only rational
rule-following conduct is conduct to which there is an alternative. At the
same time, to be able to acquire (causal) knowledge by comparing the
results obtained with the results expected (Popper) is equally a condition
of being able to learn from experience. Both conditions necessarily apply
to the case of learning from political experience: we follow the rules of
political behaviour established in our democratic society, and we try to
compare what happens with what was intended in a methodical quasi-
scientific way. Popper's abstraction isolates the social operator in the
practice of his art, but his art has no possibility nor meaning without
reference to others on whom he is dependent and who have different
interests and purposes; this is the political situation and involves the rules
of political behaviour. By following both the political rules and the
scientific rules more intelligently and methodically, practice can be controlled and perfected to the limit of what is possible in this field. On these
lines methodical social progress can be achieved; and it is progress in the
discovery, reconciliation, and realization of actual human purposes.
Cp. Butler's *The Study of Political Behaviour*, pp. 19-25.

4. *Knowledge was inseparable from freedom:*
of course to speak merely of 'enlightenment and emancipation' begs a big
question. For instance Comte's whole contention was that as understood
by the revolutionary philosophers these ideals produced not order and

progress but anarchy, extravagance, and endless oscillation: to produce order and progress required an historical development which, having dissolved the theocratic absolutist regime, would bring about by the division of labour and the social discipline and solidarity of the industrial order the natural preponderance of social feeling and public spirit, which would be directed to human welfare by the systematic organization of scientific knowledge, completed in man's historical consciousness of himself, and applied to the organization of society and industry, and even art and philosophy, for the sake of the continuous extension of liberty understood as the gradual expansion of human powers through rational submission to the laws of nature. Thus for Comte, heir to the *philosophes*, 'enlightenment and emancipation' meant the due replacement of the will of God and of metaphysical entities and essences *and of human wills* by laws of nature.

5. *an increase in the resources of mankind:*
Condorcet makes it clear that by the perfectibility of the species he is thinking mainly of the development of culture, the cumulative increase of transmissible resources. In the first stage of civilization: 'The uncertainty of life, the difficulty man experiences in providing for his needs, and the necessary cycle of extreme activity and total idleness do not allow him the leisure in which he can indulge in thought and enrich his understanding with new combinations of ideas. The means of satisfying his needs are too dependent on chance and the seasons to encourage any occupation whose progress might be handed down to later generations, and so each man confines himself to perfecting his own individual skill and talent.' With the development of settled agriculture, property, industry, 'the dawn of science had begun to break; man revealed himself to be distinct from the other species of animals and seemed no longer confined like them to a purely individual perfection' (p. 6, 7). This form of perfectibility of the species is indubitable; and if you think that this predictable increase in the resources of mankind will become available for dealing with the problems you face, human progress seems equally indubitable. Unfortunately the problems do not stay still either.

6. *consonant with the analysis of . . . Myrdal:*
see *Economic Theory and Underdeveloped Regions*, ch. 2.

7. *'historicism':*
there is a full discussion in Karl Popper's *The Poverty of Historicism*.

8. *'the meaning of history':*
There is a better way of seeing it. 'Progress' is unequivocally thought of in terms of discovery: the physical exploration of the globe — and of space; the mental exploration of the cosmos. There is here spectacular achievement and prodigious performance, accompanied, as always, by fierce rivalry, secrecy, destructive conflict and competitive pressure. The source of this enterprise is in human needs and instinctual urges, to satisfy curiosity, to make comparisons, to solve problems, as well as greed and the desire to get ahead. And the achievement, whoever enjoys the glory and the firstfruits, is human achievement; the discovery or invention goes eventually into the human stock. Such achievement is always a beginning as well as an end, and there is no limit. This progress in physical exploration and knowledge and its applications is a paradigm of history. Idealized, it is the concept of man growing in self-consciousness and in the power of self-determination: collectively, in terms of science and

technology, education, free institutions; personally, in terms of private choices and the creation, interpretation, and sharing of personal experience. This is not a blind faith in so far as it is grounded in real tendencies and actual trends to which the paradigm in its comparative simplicity and regularity gives perspective shape.

9. *such forecasts:*
a good example of a long-term forecast is the book produced by three members of the Californian Institute of Technology as an outcome of conferences with industrialists: *The Next Hundred Years* by Harrison Brown, James Bonner, and John Weir, 1957.

10. *Such social plans:*
Popper's 'piecemeal social engineering'.

11. *for humane values, for life:*
a period of rapid and intensive scientific and industrial expansion, such as the nineteenth century in Europe and America, is a period in which human life tends to be sacrificed to culture. With the achievement of plenty and the means of plenty, this tendency is put in question, and its reversal proposed, 'culture for the sake of life'. See Ortega y Gasset *The Modern Theme* (1931) and J. K. Galbraith's *The Affluent Society* (1958).

12. *an age-old dilemma as well as the old Adam:*
unless the two components are recognized and distinguished, the theory of progress is bound to be false; the notion that moral progress has not kept pace with intellectual progress is a most misleading idea.

13. *differs profoundly from Buber's:*
as Buber explicitly says, *Between Man and Man*, p. 88. Erich Fromm in *The Sane Society* criticizes the 'libido' concept and castigates current treatment of 'love' as a patent product, a useful and necessary dose for infants and husbands, but his generalization of love as the sanity of society is the very thing that is in question. Schneider seems more sane: 'Among neighbours it is necessary to keep self-respect and yet to be decent and equitable toward those who are not friends, or comrades, or co-workers, or even trustworthy customers. . . . Friendship is no adequate basis for public relations' (*Three Dimensions of Public Morality*, p. 135). For a resolute resolution of all morality into 'love' as an absolute, on humanist assumptions, see Dorothea Krook's *Three Traditions of Moral Thought* (Cambridge, 1959) – a model of brilliant wrongheadedness on the question.

14. *I am dependable myself:*
sounds like the formula for selfrighteousness or the tyranny of my neighbour; and that is what it might be. All the same, this two-way good faith is as indispensable as the rules themselves to any social order. It is never enough to refrain from injustice; it is always necessary also to defend oneself, and others, from injustice. Cicero here is a better political (and moral) philosopher than Plato (see *De Officiis*, I, ix).

Conclusion

The *philosophes* of the eighteenth century could not but think it was obvious that cumulative knowledge and capital, applied to the solution of human problems and the relief of man's estate, would improve vastly the condition of the people and the prospects of the race. The ignorant and indigent many were dependent and oppressed; and the rules of society were devised to remedy the unfortunate consequences of their being in that condition.[1] Educate them, which would give them the means of self-help, and all, or nearly all, would hold their own and prosper. Then the rules of society could simply reinforce with common approval a spontaneous discipline, the ascendancy of everybody's permanent interests; as in personal life reflection reinforced the spontaneous inclination to fulfil the offices of natural affection and to be a useful and agreeable member of society.[2] Cumulatively, then, knowledge and capital would carry humanity forward out of the dark past of superstition, poverty, and servility into a universal civilization of liberty, equality, and fraternity.

If in the nineteenth century thinkers learned to see more clearly the permanence of personal inequalities and the permanence of human conflict, and began to dread the ruinous pressure of population, in fact sensed the fatal element in human affairs, they were also exhilarated by the large-scale social transformations going on, like a natural tide that carried humanity forward, willy nilly, and was not the work of senates nor commanders nor any of the legendary masters of human destiny. Since science had showed that all things are regulated by laws, and with the example of the origin of species and the descent of man, the progress of humanity seemed reasonably assured, theoretically predictable.

In the twentieth century the fatalistic underside of thinking has turned uppermost: the ruinous pressure of population blights every prospect; the permanence of inequalities and of conflict is not merely a sociological fact to be noted, but mainly a daily problem to be dealt with, a continuous hazard;[3] scientific law and biological analogy are better understood, and provide no global comfort. In sum, the big human problems do not appear so obviously to be capable of being resolved by the accumulation of knowledge and of capital.

Actually, the problems which are capable of being solved in this way are being solved in this way. The problems which make the anxieties of the age are not capable of being solved in this way: the drift to nuclear war; the mounting population and diminishing natural resources; the concentration of power in the hands of irresponsible *élites*; the destruction of personal initiative and responsibility by large-scale organization; the destruction of culture and standards by commercial exploitation of mass media. Sociologists do not speak much of progress, nor of liberty and equality, nor of popular sovereignty (antiques are out of place at the ironmonger's); they talk, rather, of the 'secondary environment' (the city of technology); of 'basic personality structure', and of the relation between them. Or they compare current social disciplines with past social disciplines, 'other-directed' contemporary personalities with yesterday's 'inner-directed' and the day before's 'tradition-directed'. These are American sociologists looking at citizens of the USA, a 'people of plenty' — 'and America is the prophetic image of the rest of the urban-industrial world as it will be a few years from now'.[4] Perhaps the world is being shown in these analyses how the problems of these societies can and will be solved, at least to the satisfaction of the power *élites* and of the masses; that is to say, perhaps these societies have no major problems, and the nightmares from which intellectuals suffer are merely the result of the utopian dreams of the *philosophes*, a moral counterpart of the intellectual puzzles which worry (or amuse) only philosophers, since only philosophers are acquainted with them. Of course the threat of nuclear war and of over-population cannot be described as super-heated ideas of the over-educated; they are more like millstones hanged about the neck of every man that cometh into the world. Even so heavy a liability, however, can be made to disappear in a welfare world of social magic. Meanwhile, 'there be delights, there be recreations and jolly pastimes, that will fetch the day about from sun to sun, and rock the tedious year'[5] as in the seventeenth century. Mr Eisenhower will see there is no nuclear war. If the 'idiot' masses have made over to the power *élites* and their 'crackpot realism'[6] the final destiny of mankind, or if, *per impossibile*, the fatal clash is avoided and the 'ocracy that rules Brave New World establishes for ever the greatest happiness of the greatest number and the motto of the United States is realized (if not literally, as near as no matter), *e pluribus unum*, who is to say nay? Is it indeed the intellectuals, and especially the intellectuals of America, the scientists, writers, publicists, scholars,

S

men of religion, who alone stand between mankind and these alternatives?

The only answer is another question: what is the alternative offered by the intellectuals? Is there an alternative on which they are all lined up, or can there be?

Perhaps it does not help much to dramatize the situation. Perhaps too many have too long been sated with just that. Perhaps it is the mistake to look for saviours from any quarter. Perhaps nightmares and utopias are the poisons on which thoughtful people have gone limp and stale. Perhaps the truth is less spectacular and more complex, and the needed remedies are perhaps slower and more modest. That, at any rate, has been the suggestion of these pages. Let me recapitulate the argument.

The accumulation of knowledge and of capital, whatever problems it has brought in its train, has conspicuously solved the primary problems, and is now recognized as the solution by all mankind. The hunger of the peoples of the underdeveloped regions (or their educated leaders) for knowledge and capital, and for what they can bring, will be largely satisfied, somehow, in two or three generations. How these needs are satisfied is likely to have large consequences for mankind. An imaginative and adventurous programme on the part of the advanced industrial nations would do more than anything to redeem the past and buy the future. The two major problems of over-population in a scientific-welfare world and of national defence in a nuclear age would be far more tractable in this context; and in so far as these major problems were brought under control, the subsidiary problems of mass industrial societies would be far more manageable. Disillusionment with some of the effects of the accumulation of knowledge and of capital should not blind Western intellectuals to the primary and permanent importance of this accumulation as necessary to the solution of human problems, even those which it seems to have occasioned.

Of course an imaginative and adventurous programme linking communist and capitalist powers in the build-up of underdeveloped regions, or even generously conceived and carried out by either side, is a utopian idea rather than an encouraging hope. Those who can expect something like this have nothing to worry about, and it is because there is so little reason to expect anything like this that there is worry abounding amongst thoughtful people. To know what ought to be done, to have a scale of better and worse possibilities by which to measure actual policies and events is at least a beginning; and although the best possible is not to be expected, neither is the worst. Achievement measured on this scale, without being all that it ought to be, may well turn out a turning point in history. To begin with, something is being done, and much can be done to make it more.

The affluent capitalist democracies have their special problems; but there are in these societies, already at work or else in the making, certain social disciplines which, worked at, might reasonably be relied upon to stabilize them and to provide the conditions of the maximum attainable intelligent self-determination.

The basic relation between the structure of a society and the typical structure of personality in that society begins with the pattern of child-rearing. Democracy means explicit public rejection of an authoritarian regime and of the authoritarian personality. There are historical reasons for this, but democracy, like science, is a universal ideal, not merely an historical accident. It has permanent rational and moral justifications. On the moral side, as Hobbes insisted, without a political foundation moral rules are impracticable and lose their obligation: the primary law of self-preservation forbids one to make oneself a victim. When mutual security is guaranteed, the rules become reasonable and good faith in keeping them is required; but unless the rules are indeed reasonable, in the sense of mutually advantageous, the social order may be little better than the state of nature, may even be worse (as Bentham insisted), and therefore the reasonableness of good faith requires also rules for changing the rules. History shows in practice that moral and social rules cannot be given by nor derived from authoritarian nor transcendental sources, without rational challenge.[7] As rules agreed by actual people to regulate their real interests, they are reasonable and have the support and sanction of most people. In this way, democracy, as necessary rules for the changing of necessary rules, is morally and politically ultimate.

In a democracy, a child should be brought up to accept, sooner or later, only rules for which good enough reasons can be given; mainly, rules accepted for the sake of desired and enjoyed personal and social ends. But he is not put into a position to do this if he is left to the devices and desires of his own heart. The authoritarian personality can only dominate or be dominated, and looks for or tries to bring about situations in which these roles can be played. On the other hand, anarchy in the home and the classroom plays into the hands of anarchists (and crypto-authoritarians) in the factory and everywhere else. Without the component of authority in the child's early life, he is not put in authority over himself; he cannot become free and responsible; he cannot learn to evaluate realistically the actual world: like the dominated child, he is condemned to fantasies. Rational authority in a society begins with the child's learned acceptance of adult control as not hostile, which is what he inevitably begins by supposing it is; for fear of this hostility and of his own aggression against the power on which he depends for all good brings the danger of permanent damage from total repression and total submission. This is the first and fundamental learning from experience, and the condition of all future learning, in that it is the first condition of realistic discrimination and evaluation in self-knowledge and in the knowledge of others.

This earliest phase of complete dependence on adult help and control gives place as soon as appropriate in the individual case to self-dependence, when the child has been enabled to become competent and sociable. At a school suited to his aptitudes and abilities he is stimulated and developed, and the basis of his self-dependence is broadened with his capacities for achievement. At such a school, he does not merely have the experience of learning, but mainly he has the experience of learning from experience and of learning how to create an experience from which he can learn what he most needs to know; that is to say, he is enabled to learn how to learn what he wants to do, and how successfully to do it. On this basis, whatever his abilities, he can in the reflective last phase of his schooling be enabled to begin to learn to choose, to value, and to manage a life of his own.

The home is even more important than the school, although a good school (good in the sense of meeting real needs effectually) can go some way towards mitigating the effects of a bad home and enabling the child to make a better parent than his own. All the social services contribute to family welfare and to raising the standards of the home; and as these services are remodelled in the light of experience, and as professional training and skill improve, they will contribute more effectually. That is to say, there is in all the mass social services, including education, a complex partnership at work whose tendency is to create good patterns and traditions of marriage and parenthood.[8]

When the school leaver goes into industry he is in the hands of business management, good or bad. Here, again, firms are under pressure to improve their standards, and enlightened example, established knowledge, and trained skill are increasingly available. Good human relations, intelligent co-operation, mutuality, responsibility, are as necessary to industry as capital or technical efficiency, and can be had on the same terms—by adopting the appropriate means. Direct democracy in industry is impracticable, but the representative principle is practised, and a patriarchal or authoritarian order in industry is not a natural outcome of political democracy. This may seem blatantly untrue in view of the irresponsible industrial empires that exist and the trade union bosses who no longer serve but only stand and wait. Unhealthy as this state of affairs may be, it is not the direct result of a political regimen, and indeed the political regimen remains the available resource by means of which at any time health may be restored, whether the cure starts on the shop-floor or in the lobby of the national assembly. In so far as decisions have passed into the hands of a power *élite* not in practice answerable to anyone, this is an aberration, something which seems to have happened, not a new method of government; for government requires organized support. Of course the chain of command in the armed forces, in big industry, and in the Administration is ready-made organized support for all orders handed down, and the danger is that in a situation of cold war and an arms race, when industrial and military technologies and resources are inseparable, the top executives in the military and in the industrial fields have a league and a lead, partly secret, that give them a stranglehold on the national life. This is a real danger which will increase whilst the cold war and the arms race last. If such conditions do persist, it would seem that democracy must perish— unless aroused to do something about it.

The political foundation of democracy was the discipline by which rulers and office-holders were controlled by the people whose interests they were selected and returned to serve: universal franchise, secret ballot, frequent parliaments, freedom of the press and of association and meeting—the full complement of electoral rights. If the contemporary democratic scene is not so simple and satisfying as the one painted by Tom Paine, that does not mean that the original was a romantic lie now exposed to the cynicism of the least sophisticated. If current social criticism complains, on the one hand, of the dominance of a power *élite* (Wright Mills) and, on the other, of the subjection of the informed and responsible authorities to the pressure of the uninformed and irresponsible masses (Walter Lippmann), these judgements do not necessarily cancel one another out. Dangers from these quarters are incidental to democracy, vary with the situation, and sometimes blow up, sometimes work up. They can mount to disaster. The liability of democracy to their occurrence does not mean that there is a better practicable alternative to democracy. The body is a precarious vehicle of life, mortal and perpetually liable to a large variety of distressful minor and major diseases; and there is no known practicable alternative to it, yet. Of course there are practicable alternatives to democracy, and they are well known; but it would be rash to fly to any of them in despair of democracy because of its liability to serious distempers. A healthy democracy is hardly more hopelessly utopian than a healthy body.

The health of democracy is not secured by the punctual cast of a periodic vote, however universally and prudently performed. This is a more or less meaningless performance unless people are actively seeking personal and social ends by organized means. In that context a vote has some point: alternative teams for office, alternative programmes for the agenda, have always more or less relevance to what people are trying to do or trying to get. (To say that there is nothing you *can* do or get by these means is only not silly if there is nothing you are trying to do or get by other means.) But the rhythm of party elections is a conventional rhythm, a necessary public calendar for the ordering of political events. The vital rhythms on which the health of democracy depends are in the social initiatives taken, the ripening of the experience created, and the returns to revision of policy. Election returns and party decisions necessarily have a principal formal share in the determination of what happens in these 'natural' social rhythms, but organized interests and informed persons also have indefinite scope in the shaping of what is to come and in the remodelling that follows in due course. That events shall be shaped and policies remodelled in this way in vital social rhythms, and that the necessary procedures shall be followed and the necessary compromises and co-operation forthcoming to make this possible, these are the indispensable conditions of health in democracy. The policies which are shaped and reshaped in this way, and become more closely adapted to what people learn that they want and to the conditions of getting it, include not only educational and social welfare policies, but also foreign policy and, not least, the economic and social policies of a managed economy. It is in the context of the experiences created by such tentative, but cumulatively stable, policies that there is room for flexibility in dealing realistically with such bedevilled questions as public ownership, priorities, and wage policy. Even the cultural and moral devastation wrought by ubiquitous, high-powered, irresponsible advertising can be tackled to some purpose (with the help of, or with help to, artist, critic, and teacher) by a public made self-conscious and responsible by its own organized trial intentions in every other major field of social policy.

In the affluent capitalist democracies, then, discipline of the ruled by the rulers and of the rulers by the ruled, which in historically simple forms were the remedies against anarchy (Hobbes) and against misgovernment (Bentham), have developed into complex forms of social discipline that in some measure transform the raw wishes of real people into the will to civilization. Infant training, the processes of education, business management, democratic procedures, the requirements of common social action, under statute or otherwise, impose forms of discipline which reinforce one another and which do not repress nor replace real personalities, but enable them to learn to live together by establishing ways and habits of learning to live by experience. This is not a natural harmony of interests, nor an artificial harmony; it is, rather, a working harmony, a continuous purposive transformation, a striving that may become strife, but not without rule, not unlimited violence and cunning. The better possibilities of achieved harmony are ever open. Democratic society, fully taken up in all its resources of traditions and institutions, is indeed 'a partnership in all science; a partnership in all art; a partnership in every virtue, and in all perfection'.[9]

The results in this kind, positive, encouraging, of these social disciplines which are already at work in these societies are certainly not spectacular. Such results may be, and have been, denied. They are not certain, as certain as the operations of machines. But the point is this: employment of a sound technique can be relied on to obtain as good a result as the material allows. If these disciplines are not used when they are available, or if when used the results are poor, the liberal hopes of mankind must fade into the past. Humanity is on trial.

There is no alternative to working at these disciplines, and in these disciplines there is something to work at: that is all we know, and all we need to know. As to faith and hope, there is enough attained and enjoyed good to sustain reasonable ideals.[10]

Death, the venerable king of natural terrors, closes every personal prospect; but civilization goes marching on, and the civilized will, the will to civilization, finds satisfaction in that general prospect. Nuclear war, the factory of mass terror, dims if not damns that larger hope. Only an institutional solution, a world system of collective security, offers deliverance from the bitterly ironical dilemma in which the advanced nations find themselves locked up. On the domestic front we have the tools and can get on with the job; on the international front we have weapons which threaten to finish the job for us. The theoretical contrast between the open situation of gradualness and the closed situation of all-or-nothing could not be stronger; but in practice they are one and the same situation, for both are being determined by the dilemma of nationalism. Nevertheless, although it would be delusion to think that there can be reasonable security outside a collective system, there is now, without mutual confidence and with the determination to keep the freehand that used to go with military power, there is even now an unprecedented fear of war, perhaps strong enough to rule it out as a means of politics, perhaps strong enough to impel serious steps towards reducing the risks of war and finding means to avoid and prevent its occurrence, to make a beginning somewhere, somehow, soon.

An initiative to find this beginning, the current international initiative (pre-summit, summit, or post-summit) can lead to learning what to do with reasonable hope of success, can thereby edge nearer to success, and success is nothing more than a new starting-point. This is the natural course of an initiative, of the current initiative, and there are two things only which can stop its beneficent career: one is the transformation of the initiative from a search for the beginning of an end to war into a bid for advantage and mastery; the other is an assumption that the existing state of affairs (cold war, diplomatic deadlock, arms race) is a better state of affairs than any relevant concession would produce. Now it is this illusory preference for the security and advantages of things as they are, the assumption that this is a viable alternative, or the feeling that existing advantages can be improved or turned to better account, it is this dangerously different initiative or the turning away of the original initiative 'aloof from the entire point' that is, or ought to be, intolerable to thoughtful people—vastly more highly intolerable than was taxation without representation or any of the abominations of tyranny in simpler times. The public has no right to demand that the government make a particular concession, but it has the duty to demand that all the resources of diplomacy be put into a serious and sustained initiative to bring about conditions of permanent international security, on the never-to-be forgotten assumption that there is no reliable safety in things as they are, that disregard of the unprecedented hazards is a dereliction of a government's first duty to secure the public safety. The public has a right to demand this initiative, and to demand that it shall not be allowed to fail. After all, what is at issue is mutual security, not the most difficult bargain to conclude when the negotiators really need it.[11]

The movement of reflection that can rub out despair razes also

Utopia. We have grown up into a complex world of adult sepia; it can be warm sepia, but the black and white vision of the child and the paranoiac is too dangerous for survival.[12] To see what is to be done and how to go about it, to evaluate results in the light of intentions, and intentions in the light of results, because the intentions are practical enough and sufficiently determine what is actually done for the comparison to be useful, these are the modest limits within which it is always possible to think and act, to choose and avoid, wisely and efficaciously. They are narrow limits, like the climatic range within which human existence came into being and could remain extant; but within that genial range, what myriad life, what heavenly days befall, what blessed moments supervene.

NOTES: CONCLUSION

1. *devised to remedy the unfortunate consequences:*
   it was an assumption of eighteenth century radicalism that liberal constitutions with their elaborate checks and balances were merely an attempt to deal with the necessary consequences of an artificial society in which man was corrupted by prejudices and the ascendancy of 'sinister' interests. Laws founded on reason and nature (freedom and equality) would remove the causes whose effects most existing laws were devised to remedy. (See Condorcet, op. cit., pp. 52-3, 128-9.).

2. *reflection reinforced . . . spontaneous inclination:*
   it did not take a radical in the eighteenth century to take this view of human nature; Bishop Butler expressed it definitively in his sermons *Upon Human Nature*.

3. *a continuous hazard:*
   between nations and within nations; of course this was always so, and if it is clearer now that it always will be so, there are still hopeful ways of reducing and mitigating the attendant evils.

4. *a people of plenty:*
   in *People of Plenty* (Chicago, 1954) David M. Potter summarizes the sociological analyses of Riesman, Linton, Kardiner, and others. '*America is the prophetic image*', quoted from *Brave New World Revisited*, p. 161.

5. '*there be delights . . .*':
   Milton's *Areopagitica*.

6. *the 'idiot' masses . . . 'crackpot realism':*
   the phrases are from *The Cause of World War Three* by C. Wright Mills (London, 1959).

7. *History shows:*
   this is the meaning of the several 'Enlightenments'.

8. *a complex partnership:*
   e.g. Dr John D. Kershaw, in a letter to *The Times* (June 6. 1959), described the situation in the borough of which he is Medical Officer of Health: '. . . during the past four years a "social workers' group" has been bringing together regularly health visitors, public health doctors, child guidance clinic staffs, probation officers, hospital almoners, the staff of the children's department, and many others for discussion of each other's fields of work and sundry common problems. . . . Out of the meetings is growing the

consciousness that "social work" is really a matter of skilled people working together to help unskilled people in the science and art of living in a twentieth-century community and that some of the most vital social work is being done by people who would never claim the title of "social worker".'

See also 'Overcoming Inertia', main leader in *The Times* of June 8, 1959, for another aspect of this partnership.

9. *a partnership in all science . . .':*
Burke's *Reflections on the Revolution in France*, Rivington ed., v., p. 183; Everyman ed., p. 93.

10. The above three paragraphs may be taken to express the political philosophy of this book, if they are not taken out of the context of the preceding chapters. The argument might be summarized thus:

A. The *philosophes* and the Utilitarians started from the assumptions that 'men cannot change their natures; all they can do is to change their situation'; and that 'men are in every respect what the laws make them to be'. They expected by specific (constitutional) changes in the law to improve human behaviour and promote happiness.

B. Those dominant philosophers of the succeeding generations who were convinced that there was an order of things as a whole which was regulated by unchangeable laws were therefore convinced that men could not change their situation more than their natures; but these philosophers believed that the actual situation was the best possible, and that the unchangeable laws were ultimately beneficial.

C. Contemporaries are inclined to agree that men cannot change their natures nor their situation, and they know there are no laws of general development, beneficial or not. Therefore they fear the way in which human life is being determined is neither controllable nor hopeful. For they see that the general situation which cannot be changed has become worse, in the sense that the exigencies of national defence which have always occasioned wars threaten now to occasion general catastrophe, and that new dominant institutions (like advertising) are socially irresponsible and exert a pervasive demoralizing influence.

D. If the view taken in this book is that human life is in fact being determined in a way that is controllable and can be hopeful, this depends largely, if not altogether, on ourselves. Men certainly can change their situation, and in the present international predicament they certainly must as a prerequisite of anything worth talking about. Given this much, although there are no beneficial laws of social development, it is reasonable to think that certain trends of development at present warped by nationalism from universal benefit would start down the ringing grooves of change in a spiral advancement of human conditions.

However, the truth of A and B is not exhausted in saying this, for the social determinism of A and the involuntary determinism of B can indeed become the self-determinism of which the *philosophes* and the Utilitarians wanted to see the conditions established. The following outline then emerges.

(i) The real wills of actual people are indefeasible.

(ii) They are, however, subject to agreed social rules, and this requires agreed rules for changing the rules to ensure that they are genuinely agreed.

(These two principles are traditional abstract radical political doctrine: freedom and equality, and the sovereignty of the people.)

(iii) In practice in advanced industrial democracies, the agreed changes in the rules are revisions of social plans, and the rules for changing the rules bring the established democratic political procedures under the universal rules for revising an initiative in the light of the experience it has created. If in this the way the general rules for general participation in a progressive public life are the same as the general rules by which children are enabled in due course to set out on a purposive personal life, namely, the rules for learning from experience, the indefeasible personal will is stimulated to form and become itself at the same time as it is stimulated to socialize itself by contributing to and learning from a relevant social experience; and, since the will is largely socially determined in any case, this form of interdependent personal and social self-determination is the form of the highest possible achievement.

In other words, the procedural rules and the efficiency rules together with the substantive decisions, laws, policies, plans, (not least) services, which they regulate form a continuous discipline that transforms primary drives and wishes into civilized interests capable of being maintained and satisfied. All the rules, plans, services, are informed by experience and may be improved (in the standard of efficiency or in definition of purpose) in the light of the experience they create. This cumulative improvement is not automatic, nor is it a result of merely consulting experience: it depends on deliberate conformity to the universal rules for learning from experience. And these rules apply also to the attempt to modify general social trends.

(iv) There is no term to this process, no destined achievement in history, no magic of any kind; but the universal rules by which it may be controlled are of the order of reliability of scientific procedures, and to follow them is to ascend the road of personal and social self-determination. There is no liberal hope for mankind by any other means.

11. *not the most difficult bargain to conclude:*
if both sides are seeking the peace of victory (for whatever excellent reasons), nothing is possible save war; if only one side is genuinely prepared for co-existence and is seeking for its conditions, peace is possible, and even likely if this side is genuine and persistent enough. Cp. Sir William Hayter's letter in *The Times* of May 11, 1960.

12. *the black and white vision:*
one should be open-eyed not only to the dreadful evil one is up against but also to the comparable ambiguities within; denunciation is sometimes justifiable, the language of righteousness never. Similarly with the brighter fantasies of hero-worship and golden ages and good times coming: look within.

INDEX

GEORGE ALLEN & UNWIN LTD
London: 40 Museum Street, W.C.1

Auckland: 24 Wyndham Street
Bombay: 15 Graham Road, Ballard Estate, Bombay 1
Buenos Aires: Escritorio 454-459, Florida 165
Cape Town: 109 Long Street
Calcutta: 17 Chittaranjan Avenue, Calcutta 13
Hong Kong: F1/12 Mirador Mansions, Kowloon
Karachi: Karachi Chambers, McLeod Road
Mexico: Villalongin 32-10, Piso, Mexico 5, D.F.
New Delhi: 13-14 Ajmeri Gate Extension, New Delhi 1
São Paulo: Avenida 9 de Julho 1138-Ap. 51
Singapore: 36c Princep Street, Singapore 7
Sydney, N.S.W.: Bradbury House, 55 York Street
Toronto: 91 Wellington Street West

Political decisions can be made by individuals as much as by Gov^t.—any act, by any person, which challenges/agrees with Govt. decisions must (sub) consciously be political decisions

Is there a higher order to which mankind believe or not? if there is not then politically arbitrary decisions can be made by Gov^t which will effectively define the morals of society — if these arbitrary decisions conflict with the generally held views of society then individuals, by disobeying the laws of Govt. would be immoral, but by appealing to the ~~not~~ normally accepted standards they would be acting morally. Similarly if one believes in a higher order to which mankind can appeal then political decisions made by individuals, whilst conflicting with those standards required by society, may nonetheless by moral standards according to the higher order.